THE OVERDEVELOPED NATIONS

THE OVERDEVELOPED NATIONS

The Diseconomies of Scale

LEOPOLD KOHR

SCHOCKEN BOOKS · NEW YORK

First published by SCHOCKEN BOOKS 1978

Copyright © 1977 by Leopold Kohr

Library of Congress Cataloging in Publication Data

Kohr, Leopold, 1909–
   The overdeveloped nations.

   Bibliography: p. 175
   Includes indexes.
   1. Economic development.   2. States, Size of.
I. Title.
HD82.K5973 1978   338.9   77-87892

Publishers' note: Although originally written in English, THE OVERDEVELOPED NATIONS first appeared in Spanish and German editions. It was first published in the English language in 1977 in Great Britain, by Christopher Davies (Publishers) Ltd. This present edition constitutes its first U.S. publication.

Manufactured in the United States of America

To

Mary

Jean François

Dan and Claire

DASSIER

Acknowledgements

"The classic stages of a theory's career," writes William James, are characterized by the following sequence: First, the theory is "attacked as absurd; then it is admitted to be true, but obvious and insignificant; finally, it is seen to be so important that its adversaries claim that they themselves have discovered it."

My gratitude goes to those of my friends who were with me when the theory of size advanced in this book was still very much in the first stage of its career. In particular, I want to thank A. von Breicha-Vautier, Romulo Betancourt, Severo Colberg, Sir Alun Talfan Davies, Niels Diffrient, Alexander des Echerolles, Gwynfor Evans, Yann Fouéré, Antonio Gonzalez, Norma Heine, Margaret Hemming, Helena Hernmark, my brother John R. Kohr, Broadus Mitchell, Anatol Murad, Donna Pace, John Papworth, the late Sir Herbert Read and Alwyn Rees, Franc Ricciardi, Peter Seibt, Brynmor Thomas, Robert Solo, Luz M. Torruellas, and Alfred P. Thorne. I am also indebted to Myfanwy Evans for helping in the preparation of the manuscript, and especially to Barrows Mussey for his many constructive suggestions which ultimately led to its publication in German and Spanish and for furnishing its title: *The Overdeveloped Nations*.

My gratitude for enabling me to discuss my theories is also due to the Sociological Society, The European Group, the Heretics, the Welsh Society, the Seminar of Professor James Meade, all of the University of Cambridge; to the Extra-Mural Department of the University College of Wales, the Canadian Institute of International Affairs, the 25th International Design Conference in Aspen, Colorado and, lastly, to the editors of Business Quarterly, The American Journal of Economics and Sociology, Social Science, Land Economics, Vista, the Spectator, Cambridge Opinion, Faith and Freedom, Welsh Nation, Revista de Ciencias Sociales, Zukunft, and Jahrbuch der Absatz und Verbrauchsforschung – for publishing a number of my early formulations.

Contents

Acknowledgements vi

The classic stages of a theory's career.

Preface xi

Size Interpretation of History, its 'maddening' nature (ii). Virginity of Inquiry (iii). Author's distrust of up-dating (iii, v). Statistics as History taught by Figures (iv). 'Antecedent' Literature (iv, v).

Introduction to the German and Spanish editions xv

Limits to Growth; Critical Size; Size Cycles (vi). Size as Determinant of Economic Development; objections to theory; Disunion Now (vii). Satirical manner, tentative statement, literary method (viii-ix). Economic Consequences of the Size of Nations (ix).

I. Critical Size 1

Critical size as cause of accidents (1); crime (2); vicious ideologies (3); collectivism (4). Influence of speed on mass and size (2n, 4). Size Cycles in Soviet Union (5). Cure by Devolution (6). Critical size as sole cause of war (6). Examples: Nehru *père et fille*, Dr. Connor Cruise O'Brien (7). Definitions: Social Size, Critical Size, Optimum Size (8-10). New Interpretation of History (10). Objections (11-12).

II. Optimum Size 13

Lord and Size of Castle (13). Function as determinant of size (13-20). Limits to size of Convivial Society (14); Economic Society (15); Political Society (17-17); Cultural Society (18-19). Size of Optimum Society (19). Optimum Extending Factors (20-21). Optimum Size of Committees (21n). Effect of Post-Optimum Size on Function and Individualism (21-23). Orwell's 1984; Aristotle's Ship Analogy (22). American Illustration (22n).

III. Size and Living Standards 25

Professors as Laundrymen (25). Superior Standards of Past (25-28). Progress turning Housewives into Maids (26, 38n). Remedial 'Affluence' (27). Aspirin Standard of Living (27-29). Form versus Growth (29). Bigness as Cause of Decline (30-34). Malthusian Effect of Social expansion (33). Skyscraper Analogy (34). Cure through Smallness (31, 34, 35n, 43). Deceptive Living-Standard Statistics (34-35). Need for Different Commodity Breakdown (35-49): Power Commodities (36-38); Changing Concept of Cultural Necessities (38-39); Density Commodities (39-41). New Living-Standard Measurement: Luxometer (41-44); Samuelsons'NEW (42n). Statistics in Footnotes. Diagram (45), and Table (46) showing Point of Diminishing Living-Standards.

IV. Size and Socialism   47

Role of Taste as Dterminant of Economic Systems (47). Ideologies as Rationalizations of taste (48-50). Definition of 'pure' socialist (50n). Size as Factor superseding Taste (51). Redefinition of Social Size (51n). Socialism inherent in the too small (51-52), and the too large (52-59). Socializing Factors in Big Powers: Disruption of Capitalist Self-Balancing Mechanism through Scale (52, 54); Geometric Increase of Defence Needs (53); rising dependence on economic controls (54-55); Marx' interpretation disputed (55-56); Levelling Effect of Increasing Populations (56); Intellectual Adaptation to Collectivist Mass Philosophy (57-59). Adultery by Community (58n).

V. Size Cycles   60

Chicken Cannibalism (60). Cure by Contact Lenses Narrowing Vision (61). Group-Size and Crime Escalation (61-64). St. Augustine on the largeness of Empire (63). The Saharoff Exemption (63n). From Farm to Size Cycles (64-67, 78-80). Size, not System, as Capitalism's Germ of Destruction (67). Soviet Size Cycles (69). Malthusian consequences of national Overgrowth (70, 72). Cure not by Increase in Controls but by Reduction of Size through Division, Regionalism, Devolution (71-77). Small is Harmonious (75n). One Can Not Turn Back the Clock (74). Have You Tried? (77). Gigantomania (76, 77n). Statistics in Footnotes. Diagrams (78-80).

VI. Budget Diagnosis   81

Eye Diagnistics; Budget as Measure of all Things (81). Tax Irritation — Mother of Freedom (82). State Origin Theories (82). Convivial Theory (84-88). From Feast to Inn-State (84). Samuel Johnson's 'Good tavern'; Identity of Political and Convivial Terms (85). Queen Elizabeth's Inn-State (86n). Evolution of State-Functions from Inn (86-88). Individualistic Purpose of State (87). Politics by Budget: Liechtenstein as Mirror and Tool of Change (88-91). Budget Politics and Critical Size (92-96). Bigness, not Parliament or Parties, as Determinant of Budgetary Politics (92). U.S. as World's Second Most Socialized Community (93). Totalitarianism by Growth (94). Balanced Budget — Blessing or Curse (95).

VII. Velocity Theory of Population   97

Analogy of Quantity Theory of Money (87). Effect of Velocity on Size of Population (89-101); on Emergency Exits (99). Numerical versus Velocity Overpopulation (98-100). Control of Mass through Control of Speed (99, 102, 103). Technological Distances as Prime Motive for Speeding (102). Cure by National and Urban Contraction: Richness of Pedestrianism (103-104).

VIII. Sky-Scraper Economics 105

Benefits of Smallness (105-110, 116n). Access to World Markets (106). Cost of Bigness (107, 119n, 121). Mass Production Independent of Scale (108). Diseconomies of Scale (109-114). Superior Employment Opportunities and Anti-Cyclical Resilience of Small States (110). 'Exceptions' (110n, 115n). Disemployment Effect of Bigness (111-114). Bigness as Mother of Bureaucracy and Militarism (112-104). Blessings of Secession (114-116), of Loss of Empire, of Military Defeat (116-121): Puerto Rico's Rise (117); German Miracle (118); Ancient Thebes (118). The Rowntree Figures (119n). Bismarck on the advantages of Defeat (121). Causes of 'Success' of Common Market (117-124). Law of Peripheral Neglect (121n). Butter Mountains and Wine Wars (123n). Destruction by Growth (123). Cure by Regionalism: The Heptarchy (125).

IX. Is Reason Treason 126

Ode on Indolence (126). Alienation Effect of Assistance (126). Puerto Rican Example (127n). Romantic Nature of Nation Building (128). Damage of Rationalism (128). Need for Identity Wars (129, 140, 142n). Hatred as Alternative (129). Uselessness of Love (130). Economic Hardship as Substitute (131). Irrationality of Identity Aids: Heraldic Emblems (133); National Costumes (134, 138); Initiation Ceremonies (135n, 137n); Languages and Accents (135); Ritualistic Sports (136); Doubtful Tastes (137). Rationalization of the Irrational (138). Poets as Shapers of National Identity (140). Factors determining Degree of Necessary Irrationality: Age of Nation (145); Affinity with Neighbours (146); Intellectual Eminence of Citicenry — Jews (147), Greeks (148), English (149); Size of Nation (149-152). Alexander Herzen's delightful National Types (150n). National Concepts proportionate to National Size: Examples (149-154). Social Rationality of Nonsense (155). Three Types of Rationality (157). Change of National Identity with each Generation (159). Oxford Accent as Nation Builder (160).

X. Meta-Economics 161

An Economist's Confessions (161). Overgrowth of Economics (161n, 162). Sterility of Macro-Economic Revolutions (163). Limits to Mathematical Economy (163). 'Only Second-rate Mathematicians are Economists' (164n). Need for Return to Basics (165, 173). The Meta-Economists (166, 169n-171n). Meta-Approach: the Value of Analogies (167). Examples (167-171). Transition from Growth Economics to Form Economics (171). The Meta-Approach in Other Disciplines (173).

Bibliography 175
Index of Names 179
Index of Places 182
Index of Subjects 185

Preface

That which links most of the essays assembled in this volume is the theory that a number of the worst economic problems of our time – declining living standards, cyclical disruptions, the seemingly irresistible triumph (as the penultimate step towards their own collapse) of controlled over free-enterprise systems – can be attributed to a single cause: the excessive size of nations.

This does not mean that such conventionally cited causes as lack of government control, monopolostic practices, ideological commitments, capitalist wastes, socialist bureaucracy, ineptitude of leaders, profit motive, political unrest, or Marx's famous mode of production, have lost their relevance as tools of historic interpretation. They have lost their eminence. As *primary* causal forces they have been superseded during the last few decades by a cancerous degree of social overgrowth such as could never have occurred in earlier ages when the limited size of nations placed limits too on the magnitude of their problems, and thus kept them down in scale to that commensurate with the small stature of ordinary mortals.

Because of the relative newness of this unprecedented condition, brought about by advance in the technology of communication and transportation, it is not surprising that the idea of the size of nations as the prime determinant of social, political, and economic difficulties should have been brushed aside by most contemporary theorists as whimsical speculation. Indeed, as Professor Anatol Murad points out in his original introduction to this volume, the best *The Economist* could do with one of my earlier publications, *The Breakdown of Nations*,[1] in which I had presented a more general theory of the consequences of the size of nations, was to dismiss it as "a maddening little book."[2] It was not until three years later, after the publication in 1960 of the papers of a symposium held in Lisbon by the International Economic Association on *The Economic Consequences of the Size of*

---

[1] London: Routledge S. Kegan Paul; New York: Rinehart, 1957; (paper back, Swansea: Christopher Davies, 1975).
[2] *The Economist*, June 29, 1957.

Nations, that the editors of that distinguished journal managed to overcome their curious madness.[3] In fact, they now actually praised an inquiry which even then was still so new that Professor Austin Robinson of Cambridge confessed to "a feeling of incredulity" at the thought that in all the nearly 200 years that had elapsed since the publication of Adam Smith's *The Wealth of Nations*, he was unable "to discover a volume of antecedent literature such as the subject seemed to have deserved."[4]

All this, as I said, occurred as recently as 1960. Now, sixteen years later, the 'nearly' 200 years have become 'fully' 200 years, making 1976 the bicentenary not only of the *American Declaration of Independence* but also of *The Wealth of Nations*. And though none of the thirty-two eminent contributors to the Lisbon symposium has followed up the discussion about the relationship between the welfare of nations and their size which they had considered of such profound significance, the subject has ceased to be the 'virgin field' which they had thought it still to be when they first beheld it. Indeed, preoccupation with the dangers of bigness, scale, growth, and size has since produced so many publications that a number of friends, including my publisher, have urged me to take account of them and update my own volume in the light of these newer dissertations.

Unfortunately, I do not believe in the practice of updating, apart perhaps from inserting an occasional 'the late' before the name of such persons as Dr. Nkrumah or Nikita Khruschev, who were still alive when I cited them as witnesses. Even that I do with reluctance, just as Thucidides would have hesitated to update his *History of the Peloponesian War* by referring to Pericles as 'the late' or, still worse, by replacing the names of past leaders with those of their successors. Nor do I believe in adapting my figures as I consider that the only value of figures is their ability to illustrate a philosophic proposition. If newer figures disprove a proposition, it never was any good in the first place. What should then be done is not update the figures but drop the proposition and, for good measure, tear up the book one has written about it.

[3] *The Economist*, May 14, 1960.
[4] Ed. Austin Robinson. London: Macmillan, 1960, p. xiii.

If, on the other hand, a proposition has validity, it can be illustrated by an old set of figures just as well as by a new one, for the same reason that a true analogy from one field is as good for making a point as one from any other field. As Dionisius said of history, that it is philosophy taught by examples, so one can say of statistics that they are philosophy illustrated by figures. It is the latters' rhythm that matters, not the date of their compilation. Moreover in some cases, such as in my effort to locate the time at which a given society has slipped over the 'point of diminishing living standards,' the only figures that make sense are those covering the period when the event occurred not those of the year in which the book describing it is published.

Lastly, I have resisted the advice to add to the value of a book parts of which were written in the early 1950's by taking into account writings on similar themes which have begun pouring onto the market since the late 60's and early 70's. True, these later writings have made the once discredited subject so respectable that I am constantly being told that my theories remind people of what they have already heard from Professors Galbraith, Tobin, Nordhaus, Mishan, Samuelson, Boulding and other scholars gracing the prestigious economics faculties of Harvard, Cambridge, Yale, L.S.E., or M.I.T.

For all of them I have of course the profoundest respect. How could I feel otherwise since they actually do say much of what I am saying too. Perhaps, then, I really should not resist updating a book to be published in 1976 by incorporating, for example, a discussion of the as yet tentative 1973 studies of Professors Nordhaus, Tobin, and the Nobel Prize winner Paul Samuelson on the need for a more meaningful way of measuring living standards. The only difficulty here is that my own chapter, dealing with the same subject not tentatively but definitively and illustrated with all the figures and diagrams necessary for making the point, was published in various forms twenty years earlier (in the mid 1950's) in a number of journals, and a little later in translations of this very volume which appeared in Germany in 1962, and in Spain in 1965. Nor for that matter do I see any reason for including in an 'antecedent' study the valuable findings of works such as *The Economic Consequences of the Size of Nations* even when, as in this case, the 'antecedent' volume is first published in its original English version more than a decade after the 'subsequent' one. Should one try to improve on the account of the Prophets by updating it with the story of its Fulfilment? That would be to turn prophecy into banality and risk as my friend and colleague Brynmor Thomas warned, the veniality of the trader whose epitaph reads: Born a man – Died a Grocer.

I trust, then, that I shall be forgiven for leaving my text, apart from very minor changes, largely as it was more than twenty years ago, *before* subsequent economic and political literature began to train its heavy artillery on the problems of excessive growth, bigness and scale. This, however, does not mean that I have ignored the newer work of others. As Alfred Marshall did with mathematics in his economic treatises, I have given account of it in an amplitude of footnotes. Moreover I should like to take this opportunity for expressing my admiration for Ivan Illich and E. F. Schumacher whose brilliant pioneering work on the humanity of small proportions antedates that of most who have by now come to realize too that bigger is not necessarily better.

University College of Wales
Aberystwyth
Autumn 1976   Leopold Kohr

Introduction to the German and Spanish Editions

There is no mistake. The title of this book is The *Overdeveloped Nations*. We are used to hearing only about the *under* developed nations and how to promote their development. Indeed, this has been the main topic of discussion and controversy among economists, and the concern of statesmen throughout the world, ever since the end of World War II. Professor Kohr, however, insistently reminds us that the real problems are not those of underdevelopment, but of *over*development. While the world lavishes its attention and sympathies on the countries struggling to catch up with the industrial giants, it is blind to the much greater problems and dangers faced by these already developed large industrial nations.

The problems of overdevelopment, as Professor Kohr sees them, are due to *social overgrowth*. There is an optimum social size (defined and explained in Chapter II) beyond which a society can grow only at the cost of escalating into difficulties. Each further step in the direction of integration, consolidation, automation, then begins to contribute not to the solution of problems, but only to their scale. As the weight of bodies progresses by the square of their size – which explains why an elephant's legs must be so much sturdier than a doe's – so the weight of a society's problems may be said to increase by the square of any increase in its size, once it has passed optimum size and reached "critical size" (defined and explained in Chapter I).

Social growth beyond critical size leads not to greater welfare, but to social elephantiasis. Though per capita output may continue to grow, living standards decline. Staggering under the weight of their excessive size, the economies of overgrown, overdeveloped nations are increasingly unstable. They are afflicted not only with business cycles, but with wider, less controllable "size cycles" (Chapter V). These size cycles occur regardless of the prevailing economic system, whether capitalist or socialist. In fact, Professor Kohr argues, all the overgrown elephantine nations must necessarily be socialistic, since capitalism is no longer feasible when social size has become excessive. (Chapter IV).

The concept of social size, and its implications, is the unifying thought running through the whole of the present book, as indeed it has been the central idea Professor Kohr advanced and elaborated on over many years in numerous newspaper and magazine articles and in his earlier book *The Breakdown of Nations*. Social size, Professor Kohr argues, is the ultimate determinant of social and economic development. It is not human reason which is ultimately significant, nor the choice of this or that economic system, such as socialism or capitalism, nor Marx's mode of production, but social size. All modern social, political, and economic problems are in the last analysis traceable to excessive social size.

Although many reviewers, including economists, have acknowledged and acclaimed the merits of Professor Kohr's ideas, the economics profession proper has not welcomed his size theory; that is to say, the size theory has not, up to now, been admitted to general discussion and debate in professional economic journals. One reason for this may be that economists have so consistently ignored the problem that they simply could not see the relevance of social size to economic problems.

Another, perhaps more important, reason is that the size theory strikes at one of the most cherished shibboleths of our day: the belief in the virtue of continued economic growth, of cooperation, unification, integration. One would think that the emphasis on the dangers of overgrowth, of excessive size, would find a warm acceptance and approval in our capitalistic society which professes to abhor big business, to forbid monopolies, to regard small business as socially beneficial. Strangely, however, the same people who proclaim their faith in *laissez faire* capitalism which implies competition between small enterprises, at the same time also applaud the virtues and wisdom of integration, of unification, of common markets, union now, and One World. Kohr's argument for division instead of unification, for a world of small competitive societies, for Disunion Now (as he headed one of his articles published as early as 1941),[1] constitutes an attack on the prevalent collectivist mode of thinking. No wonder that those who feel their

---

[1] *Commonweal* (New York), September 26, 1941.

sacred beliefs attacked try to discredit the arguments marshalled against them, or ignore them altogether.

It is not only the substance of Professor Kohr's ideas, however, but also the manner in which he has chosen to present them, which may account for the hostility or indifference of the economics profession to these ideas. For one thing, as the reader of *The Overdeveloped Nations* will presently discover for himself, Professor Kohr writes with wit and humour, with sarcasm and satire. From this, an academic pedant may possibly get the impression that Kohr's arguments are not serious. To confuse the humourous with the trifling is a common error. Yet some of the most profound truths have been couched in satire and presented in a humourous vein.

Secondly, Professor Kohr has a special gift, reminiscent of Thorstein Veblen, for the clever, cutting phrase, and the well-aimed thrust. Like Thorstein Veblen before him, he laughs at his fellow economists. It would be too much to expect the targets of his mirth to applaud him any more than they applauded Veblen.

Thirdly, Professor Kohr launches many of his ideas in a tentative way, without complete verification. His theory of size cycles is a case in point. He develops the general outline of the theory, but leaves many details hazy and at times offers no statistical evidence to support it. He uses what might be called the literary method of presenting his theories. This method is by no means novel in economics. On the contrary, it was until recently the only known way of proceeding in economic analysis and even today, in our statistics-minded age, it is a widely used and reputable method. Yet when a new theory is advanced – and especially one which does not fall within the range of subjects decreed by the profession as eligible for debate – the verdict is apt to be: prove it beyond a reasonable doubt or we will not consider it at all. This, of course, is an inadmissible position.

The discoverer of a new theory may not have the inclination, or perhaps the facilities, for marshalling the empirical evidence which will either prove or disprove the theory. Einstein formulated theories, but left it to others to supply experimental proof.

Professor Kohr's ideas should similarly be tested, proved, improved, or disproved, on the basis of further empirical investigation, but should certainly not be lightly discarded merely because such empirical proof has at the time of writing not as yet been forthcoming in sufficiently conclusive quantities. As Professor Kohr says, his purpose in advancing a new idea is to *start* a discussion, not to say the last word about it.

For any or all of these reasons, then, or for still others perhaps, Professor Kohr's theory which sees in excessive social size, in social overgrowth, the key to social and economic problems, has not had the attention on the part of the profession which the importance of the subject merits. For two decades this theory was developed and discussed only *extra muros*, so to speak, and was barred from discussion within the sacred precincts of the profession. This fate Kohr's size theory shares with many other new ideas in economics as in other sciences – which had to wait as pariahs outside the walls before eventually being admitted as honoured newcomers to the inner circle. One thinks of Pasteur's germ theory of diseases, which was at first condenscendingly brushed aside by the medical profession; or, in economics, of Hermann Gossen, whose theory of marginal utility, advanced in 1854, was ignored until, seventeen years later, it became orthodox doctrine in the formulations of Jevons and Menger. In fact, it seems that most new ideas and theories are developed *extra muros;* rarely do they spring from within the established schools which have a vested interest in the elaboration of their approved subjects, like to stick to established dogma, and tend to be unreceptive to new ideas.

Recently there have been indications that Professor Kohr's size theory may at last be admitted to respectability within the profession. Meeting at Lisbon in 1957, the International Economic Association directed its attention to "the relationship between the welfare of nations and their size." The papers presented at that conference by a group of top-ranking economists were published in a volume entitled *The Economic Consequences of the Size of Nations,* edited by Professor Austin Robinson of

Cambridge (London, Macmillan, 1960). It is hoped that publication of the Lisbon papers will spark a more extensive discussion of this important subject which has for so many years been the chief interest of Professor Kohr. Already the philosophical infrastructure which when presented in Kohr's *Breakdown of Nations*, was characterized by the London *Economist* (June 29, 1957) as "curiously maddening," has been declared in the same journal (May 14, 1960), "an immensly rich mine of ideas and facts" now that it has been sanctified by proper authority. This belated recognition that "the whole question of size deserves a great deal more attention than it has hitherto had," should stimulate further investigation on the subject. As the *Journal of Economic History* (June 1961) adds: "there is room for subsequent exploitation by whole brigades of economists, political scientists, historians – for anyone interested in the nature and causes of the wealth of nations."

With their attention at last directed toward the role played by social size, economists and laymen alike will find many provocative questions raised and many unexpected answers suggested in professor Kohr's fascinating volume on *The Overdeveloped Nations*.

University of Puerto Rico
Rio Piedras, 1962   Anatol Murad

THE OVERDEVELOPED NATIONS

I. Critical Size

1

A number of years ago, Puerto Rico proclaimed a Road Safety Day. It was backed by government, police, civic organizations, newspapers, and clergymen. The result: the same number of of accidents by noon that was registered on the corresponding date a year earlier by nightfall. Had the warnings against reckless driving fallen on deaf ears? By no means. All it proved was that, once a car-driving society has reached *critical* size, traffic accidents are no longer the result of recklessness but of the size of society. This is why they are predictable by statisticians whose material is not the nature but the number of men. Warning or no warning, caution or no caution, reckless or not, a given population of drivers will by statistical law produce a given number of casulties.

This being the case, accidents in societies having reached *critical* size can obviously not be reduced by road safety days or appeals to reason. What is needed is the reduction of the society of car drivers to sub-critical size, that is to proportions at which the numbers of cars become so few that they cease to enrol themselves into orderly statistical patterns. Only then are accidents the result of personal factors, and can be averted by caution or appeals to reason.

This does not mean that roads require a reduction in the actual number of cars using them. The same effect can be achieved through a reduction in speed limits. This is not because lower speeds produce greater caution but because by physical law a change in the velocity of movement has the same quantitative effect as a change in the number of moving particles. More people moving at reduced speed represent therefore the same mass as fewer people moving at increased speed. Hence the emergency exits in theatres, the use of which is unnecessary as long as people move at ordinary pace. Yet they must be kept in reserve to cope with the volume-increasing effect of people suddenly moving at an accelerated pace as under the impact of panic.[1]

What applies to road accidents applies also to crime. At *critical* social size, it is not so much the criminal disposition of man that causes violations of the law as the size of the group. This is why statisticians are able to be as accurate with their figures of crime as with those of accidents. They can tell us that during the next 30 days, Chicago, for example, will experience about 1,000 burglaries, 500 robberies, 30 attacks on women, 15 murders. Yet, Chicago is not inhabited by worse people than other cities. In fact, were its 1,545 weekly criminals living in communities by themselves, not only would their crimes be so few that they could not be predicted; most of the criminals would be engaged in wholly conventional activities, earning their living as teachers, lawyers, businessmen, college presidents and priests, with a bishop thrown in for good measure. But a population as numerous as Chicago's will produce a figure of crime proportionate to its size even if it were composed of nothing but monks and nuns. As a result, once societies have reached *critical* size, no administrative action, appeal to conscience, or change in educational policy can bring about the fall in the rate of crime. The only way of achieving this is by reducing them to sub-critical size, that is to a size at which crimes, similar to traffic accidents, depend no longer on given numerical magnitudes but on reason or the enforcement of law.

Nowhere has this connection been more dramatically illustrated than in Korea at the time of the prisoner-of-war rebellions of

---

[1] For this reason, any problem of pressure caused by the existence of an excessive number of moving particles can be solved in two ways: Quantitatively, through the reduction of particles, and qualitatively, through the reduction of the speed of their movement. As Chapter VII on the *Velocity Theory of Population* tries to show, most problems of modern overpopulation could thus be solved by the reduction of the velocity with which people move, rather than by emigration or the conquest of new *Lebensraum*. Vice versa, many generals having too small armies at their disposal, have made up for this by moving them around at so fast a pace that, like a single immense army, they seemed to be everywhere at the same time. This was the whole mystery of the military success of men such as Alexander, Hannibal, Napoleon, or Hitler. Theirs was not a strategy of numbers but of speed (*Blitzkrieg*) which produced physically the same effect of mass as greater number.

1948. Ascribing them at first to the recalcitrant nature of communists, American emissaries up to the rank of general went into the camps to talk sense. The only sense the inmates could see was that generals made good hostages. The situation was finally brought under control when it dawned on the policy makers that the real cause of trouble was not the incorrigible character of communists but the sheer physical size of prison compounds which, at a critical magnitude, leads to obstruction and hostage-taking irrespective of the nationality, ideology, or nature of inmates. Once this was understood, they ended the violence simply by breaking up the compounds into units of such small size that only a madman would have thought of getting away with continued defiance of the regulations.

But it is not only violence and crime which bears a relationship to social size. It is the same with crime-fostering *ideologies*. When a crowd of New Yorkers impatiently invited a suicide candidate clinging for hours to a window sill high on a skyscraper to "make it snappy", one might have been inclined to attribute this monstrous sentiment to the brutalized outlook of insensitive city dwellers. Yet, the first ones to arrive at the scene displayed quite a different attitude. They were terror-struck. They prayed. But as their number changed, so did their outlook. The pangs of individual conscience were insensibly drowned in the throb of socialized excitement. Tragedy turned into spectacle, terror into thrill, and the prayer to desist into the clamour to perform. Only when the spectators dispersed did they return to prayer. However this had nothing to do with their better selves. It was the simple result of the transformation of a critical into a sub-critical mass the tenuous translucency of which makes it impossible for an individual to hide his action from his own conscience. Contrary to current theory, crime-condoning and atrocity-loving ideologies such as fascism, nazism, or political terrorism, seem therefore not so much to spring from bad leadership, evil education, or metropolitan callousness as, again, from the strictly physical factor of a change in social size from sub-critical to critical dimensions.

And so it is not only with *crime*-condoning but also with *crowd*-condoning ideologies which, such as collectivism, are attributed by many to the reformers' philosophic conviction that the immense aggregate power generated by society as a whole makes it so superior to the individual human person that there can be no doubt as to its position of precedence and pre-eminence. However, though shared by many reformers, no one is *born* with this sort of revelation. It begins to make sense only when society reaches that dangerous *critical* volume at which its collective physical bulk becomes so overpowering that its individual members are reduced to particles of minor rank on that ground alone. Unable to assert themselves under these conditions, they can then just as well rationalize their degradation by becoming collectivists not only in fact but also in spirit. This explains why the United States with her enormous and highly integrated social mass is, in spite of her individualistic heritage, well on the road to becoming second only to the Soviet Union and China in the collectivist glorification of her society. How otherwise could President Kennedy have been applauded rather than impeached when he exhorted the citizen in a reversal of democratic priorities: "ask not what the government can do for you. Ask what you can do for the government."

Hence, if statesmen want to preserve a country's individualism, they will get nowhere with indoctrination, which is itself a principle of collectivisation. What they must do also in this instance is to reduce society from critical to sub-critical size, a size at which social power becomes so shrunken that the individual will once again be able to assert himself simply because he will no longer feel either oppressed or impressed by it. But as in the case of traffic problems, the reduction of *social* size does not imply a reduction in the *numerical* size of a population. A reduction of its velocity will have the same effect. And this can be achieved by less drastic means than war, famine, and disease. All it needs is the introduction of a high measure of cantonization, decentralization, or devolution as it is now frequently called. Shortening the distance between the citizen and the state, this diminishes a people's *speed* by diminishing its *motive* for moving over long distances in its effort of dealing with the central authorities administering it. And, as we have seen in the example of the emergency exits of a theatre, a *slower* moving population becomes in effect a *smaller* population as compared with one numerically equally large but forced by far-flung political and economic integration to travel at ever shorter intervals over ever longer distances at ever faster speeds.

Similar to the rise in mass-dominated ideologies or the mounting accident and crime figures, the increasingly unmanageable complexities in the world of economics have their origin no longer in the nature but in the size of things, taking the form of anything from wine lakes, beef, egg, and butter mountains, unemployment, declining living-standards, or inflation all the way up to the increasing ferocity of cyclical fluctuations. Ascribing particularly the latter to uncontrolled free-enterprise systems, most theorists suggest as a cure a switchover to either a mixed system with limited controls or to socialism with full controls. What they tend to overlook in the absence of an appropriate theory is that limited as well as fully controlled systems may suffer as much from deepening disruptions and cyclical upheavals as uncontrolled systems. Thus, though it should have been theoretically impossible, communist Russia began from the 1930's onward to experience all the economic dislocations usually identified with *capitalist* depressions: factories that could not work, output that could not be shipped, goods that could not be distributed. And in spite of the the social ownership of the means of production, the individual worker of excessively large societies has even under communism yet to see the day on which his wage will approximate the full value of his labour.

But why should this be the case? The reason is again the same. At critical size, the survival requirements of society begin to increase at a faster rate than its productivity. As a result, an ever increasing proportion of goods which were previously available for raising *personal* living standards must now be diverted to *social* use. Moreover fluctuations, which at sub-critical size were capitalist in nature and could therefore be eliminated through the introduction of a system based on government control, re-enter the stage at critical size as sheer *physical* phenomena which, like waves in the ocean, derive their amplitude no longer from the nature but from the size of the body through which they travel. It makes no difference whether the body is governed by a capitalist or communist brain. In either case it suffers from the inner instability of the overgrown. Hence no fluctuation of any kind can be contained by new or wider controls in societies which are characterized by the very fact that their oceanic dimensions have *outgrown* all human control.

Again, the only way of restoring stability and manageability is not by changing governments or economic systems but by reducing social size to a magnitude commensurate to the small stature of Man. For many this is equivalent to suggesting a reactionary step back. But it is exactly what the Soviet Union did in 1957. After four decades of experimenting with a policy of *One Country – One Factory,* it stunned the world not a little by dismantling its monolithic unity into no fewer than 105 semi-autonomous economic units (embodied in 1961 in 17 separate regions of from 8 to 15 million inhabitants, with only the metropolitan district around Moscow left with a population of 25 million), at the very moment when the rest of Europe, lacking the Russian experience, signed the Treaty of Rome in an effort to achieve its economic unification.

Finally, what applies to so many of our other contemporary social complexities, applies also to the world's most tragic problem: war. During World War II and, indeed, to this day, aggression has been attributed to German militarism. That is why we dismembered Germany. To bad leaders. That is why we hanged the war criminals. To bad ideologies. That is why we believe in re-education. To disunity. That is why we created the United Nations. To capitalist imperialism. That is why many believe in socialism. Yet, instead of creating peace, we merely discovered that war is made by peace lovers, the re-educated, the democrats, the socialists, as readily as by the militarists, the barbarians, the disunited, the dictators, the capitalists.

But, again, the paradox resolves itself if we attribute war to the acquisition of *critical* size: that mysterious social volume at which it breaks out spontaneously irrespective of the ideology, religion, leadership, culture, or economic system of the countries involved. It explains why Franco and Tito, one a fascist and one a communist whom even the Russians find obnoxious, have surpassed each other in the pursuit of peaceful policies: They have been lacking in critical power. And it explains, on the other hand, why the peace-loving Nehru's both *père et fille,* have rolled up a record of aggression that has no match since the defeat of the Axis Dictators. In his first years of power, Jawaharlal had made two wars, on Hyderabad and Kashmir; threatened a third, which was finally carried out in two instalments by his daughter Indira, against Pakistan; pushed the French, bullied the Portuguese, and intervened imperialistically in Nepal whose government he changed and whose soldiers he started to recruit as eagerly for his armies as the British had done before him.[1] Only in the face of China and Russia did the two Nehru's indulge in the practice of peace, not because they did not believe in force but because in relation to these giants India's social size was not critical. In other words, she did not convey to her leaders the impression that they could have waged war with impunity. Which means that even the problem of war can be solved only through a reduction of the social size of potentially aggressive societies to sub-critical

---

[1] A similar example was provided by the gentle representative of the United Nations in Katanga, Dr. Connor Cruise O'Brien who, not unlike Hitler, promised friendship and peace to the local government, but unleashed ferocious street battles in Elisabethville (Lubumbashi) the moment he thought he had amassed critical power over the native tribe. When he realized his error, he promptly rediscovered his love of peace, resigned, and got married. Even the United Nations, committed as they are to peace, have thus shown that they will lustily begin shooting if they think they can get away with it. And so has the People's Republic of China, which marched into fraternal India when the absorption of the Soviet Union and the United States in the Cuban missile crisis gave it briefly critical power, only to declare the venture a peaceful boundary inspection and withdraw a few days later when she was once again reduced to sub-critical size as a result of the end of the Cuban confrontation, and the ability of the two giant antagonists to give their renewed support to India. However, these are only two added examples of a theory of aggression that has no known exception.

dimensions which insure peace not through love or good-will which Oscar Wilde defines as a cheque drawn on a bank where one has no account: it insures peace by means of the sheer physical inability to wage war – a much safer proposition.

2

The preceding pages, sketching in rough outlines some of the most pressing of our contemporary problems, try to give form to a number of concepts that seem vital to our understanding of causal connections, and will therefore be extensively used in the more detailed investigations contained in the following chapters. The most important of these are:

1. The concept of *social* size or, as it might also be called, the *effective* size, of society.

This is in contrast to the *physical* size of society which is based on population number. Social size, on the other hand, rests not merely on one factor but on four: not only on the number of a population but also on its density, the degree of its administrative integration, and the velocity of its movements. For a denser society is *in effect* a larger society than one of equal numbers but lower density. It produces more energy. For the same reason, a more integrated society is *in effect* a larger society than a less integrated one; and a faster society is *effectively* larger than a slower one. Thus, while the numerical or physical size of Great Britain is very much smaller than that of India, her social size, reflected in her status as a big power, is very much larger due to the magnifying effect of both her greater administrative integration and her technologically generated higher velocity of population. However, considering that the internal pressures of numerically larger societies are bound to produce in due course first greater density, then greater integration, and finally greater velocity, the numerically largest will ultimately also be the effectively largest society. This will, in the end, make the concept of physical and numerical size identical with effective or social size. But before this stage is reached, the historically important concept is social size, not physical or numerical size.

2. The concept of *critical* size.

This may be defined as the size of society at which problems are caused by proportions rather than by institutional or human shortcomings in the same sense as at critical height breathing difficulties set in as a result of altitude rather than of individually defective lungs; or as at critical accumulation uranium explodes as a result of its mass rather than of any change in the character of its particles.

3. The concept of the *variability* of critical size.

This depends on the differing nature of the problems concerned. Related to war, a society may be said to have reached critical size when its leaders have reason to assume that their country's power has become stronger than that of any possible opposing power. Related to pickpocketings, knifings, massacres, it materializes when crowds begin to outgrow the controlling power of the variously large police forces which can be economically afforded for preventing these crimes. Related to business cycles, it is reached when the size of a market begins to dim the vision of governments charged with alleviating their amplitude. In the case of economic systems, it sets in when social overgrowth begins to curtail the choice between alternatives, leaving only socialism viable, and even this only for a little while longer.

4. The concept of *optimum* size.

This is a slightly wider concept than that of *sub-critical* size since, unlike the latter, it conveys not only an upper but also a lower limit of social growth. A community can be too small as well as too large. However, since the central problem of the age is that communities have burst through the upper limit, the concepts of both optium and sub-critical size in the context of these pages imply that the solution of their problems lies in making societies not larger but smaller. They suggest that survival depends no longer on integration and further unification but on the break-up of the critically overgrown political, social, and economic units into sub-critical optimal groups in which problems are brought back to a scale at which ordinary mortals can once again effectively deal with them with the limited talent that nature has put at our disposal.

5. The concept of *changing* social size as the *primary* cause of historic change and human evolution.

This does not mean that there are not also other forces influencing historic development such as powerful ideas, man's will, leadership, accident, or Marx's famous mode of production. There are. But they exercise a significant role only in societies of sub-critical or optimum dimensions. In societies of critical size such as the world's contemporary dominant powers, however, only social size seems to count as a *primary* force. Hence, the only thing man can do if he wants to escape the mind-levelling atrocities inherent in their sheer physical weight and resume once more the effective direction of his destiny, is to do to all of them politically what the Kremlin has done to the vastness of the Soviet Union economically – dismember them.

3

There are numerous objections to this *Size Interpretation of History* and its seemingly anarchronistic conclusion suggesting an Augustinian pluralist small-state arrangement rather than a unitarian world. It is called *simplicist*. But which theory worth its name is not? The *Providential Interpretation* assigns all historic events to the will of God. The *Great-Man Interpretation:* to great men. The *Idealistic Interpretation:* to ideas. Marx: to the mode of production. Freud: to sex. Jung: to *Angst*. I: to the size of society. Only those playing it safe, or unwilling to deduce complicated structures from simple beginnings, would hold this against it. Professor Edward Teller, the master mind behind the hydrogen bomb, confessed recently that physicists are still baffled by the mystery of the atomic nucleus. The only thing he knew for certain, he said, was that when it will ultimately be revealed, it will turn out to be very simple. And Confucius told a student admiring him for knowing so many things: "I know only one thing. But that permeates everything."

It is called *materialist*. But do we not live in a material universe? God, not Karl Marx, has made it that way. To consider His creation meaningless in the interpretation of human processes seems more blasphemous than the Marxian interpretation which may deny God. But at least it accepts the meaningfulness of His design which cannot always be said of its detractors. And what about Churchill who, when pleading for the reconstruction of the House of Commons in its oblong form, warned that *"we shape our buildings, but our buildings shape us"*? Making British democracy dependent on the shape of a crowded debating place rather than on more flattering elements such as schooling, tradition, or good sense, is this not also materialism? But does it make Churchill a Marxist or Atheist?

It is called *determinist*. Even if it were, has determinism been outlawed by the academies? But is it? True, it pictures certain of man's ideas, ideologies, behaviour patterns, mode of production, social institutions, and actions as nothing but reflex phenomena to *critical* social size, just as a doctor pictures the ideas, emotions, and actions of a drunk as but reflexes to his consumption of *critical* quantities of liquor. A person may always feel amorous after two martinis. But no alcoholic determinism compels him to drink two martinis. Similarly, from the Germans to the Israelis and Egyptians, a society will always feel aggressive at critical size. But no historic determinisms compels it to grow to proportions at which its actions are not will but size determined. Far from being determinist, the implications of the size theory hand back to man the *self*-determination and *ego* of which the pagan force of excessive social size threatens to divest him.

It is called *reactionary*. Suggesting, as it logically must, a return to a life within smaller, or what is the same thing, slower-moving communities, is this more reactionary than a housewife's suggestion to return to a smaller house where she will find the same problems but on a smaller scale? And where, instead of having to work 15 harrassed hours a day to keep the family enterprise going, 3 leisurely hours may be enough, releasing her time for more rewarding pursuits? As long as countries were of reactionary small size, they had profligate princes. But what did these cost the citizen compared to the frugal dictators and prestige-hungry leaders of great powers? In the 'retarded' intimacy of their cities you could meet Aristotle, Shakespeare, Newton, Goethe, Dante, Botticelli, Mozart. In the cities of the 'progressive' great nations of our day, who can afford hydrogen bombs but hardly an opera, huge universities but hardly a scholar, you seem to meet only one man, the average man, of whom Ortega y Gasset wrote that he is "to history what sea level is to geography." Still, a small-state world may be reactionary. So, I presume, was the Kremlin's economic division of the Soviet Union into 17 sub-critical regions.

Finally, the division, or at least the decentralization, of great powers, which the size theory requires as a prerequisite to a social existence that is sound not because it would be without problems but because problems would once more be brought back to manageable proportions, is said to be *impractible*. Is it really? Yet social division has been practised for better or for worse as the principal device of every great organizer from the ancient Persians to the modern Germans; from Rome whose motto was *Divide and Rule*, not *Unite and Rule*, to the Vatican which has extended its sway across the world in the form of a finely spun network of small bishoprics rather than a few unmanageable sub-papacies; from Great Britain which disunited her kingdoms, into counties, to France which divided her duchies into *departments*. Is it really more impractical than the plan to sail a ship through space? Or the vision of statesmen who cannot divide a village but fancy giving us eternal peace?

II. Optimum Size

You may remember this cartoon. It shows a portly English Lord at breakfast table in one of his castle's many splendid rooms. Windows reach to the ceilings, and doors open on graceful Greek statues posed under Venetian chandeliers along seemingly endless flights of corridors fading into the distant reaches of the eye. Against this background of wealth, the Lord, slightly intrigued by an item in his morning paper but otherwise wholly unruffled, turns to his equally lordly and unruffled butler, asking casually: "I say, Bartholomew! Did you know that our East wing burned down last night?"

The cartoon well illustrates the problem of oversize. For a house so large that its own occupant has to rely on newspapers to learn what is going on in it, is obviously too big. But when is a house not too big? What is the proper or optimum size?

As in the case of all questions of size, the answer depends on the function a thing is supposed to fulfil. A structure may be a railroad terminal, a factory, a school, a wharf, a home. In the case of a home, the size determining function is to provide shelter. This does not mean, however, that the proper or optimum size of all homes must be the same. For differences in taste, temperament, and culture patterns give a wide elasticity to a person's concept of shelter. Diogenes thought its sole purpose was to protect his body from the vagaries of weather. So he considered anything larger than a barrel both superfluous and bothersome. A Medieval knight, on the other hand, thought a man's shelter should extend also to his family and friends. In addition, he wanted it to provide facilities for education, worship, hospitality, song, and sport, as well as protection from enemy attack. So his home was a castle.

While the concept of optimum size, though strictly defined for each individual, thus permits a wide range between these two extremes, there are nevertheless absolute limits beyond which a home becomes not only too small or too large but loses its function. It ceases to be a home. A structure smaller than a barrel becomes a coffin. One larger than a castle becomes a community. While still providing shelter for its occupants, it begins to socialize them as well. In terms of the preceding chapter, as a home its size has become critical.

The same principle applies to the size of society. For here, too, size is determined by function. The only difficulty is that our concept of the function of society is less clear than that of the function of a home. So before we can arrive at a concept of optimum *social* size, we must first ask ourselves: what exactly is the purpose for which man should have formed or joined a community? What benefits does he derive from it which he could not enjoy by living alone?

The Convivial Society. The first and, indeed, the founding function of society seems to be strictly convivial. Pre-social man could work alone, eat alone, and sleep alone. And, considering that, in his early pioneer existence, he would rarely encounter anyone but other solitary pioneers, his strength was sufficient to defend himself alone. But he could not enjoy company alone. This required others. The impulse driving him to the formation of his first societies was therefore in all likelihood his desire for companionship. This is why terms such as *social* or *society* are to this day endowed with both political and convivial meanings; or why such authors as Hesiod or Pausanias, intuitively still close to the beginnings of human development, envisioned the first social gatherings as convivial occasions in which gods and men were joined as table companions, Prometheus serving as host.

Theoretically, the convivial function could be satisfied by a society numbering no more than three or four individuals. However, seeing nothing but the same three or four faces would soon become unbearable. To fulfill the companionship function to the fullest, that is to ensure both variety of contacts and constancy of relationships, in addition to the upkeep of a communal meeting place such as a public house or commons, a membership of perhaps 80 to 100 may be necessary. A larger group would increase variety but hurt constancy. A smaller group would strengthen constancy but curtail variety. In addition it would make the individual share of maintaining the communal meeting place more burdensome. As far as the purpose of society is convivial, a membership of from 80 to 100 adults (a figure not much different from that of a well functioning club) might therefore be considered as constituting optimum social size.

The Economic Society. However, this picture is not quite complete. For, so that a hundred persons can enjoy each other's companionship more generously than perhaps once or twice a year, a society must almost simultaneously with its convivial role assume also an economic function. As long as each member must chase his own food, cook his own meals, build his own hut, mend his own shoes, weave his own cloth, till his own fields, he will be able to exist. But he will be so busy that he will have no time for convivial purposes even if surrounded by an otherwise large enough group. To liberate some of his time for convivial purposes, it is therefore essential that he increase his productivity. And to increase his productivity, he must specialize in activities in which he is particularly proficient, and then exchange his surplus product for that of other specialists.

But specialization requires a more numerous society than conviviality. If it takes a shoemaker one day to make a pair of shoes, and if one pair of shoes is worn out in a year, a society numbering 100 members would obviously be too small to support a specialized shoemaker. He would be idle and starve during 200 out of 365 days. Taking shoemaking as a typical activity, a society beginning to fulfill its economic function would therefore have to number about 365 adults or – if we make allowance for reduced working time and free holidays which specialization yields as the first and most cherished benefit of increased productivity – at least 300. But since a full and rich material life must also provide for children, and since not all commodities can be produced at the rate of one unit per day, economic *optimum* social size requires actually an adult membership of perhaps 1,000, or a full membership of 4,000 or 5,000 inhabitants – a little less than the population of present-day Andorra or Anguilla.

At this size, society seems capable of furnishing its members not only with most of the commodities we associate with a high standard of living, but also of surrounding each person with the margin of leisure without which it could not properly perform its original convivial function. This does not indicate that, contrary to our initial assumption, convivial and economic optimum social size are actually identical. Nor does it mean that the larger economic optimum can be accomplished only at the expense of sacrificing the smaller and more important convivial optimum. It merely means that one optimum economic society nourishes, let us say, ten optimum convivial societies, and that convivial societies cannot reach optimum size singly but severally in the form of a loosely knit federation.

The Political Society. But while specialization answers both the convivial and the economic optimum needs of a community, it breeds previously nonexisting complexities. For once man acquires his means of subsistence by exchanging goods, disputes begin to arise regarding their value. And once disputes arise, men joined convivially may come to blows. To preserve the benefits of their life in common, judicial and police authority must therefore be established. And since a prosperous society is likely to be attacked by envious neighbours, defence measures must be taken. But none of these new tasks – peace, justice, defence – can be discharged by individuals. As a result, just as the convivial function leads to the economic function, the economic function leads in turn to a third function which only society as a whole can perform – the political function.

To discharge this effectively, however, neither convivial nor economic optimum size is sufficient. For while the margin of leisure emerging from specialization relieves every person of part of his work, giving him time for enjoying the pleasures of convivium, it is too narrow to release anyone wholly. Since the discharge of the political function requires not only the maintenance of a communal meeting place but the full-time services of human agents, society cannot reach political optimum size before it has grown to the point where specialization begins to support an idling ring not only *around* individuals but also *of* individuals. For only when a sufficient number of individuals can be spared from participation in the chores of basic economic production, does it become possible to appoint from amongst them the judges, policemen, and soldiers necessary for the fulfillment of the political function of society (whose assumption, incidentally, implies the transformation of a stateless society into a state).

Thus, if economic optimum social size requires a population of around 1,000 adults, political optimum size will need one of around 1,500, or a full population of between 7,000 and 12,000 – a figure existing in such flourishing contemporary states as Andorra, Monaco, San Marino, or Liechtenstein.[1] At this size, the 150 to 200 persons needed for the tasks of peace, justice, and defence can be liberated without thereby depressing the level of individual living standards obtainable at the less costly smaller economic optimum. Once more, the larger optimum does therefore not need to come into conflict with the size requirements of a smaller optimum. For just as the seeming contradiction between convivial and economic optimum size resolved itself through the federal instead of the centralized pattern of growth, so does the contradiction between economic and political optimum size. Rather than stretching one economic society beyond its optimum to the proportions required by the political society, the number of economic societies, in the form of villages and cities, is multiplied until their total is large enough to constitute one flourishing political society, the state. In this way, the new political optimum is accomplished without affecting the optimum proportions of its several constituent economic societies.

The Cultural Society. The convivial society offers its members

---

[1] Strangely enough, most utopian authors envisioned similar populations for their perfect societies, varying in their estimates according to whether they had merely convivial-economic, or also political functions in mind. Plato thought a population of 5,040 was the best. Thomas More's towns held 6,000 families. Charles Fourrier's phalansteries contained 400 to 600 families or 1,500 to 1,600 individuals. Robert Owen's paralleiograms comprised 500 to 2,000 members, and Horace Greeley's associations from "some hundreds to some thousands."

companionship, the economic society – leisure and wealth; the political society – security. But if man is to enjoy the fullest measure of a good life, he must also have culture. True, culture is not created by society. It is created by individual poets, musicians, artists, and scholars. But society alone offers the environment which permits these individuals to exercise their talents. This leads to the fourth and last of the life enhancing functions which only society can perform – the cultural function.

As a result, the concept of optimum social size must once more be extended. For, populations of 7,000 to 12,000 may be large enough to furnish all the material amenities of life and, in addition, constitute vigorous political communities. But if we are to have theatres, galleries, museums, churches, universities, as well as the poets, composers, artists, and scholars to give them life and variety, our social enterprise must be capable of producing a second and deeper margin of leisure than is necessary if all we need is a reservoir from which to draw 200 policemen, soldiers, and judges.

The optimum cultural society will therefore require a membership from perhaps 50,000 to 200,000. The city states of ancient Greece, or of medieval Italy, Germany, and Flanders produced all the culture the heart could desire and the mind absorb with populations rarely exceeding 100,000. For at this figure, a society is statistically large enough to contain not only the greatest variety of talent but also the necessary number of ordinary citizens sufficiently interested in the variety of cultural offerings to provide for its material support.

As in the other cases, the larger cultural optimum size does not need to push the smaller political society suporting it beyond optimum limits. This in spite of the fact that the federal pattern of growth by duplication is less useful culturally than economically or convivially. For the concept of the political society implies sovereignty. It might therefore not be entirely satisfactory to have one opera or one university serving several political societies (though in the case of ancient Greece a number of sovereign city states actually did constitute a single cultural society with respect to a few common institutions such as language, oracles, or Olympic games.)

But fortunately, the concept of political optimum, unlike that of the economic or convivial optimum, is sufficiently elastic to permit a large enough extension to cover optimum size without affecting the optimal functioning of the political society. For though a community of a few hundred thousand members needs a somewhat larger political apparatus than a society of ten thousand, its social complexities do not grow at a rate that could not be offset *at this stage* by the more than proportionate growth of intellectual and economic resources which can still be made available by its now more numerous constituent economic societies. Thus while a society begins to fulfil its expected political function at a membership of around 10,000, it will still give optimum service at 200,000 and more.

The Optimum Society. However, this is about the size at which it is large enough to give man everything he expects from it. It gives him taverns symbolizing the convivial function; factories and market places symbolizing the economic function; courts, city halls, armories, symbolizing the political function; and finally theatres, churches, museums, universities, and stadia symbolizing the cultural function. Together they constitute the aggregate social function of providing man with the supreme content of Aristotle's *summum bonum,* the good life. And since there is nothing left that man could wish for, a society of about 200,000 can be thought to represent the ultimate concept of optimum social size.

Societies growing beyond this figure no longer can add significantly to human happiness. True, at larger size they can give us airplanes, cars, television sets. But these are principally size commodities, not happiness commodities, which we need only if our communities have grown so big that we can no longer reach the inn, the theatre, the market, the fields and streams simply by walking around the corner. From a personal point of view, larger societies are therefore not necessary.

Nor, however, are they necessarily detrimental. For though a community growing larger can no longer add to man's individual happiness, it does at first not detract from it. This indicates that the boundary of optium is in the nature of a ribbon rather than a sharp line. And the width of the ribon permits considerable stretching before it reaches the outer limit at which optimum size turns into critical size.

Optimum Extending Factors. The degree to which the boundary ribbon can be stretched depends on three variables connected, this time, not with any further function of society but with man's capacity to administer the original functions on an enlarged scale. One of these variables is technological, one educational, one organizational. During the Middle Ages, a society could not have extended its optimum far beyond a few hundred thousand without becoming critical. For its rising complexities would soon have grown to such proportions that proper administration could have been achieved only at the price of sacrificing the cultural and economic optimum. This is why smaller medieval societies developed faster than the larger ones.

With technological progress, however, tools came for the first time into the possession of the political administrator enabling him to extend his sway as economically over societies of, let us say, two or three million members as over pre-technological societies numbering two or three hundred thousand. When technology began to run into the barrier of diminishing social productivity, a second extension to perhaps five or six million became possible by improving the individual administrator's vision through education. When this, in turn, reached its limit considering that even the best education can enlarge our individual horizon only up to a point, one last boost to perhaps ten, twelve, or fifteen million could be achieved through integration and the organization of efficient team work. But this, too, had its limit. For once the team necessary to administer a growing social enterprise becomes itself so large that it can no longer be encompased by the vision of its presiding officer, any addition to the team would henceforth

OPTIMUM SIZE 21

not enhance but diminish administrative efficiency.[1] This being the case, the absolute limit to which a society can be extended beyond a membership of 200,000 or 300,000 without adversely affecting the optimum performance of its functions seems to be in the neighborhood of populations from 12 to 15 millions.[2]

Post Optimum Societies. This does not mean that societies cannot grow beyond this limit. What it means is that if they do, their size becomes critical; that further growth increases their complexities faster than man's ability to catch up with them. Continued administrative efficiency can therefore be maintained after this point only through either the distortion or the repression of one after the other of the original four social functions. First the political function, swelling now beyond its founding intent, leads to such curtailment of individual freedom that it ceases to be compatible with the *summum bonum*. For the proper material of an overgrown state is not the free but the organization man.

[1] By this figure is meant the population of a fully developed, centralized, administratively and technologically integrated society. In the absence of one or more of these qualifying conditions – if a society is for example highly decentralized (in which case the figure would apply to its subordinate units), or if integration, as in the great powers of the past, remains relatively tenuous and movements amongst its citizens consequently slow – the size of its populations can be much larger and yet not violate the demands of optimum. Thus, the same population of London, which now suffers severe overpopulation problems, enjoyed quite pleasant optimum conditions as recently as 50 years ago, when it was barely smaller in size but still living in a number of decentralized, socially almost selfsufficient communities. See in this connection the definition of the concept of social size on p. 8, the argument of chapter VII (*Velocity Theory of Population*), and the various attempts at defining the concept in E. A. G. Robinson, *The Economic Consequences of the Size of Nations*. London: Macmillan, 1960. – It should also be stressed that none of the figures above represents dogmatic magnitudes. Their significance lies not in their size but in the idea of limitation they imply.

[2] This point has been dramatically illustrated by the French management consultant V. A. Graicunas who, in the early 1930s, worked out the mathematical aspects of the gallopingly rising complexities of growing team size. "Just why," he wrote, "an executive already having four subordinates should hesitate before adding a fifth member to the group which he controls directly, becomes clear if it is realized that the addition not only brings twenty new relationships with him, but adds nine more relationships to each of his colleagues. The total is raised from 44 to 100 possible relationships for the unit, an increase in complexity of 127 per cent in return for a 20 per cent increase in working capacity." (Quoted from B. Y. Auger: *How to Run Effective Business Meetings*. New York: Grosset & Dunlap, 1964, pp. 21-22).

Secondly, culture must be starved. For whatever there is in creative talent must now be employed in the purely technical task of keeping the growing social enterprise from collapsing. At the third stage, when further growth, like cancer, leads to continuous crisis, the economic level of the citizen must be lowered to free the material product necessary for the now geometrically rising requirements of social survival. And lastly, when the internal pressures of oversize are joined by the external pressures emanating from equally large rival societies, even convivial leisure time may have to be sacrificed.[1] A structure such as a mankind-embracing world state could therefore be successfully maintained only if it were organized, if not like a beehive, at least like George Orwell's 1984.

However, long before this state is reached, social overgrowth begins to produce insensibly a change in social functions. As we suggested at the beginning of this chapter, when a home becomes larger than a castle, it ceases to be a home. Its new size changes its function as well as its nature. It becomes a community. Or as Aristotle points out in a well known analogy to the changing size of states: "There may be a ship of a certain size, either too large or too small, which will still be a ship, but bad for sailing." But "a ship which is only a span long will not be a ship at all, nor a a ship a quarter of a mile long."[2]

---

[1] The crescendo of claims on the citizen in post-optimum societies is well illustrated by the following three successive policy statements of three successive presidents of the United States. President Truman's Director of Defence Mobilization forecast in 1952 what the *New York Times* headlined in lapidary simplicity "Higher Production but 'severer' pinch." President Eisenhower followed this up with the consoling prospect that "there is no sacrifice – no labour, no tax, no service – too hard for us to support the logical and necessary defence of our freedom." Whose freedom? Clearly society's, not the citizen's for whom there is nothing left but labour, tax, and service – a triumvirate which has never before been associated with either a particularly high degree of freedom or a particularly high standard of living. And finally, President Kennedy has given the unpalpable truth the last in stylistic elegance when he told in his masterful inauguration address his sorely tried fellow Americans: "Ask not what the government can do for you. Ask what you can do for the government."

[2] *Politica*, VII, 4. The full text of Aristotle's analogy is as follows: "To the size of states there is a limit, as there is to other things, plants, animals,

Footnote continued overleaf

Similarly, a society outgrowing certain proportions will at first become a bad, or critical, society by the standards of its original purposes, and ultimately cease to be a society in the individualistic sense at all. For though it may still be called such, its functions will now be so different that it no longer fits its founding definition. The cultural society now becomes in turn a welfare society, a military society, perhaps a space or sputnik society, and finally – as was the case in even the most enlightened, cynical, and sophisticated mass states of antiquity – a divine society, the spark of divinity being lodged not in the individual but the group. Instead of serving the *summum bonum* of its members, it serves from now on the *summum bonum* of itself. But along with its new collectivist function emerges a new concept of optimum social size which, unlike the earlier individualistic optimum, has no limit. In fact, the more subject members it has, the better it is. Paradoxically, then, at the last stage of social overgrowth, a new concept of optimum is achieved. Moreover, being synonymous with the social maximum, this new optimum can never again be disturbed by growth. But the structure it reflects is no longer man's society but society's society – a corporate entity entirely divorced from the purposes of its members, a summit stage reached long ago by the bees.

In conclusion the preceding pages may be summarized in the following terms:

The size of society, as the size of everything, is determined by its function, and its function depends on whether we give it an individualistic or collectivist content. From an individualistic point of view, society must fulfil a fourfold purpose: ensure to

---

implements; for none of these retain their natural power when they are too small, but they either wholly lose their nature, or are spoiled. For example, a ship which is only a span long will not be a ship at all, nor a ship a quarter of a mile long; yet there may be a ship of a certain size, either too large or too small, which will still be a ship, but bad for sailing. In like manner a state when composed of too few is not, as a state ought to be, self-sufficing; when of too many, though self-sufficing in all mere necessaries as a nation may be, it is not a state, being almost incapable of constitutional government. For who can be the general of such a vast multitude, or who the herald, unless he have the voice of a stentor?"

its members companionship, prosperity, security, and culture. For these are the only four blessings man cannot obtain except by joining society. We may therefore distinguish between four individualistic societies – the convivial, economic, political, and cultural society. Each may exist separately, and each has its own optimum size. To enjoy the *summum bonum*, however, all four are needed. As history has shown and logic suggests, a society numbering from 100,000 to 200,000 members seems sufficient to furnish it.

A society of this size may therefore be said to constitute the relative optimum. Three factors – technological progress, education, organization – may, however, permit social growth beyond this figure to perhaps 15,000,000 without affecting optimum conditions. With this the outer or absolute optimum limit seems reached. Beyond this point optimum size turns into critical size, with social difficulties now tending to increase faster than the human talent necessary to cope with them, so that further growth can be sustained only at the price of diminishing the services connected with the original four social functions. Moreover, growth now not only begins to entail a distortion of functions but an insensible change from individualistic to collectivist purposes. The four individualistic societies are thus supplanted by collectivist societies such as the welfare, military, space, or divine society. Their purpose being social health, power, glory, conquest, empire, sputniks, or anything pleasing to their collectivist ego produce a new concept of social function, changing the original character of society. This, in turn, creates a new concept of optimum size which, unlike the individualistic optimum, can no longer be outgrown. For the collectivist optimum is synonymous with the maximum. A larger society is then not only automatically better than a smaller one; the larger is actually the best; the world state – the pinnacle of human accomplishment.

Why the farmer in his cottage, the fisherman by the pond, the father playing with his child, the poet admiring nature, the worker enjoying his beer, should require it in their pursuit of happiness is, however, another question.

III. Size and Living Standards

At a recent cocktail party, two middle-aged men became involved in conversation. One was a professor of economics at a major American University. The other was a professor of mechanical engineering at a famous Institute of Technology. Their talk touched upon both their fields. They discussed the economics of progress.

"How do *you* wash your nylon shirts?" asked the one.

"Very simply," answered the other. "I wash them with a nylon tooth brush. Nylon on nylon is very gentle. And it gets the smudges off collars and cuffs."

They also discussed plumbing, floor polishing, and cooking, glorying in the fact that progress had so simplified matters that all these things could be done by themselves. But in the end, one of them gave off an inadvertant sigh.

"Why the sigh," asked the other.

"Well," was the reply, "I thought that fifty years ago, we would have had maids. Instead of having to wash, plumb, and cook like unspecialized pioneers, we might have been better engineers and economists. Moreover, our shirts would have looked pressed, and our meals have tasted better. And instead of discussing housework at a party of scholars, we might have discussed our subjects."

1

The experience of the two professors is shared by an increasing number of people in all walks of life. On the one hand, we witness the gigantic pace of progress and continuously rising output figures. But on the other hand, we have the strange feeling that, instead of getting ahead , we have to give up every year something we could afford when, according to living-standard experts, we must have had less. When I was a student in the early 30s' I drove a racy sports car. As a university professor in America, with an income that ranges me according to my own textbooks into the upper 30% of the richest people on earth in the richest period of history, I managed to acquire in 1955 a 1937 model *Lasalle*, only to return to the use of a combination of bus and feet by 1956. And the income classes above me have fared still worse. Mr. DuPont, in a much publicized story a few years ago, had to abandon his palatial residence in Winterthur, Delaware. Now it is a museum, impressing the visitor with the high standards of Mr. DuPont's ancestors, not his own. Similarly, in England, Lord Halifax, at about the same time, had to give up his castle and move into his stable. Though this was hailed as a great victory of democratic living, all the story demonstrated was the existence of superior standards in the past, considering that the stable of then was found good enough to house a lord today.

However, it is said that, while the living standards of the upper strata of society have admittedly declined, those of the lower strata have risen. But have they? Where are the persons who have become richer as a result of Mr. DuPont having become poorer? On the contrary. Most have been carried along the same road: downhill. For as those who previously lived in palaces now live in houses, many of those who lived in houses now live in smaller ones or in appartments. Those who previously drank wine with their meals now drink water, and those who had maids now have none.

As to maids, it is said that their disappearance is precisely a sign not of declining but rising standards. For maids of former days are now housewives or business women. Quite. But why should maids have aspired to these higher levels except in the hope to have ultimately maids themselves? Yet, all they discovered was that, instead of escaping the chores of housework, they had to add to them. For, progress had given them not leisure but time to take on another job. As to housework, they still must do all themselves. Instead of having turned every maid into a housewife, progress has turned every housewife into a maid, with the difference that formerly she was at least paid for it.

And workers have fared only outwardly better. True, they have record incomes and record quantities of goods to spend them on. But if all is taken into account, can they really be said to be better off than workers of earlier times? They can write and read. But what is their main literature? The comics. They can send their children to college. But what has college education become under the levelling impact of intellectual mass production made necessary by the unprecedented numbers of those now able to afford it? Though the greater number of students has produced an ampler supply of professors, the very increase in teaching personnel has paradoxically become one of the principal causes not for the improvement but for the lowering of the level of academic offerings. As one of my colleagues, anxious to keep track of every development in his field, complained: "I read journals day and night. But so much is being written these days, that I have no time left to do any thinking myself." And what does the worker gain by the higher education of which we are so proud? Almost nothing. With so many other workers going to school, higher education, already intellectually sterile, seems even materially without added benefit, having become the competitive minimum requirement for almost any job.[1]

And so it is not only with many intangible but also with many tangible commodities which progress has showered on us. To an increasing extent they have assumed the character of *remedial* goods whose possession, instead of improving conditions, merely prevents them from becoming worse. They are like aspirin tablets, whose invention has certainly improved our headaches. But have they improved our health? Hardly, if one considers that the less harassed and less progressive earlier periods seem to have suffered not only from fewer aspirin tablets but also from fewer headaches.

[1] Comparing modern living standards with those of the past, it would occassionally be useful to remember periods dominated by men such as Lorenzo the Magnificent, of whom Pasquale Villari writes (*Life and Times of Savonarola*. New York: Charles Scribner's Sons, 1896, p. 45) that he "encouraged all the worst tendencies of the age and multiplied its corruption. Abandoned to pleasure himself, he urged the people to lower depths of abandonment in order to plunge them into the lethargy of intoxication. In fact, during his reign Florence was a continuous scene of revelry and dissipation." But surely, a time that could afford such revelry and lethargy of intoxication, at both princely and popular levels to say nothing of countless workfree saint's days, even the lowest beggar must have had a jollier time than the car and bathtub owning member of a modern labour union.

As a result, what has actually risen under the impact of the enormously increased production of our time is not so much the standard of living as the level of subsistence. We swim in more water, but we are still in it up to our necks. In addition, along with the rising water level, many who previously enjoyed the luxury of the dry shore, are now up to their neck in water too. Hence, the question is no longer whether we would be worse off without our supermodern electronic gadgets, our cars, radios, or television sets. They have become our swimming equipment. They are the remedy of the flood conditions we have created. The question is whether without them many of us could still exist at all. In other words we must produce the bulk of our fabulous 'progress' commodities in such record quantities not for the sake of progress but for the same reason earlier ages needed to produce much less: just to live.

2

Up to this point, the presentation of what might be called our *aspirin standard of living* has, perhaps, been too sweeping to be acceptable as more than at best an exaggerated generalization to be disproved once further economic growth will have accomplished the full transition to higher levels. I might not even be permitted to plead with Diogenes who "used to say that he followed the example of the trainers of choruses; for they too set the note a little high, to ensure that the rest should hit the right note". But even if it should be granted that there is a grain of truth in my portrayal: What about the dazzling nature of an array of recent production and consumption figures which convey so irrefutably the opposite impression?

It is because of this legitimate question that I must carry the analysis from generality to detail, from the surface to the root. In particular, the cause must be found explaining why, in the first place, the virtual decline of living standards is not merely a phenomenon of transition but the corollary of the very economic growth producing our dazzling output figures; and, secondly, why these figures may be correct, and yet convey a wrong impression.

In a superb study on the interrelationship of growth and form, the great English biologist W. D'Arcy Thompson has shown why nature puts a stop to the growth of things once they have become large enough to fulfil their function.[1] A tooth stops growing when it can effectively bite and chew. If it grew larger, it would violate its function. It would impede the organism it is meant to strengthen, and would have to be pulled out. Similarly a snail after having added a number of widening rings to the delicate structure of its shell, suddenly brings its building activities, to which it has now become accustomed, to a stop. For, as D'Arcy Thompson points out, a single additional ring would increase the size of the shell sixteen times. Instead of adding to the welfare of the snail, it would burden it with such an excess of weight that any increase in its productivity would henceforth be absorbed by the task of coping with the added difficulties created by enlarging the shell beyond the limits set by its purpose. Moreover, since from that point on the problems of overgrowth begin to multiply at a geometric ratio while the snail's productive capacity can at best be extended at an arithmetic ratio, it follows that, once overgrowth sets in, the snail will never be able to catch up with the added problems created by it.

This is the fundamental philosophic reason why there is a limit to all growth. Though highly beneficial up to a certain point, beyond it, it not only becomes life's chief complexity; it becomes nature's principal tool by which it leads its organism to obsolescence and destruction.

But nature puts limits to growth not only on its biological organisms. In particular, it puts them also on its social organisms such as firms, cities, or states. The only difference is that natural instincts which guide the behaviour of animals have become so dulled in the case of the human species as a result of educational sophistication and mechanical progress, that the social and economic implication of the limiting principle imposed on growth by function and form is not grasped with half the lucidity with which

---

[1] W. D'Arcy Thompson, *On Growth and Form*. Cambridge University Press, 1942.

it has long been recognized in its bioligical context. Hence the constant emphasis with which the bulk of our political and economic theorists continue to stress the need for further growth in spite of the handwriting on the wall that has been warning the world since the 1940's that the problem for the developed part of the globe is no longer one of how to *foster* growth but how to *stop* it.[1]

For just as the tooth or the shell of the snail are determined by the function they are meant to fulfil, so is the size of a firm, of a city, or a state. As I have tried to show in the preceding chapter, the social function of a thing may have different aspects according to whether our philosophy is collectivist or individualist. However, since living standards are meaningful only in an individual context, we may dismiss the collectivist aspect from this analysis. And as to its individualistic implication, we need but re-state the previously cited Aristotelian idea that, the function of the state is not expansion or glory but to provide the individual citizen with the essence of the good life, the *summum bonum*.

In other words, once a society has become large enough to furnish the convivial, economic, political and cultural needs of man in satisfactory, though not necessarily gluttonous, abundance – leisure to think, taverns to debate, churches to pray, universities to teach, theatres to inspire, the arts to enchant – further growth can no longer add to its basic purpose. We have reached the point of diminishing living standards. In Aristotle's terms, this is represented by the largest number of a population "which suffices for the purposes of life, and can be taken in at a single view."[2]

---

[1] I admit that a number of social theorists have recently joined the cry *against* growth. Indeed it has become fashionable to berate the Roman cardinals for insisting, in the age of exploding populations, on opposing contraception merely because they opposed it in earlier centuries when the practice would have led to the extinction of the human race because of the high death rates then existing. But aside from the cardinal-bashers, the voices warning against further growth which have begun to emerge since the early 1970's (E. J. Misham of the London School of Economics, Professor Meadows and his team from M.I.T., and especially Dr. E. F. Schumacher in his *Small is Beautiful*), can still be counted on the fingers of two hands. See in this connection also Colin Clark's *Growthmanship* (London: Hobart Papers, No. 10, 1962), and Schumacher's earlier writings in the 1960's in *Resurgence*.

[2] Aristotle, *Politica:* VII, 3.

This does not mean that the optimum limit of society is a rigid magnitude. As the preceding chapter has shown, it is subject to modification in proportion to man's ability to enlarge his administrative vision. In Antiquity or during the Middle Ages, the Aristotelian optimum was probably confined to cities and states containing between 20,000 and 500,000 inhabitants. This amounts to a population whose entire voting citizenship could be seated in a single theatre. It could therefore at all times be kept fully informed of the affairs of state by orators whose voice was capable of reaching the last seat. In our time, the three size extending factors of education, administrative integretation, and technological progress particularly in the field of communication have extended this limit to populations up to perhaps 10 or 15 millions. But wherever the exact point of diminishing living standards may now lie, one thing is certain: it still is located within the relatively narrow boundaries set by the small stature of man: by what he can take in "at a single view." Once this point is passed, further growth of a community will add not to its individualistic function of providing its members with the good life but to the collectivist function of maintaining itself for its own reason. And the individual, instead of being assisted by further social growth, will henceforth be impeded by it

Ancient Greece – which, with its emphasis on the individualistic purpose of existence, has given Western man the essence of his civilization – had its political instincts finely attuned to the question of optimum size. As a result, whenever a state reached the point of diminishing living standards, a delegation would be sent to the Delphic Oracle and, after the rendering of due sacrifices and the deposition of appropriate gifts, Apollo would communicate the following advice through the mouth of his priestess: "Cut trees. Build ships. Man them with young women and men. Then send them forth to found new cities across the seas." There, growth could set in anew until the maturing societies could produce once again in creative competition with mother and sister lands the prerequisites of the good life – inns, theatres, universities.

In more recent times, however, the Greek way was no longer so easy to duplicate, considering that the world's supply of available territory had in the meantime nearly come to an end. As a result human societies, instead of growing in the biological way by splitting, duplicating and multiplying, have long begun to grow in the cancerous way of expansion and integration. Instead of becoming more numerous in order to keep the size of the state adjusted to the small stature of man, they have become fewer and larger.

At first, this process did not greatly interfere with the continued development of higher personal levels of living.[1] For the simultan-

---

[1] Before the point of what may be called 'diminishing social productivity' is reached, social expansion and its resulting increase in both government and private investment will always result in a corresponding increase in consumption spending and consumer enjoyment, indicating that up to this point social and personal welfare are complementary. More guns will also furnish more butter. Beyond that point, however, the two become mutually exclusive. Then it is a question of either guns *or* butter, of increasing either national of personal welfare. Since an overgrowing society cannot afford to forgo the former, it must necessarily sacrifice the latter, causing thereby a gradual and inevitable decline in *personal* living standards in spite of increasing production and *social* consumption. Most great powers have already passed that point. The question is whether the rich United States has passed it too. The as yet all too incomplete figures seem to indicate that, if she has not passed it, she seems to have been closely pressing against it since 1944. Analyzing changes in total personal consumption in relation to changes in gross national product between 1939 and 1951, it is interesting to see that relative to the increasing rate of increasing national product the rate of consumption increase was declining and that, since 1944, the two have actually begun to move inversely, showing increasing total consumption only when national product, as a result of attempted reduction of national power, was temporarily reduced through curtailment of government spending. To obtain an objective picture, more years will have to be compared so that temporary trends may be separated from long-term development. Yet, even a comparison of only the preceding and following decade puts the years 1944-1945 into such a peculiar relief that the possibility cannot be outruled that these two years represent indeed the dividing line at which the United States has reached the point of diminishing social productivity, sometimes going beyond, sometimes falling below, but always hovering so close that, considering the general social and political forces influencing economic development, a significant reverse trend seems unlikely. For more detailed figures see appended table on p. 46. – P.S. Working on the figures used above and in the appended table in the early 1950's I have not taken the trouble to carry them into the 1970's to bring them up to date, considering that the subsequent years have confirmed the assumption that 1944-45 represent historically the great divide, and my purpose was to locate the crest of the development, not to follow it downhill.

eous advance of technology, accompanied in addition by improvements in techniques of social administration, made it for a time possible to keep abreast of the rapidly multiplying problems of unrestrained social growth. But with no *biological* law to check continued *social* growth, and with political instincts deteriorating in proportion as social complexes became larger and more difficult to encompass, the limit had sooner or later to be reached at which the different growth ratios governing social problems and human talent became caught in the same insoluble discrepancy which Thomas Malthus had assigned to the relationship between increasing populations and food supply. For, as in the case of the shell, once optimum size was exceeded, each arithmetic increase in the size of the community tended to produce a geometric increase in the magnitude and number of the community's problems, without being able to furnish a corresponding increase in technological facilities and administrative talent to keep up with them. Not even an Oxford or Harvard education could compensate for the pace at which, beyond a given social development stage, problems began to outrace their solutions.

There was only one way left by which, at least temporarily, the overgrowing political complexes of our time could be spared disintegration under the impact of their increasing growth problems. This was by reducing the share of the citizen's production which previously could be retained by him to serve his own *summum bonum,* and making it instead available to a government whose powers had to be increased in proportion as human administrative talent fell behind. The new *summum bonum* was therefore no longer that of the citizen but of society as a whole, with the paradoxical result that, the more splendid the social apparatus became after having outgrown the form and size best suited for sheltering the individual, the poorer became the individual. The more he produced, the less could be left in his hands for his enjoyment. For states are like skyscrapers. The taller the latter become, the larger becomes the *social* space (occupied by lifts, stairs, etc.) necessary for keeping the structure serviced, and the smaller becomes the *personal* space available for individual purposes. In the end, if a building were to rise on the area of a city block to a height of 400 floors, there would be neither office nor living space left at all. For, as architects have calculated, the entire structure would then have to be occupied by lifts in order to transport the people who could dwell or work in it if the lifts would not have robbed them of all space. One might also use the example of our giant jumbo jets whose capacity could be enlarged only if every seat could serve as toilet at the same time. The greater capacity would be most impressive, but hardly indicative of a higher standard of travel.

3

That much as to the philosophic argument supporting the proposition set forth in the first few pages of this chapter. It explains why the experience of a declining living standard felt by so many citizens of the seemingly most advanced and powerful societies is not a phenomenon of transition, to be *conquered* by further growth, but a phenomenon of growth, to be *aggravated* by it, and it explains why the rate at which living standards decline varies from country to country. What I have stated with particular reference to great powers such as the United States or Great Britain, is not half as manifest in smaller powers such as Canada. In fact, in the case of the latter, the descent to lower levels might be averted altogether if the government were to put a stop to the integrated growth of its federally loosened society before letting it fuse across the limits of optimum size set by provincial subdivisions. And it need not at all occur in such happy smaller states as Switzerland or Iceland, whose cantonal structure and narrow political boundaries automatically insure optimum size as long as their governments continue to resist the lures and dangers of excessive economic integration.[1]

---

[1] Social growth takes place either through the influx of new populations or, as pointed out before, through the centralization, integration, and the attendant increasing velocity of existing ones. One way of preserving

But what about the figures? Philosophic deductions to the contrary, these show not only an increase of net national product proportionate to the increasing size and needs of great powers, but also an increase in national income and national consumer expenditures. And they still show these increases to a dramatic extent on a per capita basis, and after rising price levels and population changes have been taken into account. As a result, it would appear that, though beyond a certain point of social expansion a continuously rising proportion of increasing national output may have to be diverted to the support of society as a whole, enough is left to improve, even if only at a declining rate, also the position of the individual.

And yet, in spite of the dramatic rise particularly in the field of per capita consumption, the portrait of improvement conveyed by it is highly misleading. Not that the figures are wrong, by any means. The error arises from the fact that they are not broken down into more significant and revealing categories. For not all consumer goods can be included in living standard computations. Many of them must actually be subtracted if they are to give proper information, since their increased consumption measures our multiplying complexities rather than our advance in well being.

A more realistic picture of living standards depends therefore on a new commodity breakdown. In the first place, we must distinguish between two general categories of goods: *social* and

---

optimum social size in the midst of growing populations is therefore through decentralization. A federal structure greatly facilitates this. The present Canadian population of 22 million inhabitants, spread across half of North America, would undoubtedly be too large to be administered centrally without a disproportionately costly government. It is not too large in its present division into ten provinces. And if decentralization and federalization are permitted to continue as the population rises, the optimum size of Canada's population, divided into an increasing number of highly autonomous provinces (perhaps 20 or 30 in the place of the present ten), might be extended far beyond present limitations. If, on the other hand, the American example of increasing national unification and integration is followed, the consequences of slowly declining living standards will be as inevitable as those experienced in the United States.

personal consumer goods.[1] Social consumer goods — goods consumed by society to maintain its political and economic apparatus, and represented by government expenditures at all levels as well as by a large proportion of private investment expenditures — may, however, be largely discounted in this analysis since they measure not personal but social standards. In addition, being largely paid for by taxes, they are so clearly idenidentifiable as not the fruit but the cost of existence that there is no danger of having their greater availability confused with greater welfare. Nevertheless they are indirectly of significance since their seemingly geometric rise with every arithmetic increase in the size of a state is responsible for the declining proportion of increasing output that can be diverted into personal channels. Since their ratio of increase depends on the increasing size and power of societies, social consumer goods might also be called *growth* or *power commodities*. They are remedial in nature. Their hallmark is that their production does not improve the status of the individuals producing them. Examples of such commodities are: general government services needed to administer increases in power,[2] safety, traffic, and police services; and particularly military expenditures whose geometric relationship to social size is clearly indicated if we compare, for example, the defence figures of various countries according to their size.[3] The production increase accomplished by the Unitel States between 1950 and 1951 in the area of power commodities alone, as

[1] Though goods consumed by society, either for maintaining government or for building, maintaining, and expanding capital needed to feed private consumption, are not usually referred to as consumer goods, the term is useful in modern living standard analysis to emphasize the similarity between the natural personality of the individual and the corporate personality of the state. It is increasingly the latter that reaps the chief advantages of material progress.

[2] An item which could be mentioned here is the cost of increasingly distant airports becoming necessary as a result of the rising power of both Russia and U.S. According to the Senate Preparedness Subcommittee, American workers taken to Greenland to build the airbase at Thule were paid $3,000,000 in wages before they even reached the site.

[3] According to figures compiled in 1956, the following countries, approximately though not quite arranged in the order of side, spent the following percentages of their Gross National Product on defence: Luxembourg, 3.9%; Denmark, 3.9%; Belgium, 4.4%; Norway, 4.7%; Italy,

expressed in government expenditures, amounted to no less than 18 billion dollars, or 72% of the much-advertised 25 billion dollar increase of our total national product of the same period. This means that nearly three fourths of the fruit of our production increase was consumed by the unparalleled needs of our power.[1]

The most important category of commodities for a meaningful living standard analysis is, however, the category of *personal consumer goods*. For if the latter registers an increase on a per

---

4.8%; Portugal (and its empire), 5.1%; Greece, 7.2%; Netherlands, 7.4%; Turkey, 8.0%; France, 8.1%; Canada, 8.8%; United Kingdom, 10.1%; United States, 11.6%. In terms of billions of dollars, the progression is even more evident if we take a characteristic series of countries: Luxembourg, .01; Belgium, .27; Canada, 1.62; France, 3.13; United Kingdom, 4.58; the United States. 40.54. Canada, twice as large as Belgium, spent four times as much on defence. The United States, a little more than three times as large as Great Britain, spent ten times as much. A similar phenomenon of disproportionately rising social costs can be seen if we compare cities of various sizes. According to Professors Schultz and Harris (*American Public Finance*. New York: Prentice-Hall, 1949, p. 34), city expenditures were found to be "directly and closely related to population, increasing steadily with the size of the population." As reasons for this is mentioned the fact that "increasing density of urban and suburban population also necessitates special 'remedial' public functions. City crowding breeds problems of sanitation, crime, social welfare, and traffic, which are less pressing in the country side. . . Some of the cost of city government results from 'remedial' functions that ward off the social disadvantages of urban growth rather than confer added social benefits." Minor unevennesses in the series cited in this footnote are due to conditioning factors such as war consequences, which space limitations prevent explaining. The fact that figures are drawn from studies made in the 1940's and 50's does not affect their continued relevance in the 70's. The relationships they illustrate are still the same.

[1] As to the argument that the period of 1950-1951 represents an exceptional rise in government expenditures due to exceptional defence outlays, it would seem that, in spite of the subsequent insignificant though overemphasized reductions, *high and increasing defence expenditures will in future not be exceptional but normal considering that the danger of war resulting from the uneasy balance maintained by the two overgrown political entities of East and West will henceforth be the normal and not the exceptional condition dominating the world.* To judge from all similar historic two-power constellations, it would seem more plausible to consider as exceptional the optimistic illusion (prevailing between 1945 and 1950 as a result of unwarranted peace hopes, and in 1954 as a result of our excessive reliance on the economy of atomic defence) that occasional reductions in defence spending could in future ever be maintained again for any length of time. — Instead of updating my figures of the early 1950's, when the article was written on which this chapter is based, I am italicizing the conclusions then drawn from them to indicate that not an iota needs to be changed for arriving at a description of the situation prevailing in 1976, or 1984 for that matter.

capita basis, it becomes, at least theoretically possible to deduce that also the living standard has risen. But even then, the conclusion is not automatic, since greater personal consumption is not necessarily a sign of better living. If changed social conditions force a person to walk twice as far to his place of work, the availability of a second pair of shoes can hardly be said to have made him any richer.

As a result, if we are to bring the problem into its proper focus, it is necessary to resort to a further breakdown of personal consumer goods into the well-known sub-categories of *necessities* and *luxuries*. But since the increase in necessity consumption merely reflects an increase in our needs, the only truly relevant category for living standard appraisals is that of *luxury commodities*. In other words, the goods measuring our welfare are not goods *within* the subsistence level, but the changing quantities of goods available to us *above* it.[1]

But here the principal difficulty sets in. For, what are luxuries? Mathematically, the answer would be simple. Luxuries are total personal consumer goods minus necessities, just as luxury

[1] It may be said that living standard appraisals must take account not only of improvements above but also within the subsistence level: that the acquisition of an electric stove or a vacuum cleaner, even though they may now be considered essentials, has nevertheless left the housewife in a position of greater comfort. At first this is undoubtedly true, but as long as it is true such goods qualify as luxuries and are located above the subsistence level. But modern life has a tendency to find soon a substitute burden the moment an improvement has reduced the burden in another area, insensibly translating the previous luxury into a now indispensible necessity so that, once the cycle of improvement is completed, the person concernd is often just as deep in chores as before. What he has gained in working less in the improved field, he has lost by having increased the number of work fields. Two housewives, Jane Whitbread and Vivian Cadden, have, in a humorous way, well described the doubtful blessing of working just as hard, but on a higher level, when they write in *The Intelligent Man's Guide to Women*, (New York: Schuman, 1951) that every laboursaving device of the past century has added to women's work. . A man invents a vacuum cleaner and . . . a co-conspirator popularizes Venetian blinds, so there will be something else for the vacuum cleaner to do in a jiffy. A man turns out a simple little mechanism to make melon balls, and it's no longer *comme il faut* to toss a plain hunk of melon into a fruit salad. In the period when beer came in kegs, the man of the house hauled it himself. Now that it comes in handy little cans, even a woman can lug a dozen from the delicatessen. The man who speeds by a woman, stopped by a flat tyre, can't be accused of lack of chivalry. He knows that the way they make jacks these days, even a woman can change a tyre."

consumption is total personal consumption minus subsistence level consumption. But mathematics does not tell us what is meant by subsistence level. For just as it cannot define the concept of luxury, so it cannot define the concept of necessity.

However, where mathematics fails, logic may succeed. All that is needed to discern the elusive boundary between luxuries and necessities is to carry the process of categorization one step further. For necessities can again be subdivided into three kinds, two of them long familiar. In the first place, there are the *biological* necessities, such as food, clothes, and shelter. Without them, physical survival is impossible. Secondly, there are the *cultural* necessities imposed by social environment, such as the *style* of food, clothes, and shelter. An example of the former would be a coat or a raw chicken, of the latter a tie or a cooked meal. As already men such as Petty, Ricardo, Marx, Pigou, or Heller have pointed out, it is due to the changing nature of the second category that the socially imposed subsistence level may be pushed upwards, and that consumption may rise above biological requirements, without indicating a rise in living standards.[1]

But there is a heretofore neglected third category whose existence explains why consumption may rise above both biological and cultural necessities, and still not entail a rise in living standards. The necessities of this third category, resulting from the technological difficulties caused by the scale and density of modern life, might be called *technological* necessities or *density*

This is perhaps an exaggerated picture. But similar experiences seem to be shared by so many, that a detailed study and reappraisal of the entire living-standard problem, as suggested in this chapter, would seem highly revealing even if it were to contribute nothing to the solution of the question.

[1] Karl Marx, in *Value, Price and Profit*. Chicago: Kerr, pp. 116-119, and A. C. Pigou, in *The Economics of Welfare*. London: MacMillan, 1938, pp. 758-767. I have made little reference to Marx, Pigou, Heller and others who dealt with the question of changing subsistence levels or minimum standards as both the basis of my argument and my conclusions are quite different from theirs. The theory advanced in this chapter tries to analyze the phenomenon of the rising subsistence level primarily against the background of the physical overgrowth of the social unit, not of the growing demand for additional minimum comforts on the part of workers as suggested by the others.

commodities. And these have become the most significant of all. For while cultural necessities were responsible for introducing the concept of a rising subsistence level, density commodities are responsible for the acceleration of that rise. It is primarily due to them that, in spite of the increase in overall consumption, the line, beyond which luxurious ease sets in, is constantly receding, and that the luxury margin, in spite of increased overall production, is constantly diminishing.

Typical examples of density commodities which, in contrast to the aforementioned power commodities, swell our *personal* consumption figures without adding to our welfare are: driver's licences, signal lights on cars, urban parking space, commuter services, a large part of what *Punch* has called *stimulants for self,* not all but a major proportion of privately purchased legal and medical services, or replacement goods for wear and losses such as would never have occurred in less harassed smaller societies. To have an idea of the magnitude of the increasing consumption of unwanted density commodities, we need but bring a few facts before our eyes. Replacements rendered necessary in 1950 as a result of fire losses in the United States, for example, amounted to almost $7,000,000,000.[1] Costs caused by the nine million casualties of the same year — of which 35,000 were fatal car accidents, more than the loss of life incurred in many a major war — to $7,700,000,000.[2] Private medical costs amounted in 1953 to $10,200,000,000,[3] though not all of them can be classified as

[1] *Facts & Trends,* National Board of Fire Underwriters, Vol. VIII, No. 4.
[2] *National Safety Council Report,* 1950. The connection between the size of a country's population and the loss in health and life seems to emerge with particular clarity also from a survey conducted in 1951, showing that in the United States the "death rate as a whole is one of the world's lowest, but after the age of 45, Americans cannot expect to live as long as their contemporaries in many other countries, e.g., England, Canada, the Netherlands, and especially Denmark and Norway. . . A dig into the records shows that American men have more fatal accidents and more heart disease. American women have more accidents, more diabetes." *Time,* December 3, 1951). Though the survey does not stress the point, it is highly revealing that the order in which the countries are mentioned as relatively better off in this respect, "especially Denmark and Norway," coincides with their decreasing populations: United States (230,000,000), Great Britain (56,000,000), Canada (22,000,000), the Netherlands (13,000,000), Denmark (5,000,000), and Norway (4,000,000).
[3] New York Times, January 24, 1954.

density expenditures. And the annual repair work resulting from driving cars in the dense streets of the City of New York was reputedly in excess of $1,000,000,000 at a time when the entire budget of the State of New York, then the largest of the union, was still below that figure.

4

As a result of the preceding considerations, it seems clear that the existing method of evaluating living standard changes has lost much of its usefulness. It was satisfactory as long as societies were within optimum size. Up till then, additional economic growth meant indeed that much of the new product could be made available for increased personal consumption not only within but also above the subsistence level. Once they developed beyond optimum to critical size, however, increased consumption ceased to reflect changes in living standard levels. It could now just as well be a sign of worsening as of improving conditions.

To obtain a correct measure of our wellbeing, a new measure must therefore be developed which emphasizes changes not in total consumption but in luxury consumption. For only changes in the latter reveal with precision whether we move upwards or downwards. Since it is luxuries which really count, the new living standard measure might therefore, in anology to a thermometer, be called a *luxometer*. Relevant changes would be expressed in degrees of *luxes* rather than in percentages, a *lux* representing a unit of above subsistence level consumption.[1]

But to arrive at a workable concept of luxury, it is important, as we have seen, to subtract from total consumption not only biological and cultural necessities, but above all the heretofore neglected category of technological necessities or *density commodities*. Unlike the other two categories, which are both needed *and* desired, they exert an undisguised depressing effect

---

[1] The *lux* unit is based on the same idea underlying the unit of the recently developed *discomfort scale* which, instead of confining itself to temperature which expresses only heat, measures the more meaningful degrees of comfort which is a composite of heat and humidity – an infinitely more relevant concept of human well-being.

since they are needed *without* being desired. The only difficulty is one of definition. For, most density commodities such as travel services, cars, or *stimulants for self*, set out as luxuries before social overgrowth transformes them into headache-producing necessities. And, depending on the density, integration, and technological development of a society, the transition from one to the other category may take place at quite different times. A car may be a necessity in one region and a luxury in another, even within the same country.[1] However, just as a zoologists have no difficulty discerning when a caterpillar becomes a butterfly, so economists, psychologists, and statisticians should have no difficulty to discern the time and place at which a good turns from luxury into necessity.

Once density commodities are properly evaluated, and a new breakdown of consumer expenditures on lines suggested in these pages is adopted, an entirely different living standard picture will emerge. We may then be able to tell that, while consumption may have increased by, let us say 10%, our living standard may at the same time have declined by 3 *luxes*. Moreover, we shall be able to discover not only the functional but also the exact economic location of the point of diminishing living standards. It is reached whenever subsistence level consumption begins to rise faster than total personal consumption, or when *percentage* changes of personal consumption begin to move inversly with changes in *luxes*.[2]

[1] Many goods which have become necessities in the United States are still luxuries in Switzerland, with the paradoxical result that their diminishing availability in the latter may indicate a better life than their abundance in the former. Also climate and other differences between countries and regions are of significance in determining the nature of the transition from luxury to density commodities but, other things being equal, none more so than effective social size as expressed by population number, density, integration and velocity.

[2] The new measurement which I suggeseed originally in 1952, and elaborated in two articles, "Towards a New Measurement of Living Standards" (*The American Journal of Economics and Sociology*, October 1955), and "The Aspirin Standard," (*Business Quarterly*, Summer 1956) is not unlike the one proposed in the early 1970's by Professors James Tobin and William D. Nordhaus of Yale University. As the *New York Times* of July 23, 1973, reports: "By juggling the ingredients of G.N.P. they have fashioned a new index called MEW or Measure of Economic Welfare" rather than

5

But will this not destroy many an illusion? Undoubtedly. This should however not detract us from the introduction of a new method of measurement. For once it provides us with facts instead of illusions, we may turn it to good account. Being able to discover a community's point of diminishing living standards, we shall be in a position to call a halt to further development instead of pushing it over the crest. This does not mean that stagnation should then be cultivated. It merely means that, beyond that point, growth should be fostered along ancient Greek lines, in the biological way, through splitting, multiplication, duplication, not through integration or unification — the great modern ideals.

In a country like Canada, as yet full of vast unexploited regions, the conditions for such a development of growth without the danger of depressing living standards are still great. A tool such as the *luxometer* would therefore be a highly useful instrument, helping to determine when optimum size is reached in a given province, and when subdivision should take place. In countries such as most of the world's great powers, where the point of diminishing standards has already been passed,[1] the road of regional rather than centralized development, with the possibility of entering another era of rising living levels, will be more difficult to pursue. For, ingrained trends of thought have for too long stressed that progress and salvation lie in the opposite direction.

---

of mere quantitave outputs. "Still very tentative, MEW has more recently been endowed with a certain legitamacy by Paul A. Samuelson, the Nobel-Prize winning economist" who included MEW in the 1973 edition of his famous textbook "and, with his flair for phrases, redubbed it NEW for Net Economic Welfare," which is the same as I express by the term LUX. The only difference is that neither MEW nor NEW takes into account the vital concept of size or density commodities which suggests that, if future living standards are to become higher, states and nations must be made smaller. However, with men like Samuelson recruited behind the idea, the *N.Y. Times* is right by saying: "We are going to hear a lot more about NEW." And about LUX too, I hope.

[1] See table and diagram on pp. 45 and 46.

But also here, the *luxometer* should prove a useful tool. For in spite of their love of integration, even the great powers have shown signs of awaking to the deeper designs of nature. Some of their giant firms have begun to abandon their monolithic structures in favour of smaller regional development. Cooperative enterprises have gained ground with their emphasis on local rather than national or world markets. And the idea of decentralization and devolution has almost become acceptable,[1] if not as targets of action, at least as legitimate subjects of debate.

This suggests that even the big powers have become mindful that greater degrees of unification and integration are no longer the answer to everything. But there is as yet no firm policy behind their groping since, in the absence of a sharper analytical tool, the connection between growing social size and declining living standards is still far from being properly understood. A new scale of measuring welfare would bring this into the open. But while it might not enable the great powers to move back to a position of actually rising standards, the information gained by it might lead to patterns of economic and political organization which could at least prevent there further deterioration.

---

[1] Characteristically, when the Ford Motor Company of England got ready for Britain's entry into the Common Market, it did not, as one might have assumed lay the ground for joining *Taunus*, its German sister company. It split itself into 5 self-contained 'profit centres' in order to increase, not diminish, its chance to survive competition from the smaller and therefore highly efficient Continental manufacturers. This is similar to the proposal of Robert Margolin, former Vice-President of the Common Market (referred to in Chapter VIII), that the larger members of the European Economic Community, now fused in their colossal enterprise, should likewise be split into small self-contained profit-centers in the form of regions not exceeding 5 million inhabitants. (See in this connection my article in *Cambridge Opinion*, November 1962).

SIZE AND LIVING STANDARDS 45

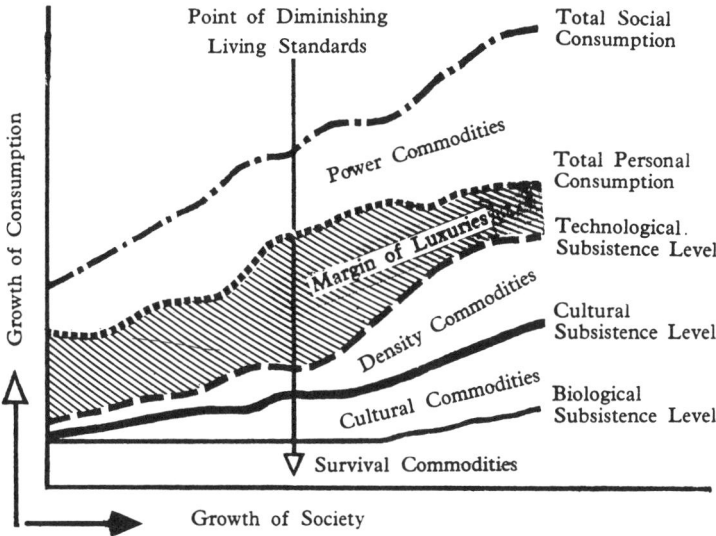

The diagram shows the changing ratios at which the various segments of total national product are consumed. Up to the point of diminishing living standards, increased national product (total social consumption) indicates the possibility not only of rising overall personal consumption but of rising per capita luxury consumption as well. The level of living improves. But beyond it, the picture changes. Under the combined pressure of now disproportionately rising socially consumed power commodities from above, and of personally consumed density commodities from below, the margin of luxuries becomes narrower in spite, and partly because, of an increase in overall production and consumption. Discounting power commodities, the crux of all the mystery of declining living standards in the midst of rising consumption thus lies in the disproportionate rise in density consumption which sets in when population numbers, technological advance, and population movement (velocity) have pierced the boundary of optimum development. — The diagram above is applicable to all countries. But not all have developed beyond the point of diminishing living standards. In addition, smaller countries, unless they adopt excessive programmes of social glory, never need to go beyond it in the first place. As a result, the part of the diagram located to the right of the line of diminishing living standards applies really only to large scale societies. Of these, the United States and Great Britain seem, on the basis of available figures, almost certainly to have passed this line. But since this happened only recently, in the United States probably between 1945 and 1950 (see table on following page), little mental adjustment has been made so far to permit a proper appraisal of the new situation. The steady downward development is therefore still often considered as merely temporary though everything indicates its permanent nature. — As long as the point of diminishing living standards has not been passed, one may say that the closer a country is to it, the better. When it is at the point of passing, as is perhaps the case in Canada, growth through division and duplication rather than through integration may postpone the need of crossing if for a very long time. Where, as in Great Britain, the point has been passed, federal devolution suggests itself for halting the downward trend.

Table 1.

Year	Gross Nat. Prod.	Pers. Cons. Exp.	Increase in Gross Nat. Prod.	Increase in Pers. Cons. Exp.	Percentage Increase in Gross Nat. Prod.	Percentage Increase in Pers. Cons. Exp.	Per Capita Disp. Inc.	Per Capita Cons. Exp.	Total Gvmt. Exp.	Defence Expend.	Cost of Society	Percentage Cost of Society
	1	2	3	4	5	6	7	8	9	10	11	12
1939	179.3	129.4	15.4	7.1	9.3	5.7	1,027	988	28.8	2.7	49.5	27.8
1940	197.3	137.0	18.3	7.6	10.2	5.8	1,089	1,037	30.5	4.9	60.3	30.5
1941	229.6	147.6	32.3	10.6	16.6	7.7	1,237	1,106	46.7	25.2	82.0	35.7
1942	262.4	145.5	32.8	-2.1	14.2	-1.4	1,381	1,079	100.3	81.5	116.9	44.5
1943	296.6	149.3	34.2	3.8	13.0	2.6	1,413	1,092	143.7	121.1	147.3	49.6
1944	320.0	155.3	23.4	6.0	7.8	4.0	1,477	1,122	159.5	144.2	164.7	51.4
1945	309.4	165.6	-10.6	10.3	-3.3	6.6	1,454	1,183	135.2	120.6	143.8	46.4
1946	272.9	184.1	-36.5	18.5	-11.7	11.7	1,409	1,301	43.4	25.3	88.8	32.5
1947	271.5	188.6	-1.4	4.5	-0.5	10.0	1,339	1,308	35.5	14.5	82.9	30.5
1948	280.4	191.9	8.9	3.0	32.7	1.6	1,386	1,309	42.4	18.1	88.5	31.9
1949	280.1	196.6	-0.3	4.7	-0.1	2.4	1,363	1,318	49.1	21.6	83.5	29.7
1950	301.2	207.5	21.1	10.9	7.5	5.5	1,444	1,367	45.8	20.4	93.7	31.1
1951	326.8	204.4	27.0	-3.1	8.5	-1.4	1,443	1,323	63.5	37.8	122.4	37.4

Columns 3, 4, 5, and 6 show the declining rate of personal consumption expenditures relative to increasing gross national product of the United States from 1939 to 1951, the critical years when the country passed the point of diminishing living standards. Since 1944, the two (personal consumption and gross national product) have actually begun to move inversely, indicating that after that year it was no longer a question of guns *and* butter, but of guns *or* butter. Columns 11 and 12 show the cost of society as it becomes both richer and more powerful. The figures include government expenditure plus capital investment but do not include density and progress spending as no measurement has yet been developed for their appraisal. They show the colossal share society as a whole, not only government, takes from our total product, as well as the increasing rate, even if we discount the war years, at which this share grows with each growth in the national product, indicating that at our level of development, increasing productivity accrues in its benefits primarily to society, not to the individual. Columns 7 and 8 show two aspects of the personal standard of living: per capita disposable income and per capita consumption expenditures. The principal trend of the former indicates a declining tendency since 1944, though the latter, showing a rise, seems to disprove the contention of this chapter (if not our personal experience). However, the figures fail to express what proportion of our additional per capita expenditures was incurred in the purchase not of desired commodities, which alone should count in meaningful living standard evaluations, but of unenjoyed necessities heaped on our shoulders by the increasingly exacting conditions of living in great multitudes. Though personally spent, these are, such as density commodities, nevertheless primarily social in character and should, like a tax, not be added but subtracted in living standard computations. Negative expenditures of this kind would include those incurred in the purchase of commuter services, parking facilities, or in the repair of phenomenally multiplying damages from frictions and accidents caused by conditions of overcrowding. Thus, while we obtain goods and services for all our expenditures, the paramount question is: what is the proportion for which we obtain goods and services which none of us really cares to have? All figures shown are in 1951 prices and, with the exception of percentages, express billions of dollars. Sources are official U.S. government reports.

IV. Size and Socialism

1

What determines the size of an economic system? As in the case of all things subject to choice, it is in the first place a matter of taste and temperament. There are many roads leading to Rome, but no one can say objectively that one is better than the other. The lover of speed will consider air travel most satisfactory, the lover of luxury — a journey by boat. A woman anxious to display her furs will prefer a route via Iceland, one anxious to display her figure — a route via the Azores. A military man will wish to go in company, a poet alone. Each will consider the other's method worse, but objectively no one choice is superior. Each arrives in his preferred fashion at the terminus common to all — Rome.

And so it is with economic systems. Whether they are capitalist or socialist, they all lead to the same goal — the best possible satisfaction of human material wants. Different are only the highways they choose. But, though to a capitalist nothing seems worse than socialism and to a socialist nothing worse than capitalism, the system of neither has any intrinsic superiority over that of the other. Their choice, as in the case of the roads to Rome, is in the first place a matter of taste and temperament. For, seemingly objective criteria such as superior productivity mean little to a community cultivating frugality. And a system providing everyone with work means nothing to a community striving for a life of contemplation. Whatever this entails, it indicates that the value of an economic system, instead of being measured, as is frequently done, in terms of maximum productivity, must be measured in terms of maximum satisfaction, two concepts which, though linked at their base, assume a vastly different significance once the production of goods has begun to exceed the requirements of bare physical survival.

Though this dependence on taste and temperament seems to remove the question from the possibility of objective appraisal, few subjects instill in the partisans of the one or the other a greater determination to make personal preference appear as the manifestation of superior virtue and truth. Yet there is nothing peculiar in this for, while nature has provided each man with a certain taste, his vanity demands that he give a good account of it. He must rationalize and praise the very things which he suspects might appear in the eyes of others as unforgivable shortcomings, just as the gourmet must rationalize and praise as perhaps the ultimate in civilized refinement what others might consider his base appetite for such seemingly unsavory substances as rotten milk (cheese) and rotten grapes (wine).

The attempt to rationalize economic preferences in a way satisfactory to man's intellectual vanity invariably leads, as every rationalization must, into the realm where all our tastes are shaped and from which all our reasons flow. This is the realm of philosophy. Every battle between systems is therefore in the ultimate a battle between ideas or, rather, between rationalized ideas, between ideologies. As a result, the most effective defender of capitalism will not merely argue his case on economic grounds by contending that the profit motive is a more reliable incentive to production than social service, and that private ownership of tools leads to better results than disinterested public ownership. He will give as the basic reason of his choice his adherence to the philosophy of individualism, which links the institution of private property not so much to productivity as to the precedence of the individual over society. For, if the individual outranks society and occupies the center around which everything else revolves, it follows that he must be given title to the instrument with which alone he can defend this position not only against all other individuals but also against the society of which he is a part. This instrument is private property. By definition, it is the exclusive right of a person over things. Only if an individual owns something to the exclusion of everyone else is he *able* to be free within the limits of his property, and only if he adheres to the philosophy of individualism, is he *entitled* to be free. And only if he is *philosophically* an individualist do such principles as the profit motive or the pursuit of his own rather than the community's interest become justifiable *economic* propositions. The incidental benefits accruing from their application also to society may strengthen his argument but are irrelevant to the justification of his system, which he chooses for the sole reason that it fits his philosophy.

Similarly, a socialist will base his advocacy of public ownership and all that goes with it not so much on the claim of greater distributive justice or superior productive efficiency as on the philosophy of collectivism. For only those giving precedence to the community over the individual can defend such ideals as economic equality on the assumption that everyone, unequal in endowment and merit, represents an equal and equally important fraction of the communal parent body, or advocate in preference to the private-profit principle the social-service concept according to which the citizen's economic effort should primarily be dedicated to the glory and benefit of the group rather than himself. And only to those placing the community into the center of all things does it become a defensible proposition that, irrespective of its productive and economic consequences, the community alone should be vested with the exclusive title over the tools necessary for the attainment of social welfare. Again, the incidental benefits accruing as a result of the general welfare also to the individual may strengthen the position of socialism but are irrelevant to its justification. There were numerous communist utopias, such as Plato's, More's, or Campanella's, which advocated communal property as a device for enriching man's social experience not by increasing his wealth but by reducing his desires. Thus, the true socialist, like the true capitalist, will choose his system not because of its economic but its philosophic implications. He is economically a socialist because he is philosophically a collectivist.¹

But if the choice of an economic system depends on the philosophy of the person making the choice, on what depends his philosophy? What are the reasons inducing one to become an individualist and the other to be a collectivist? The question will cause a second wave of rationalizations, each proving all over again the superiority of his preference. But in this case there is no longer a philosophy behind a philosophy. There are excellent arguments for the one, and there are excellent arguments for the other, but the reason one is an individualist and the other a collectivist is simply because in each case his philosophy fits his peculiar temperament, his disposition, his taste. The one is warmed by communal experience, the other is chilled by it. So we are back at taste as the ultimate determinant of economic systems and, though we argue about nothing more heatedly, there is nothing more futile than to argue about taste.

---

1 By socialist in the true sense I understand a *voluntary* socialist, a person animated by the philosophic conviction that the welfare of the community should precede the welfare of the individual because the community is greater than the individual. He wants to help his anonymous fellowmen out of purely altruistic reasons. He feels he ought to help them. The true capitalist may pursue the same end, but for basically different reasons. He is an altruist out of sheer egotism. He helps others because he wants to help himself. To the true socialist, who is philosophically a collectivist, social welfare is the end of all purposes, to the capitalist, it is simply a means. In this I simply restate Adam Smith's proposition. Many friends of the common man, disclaiming the implication of collectivism, assert that social justice — a concept very different from unprefixed justice — may animate also a non-collectivist and non-socialist person. True, but to the extent that he is animated by it, he reflects a particle of collectivist philosophy, since to an individualist a concept such as justice, in contrast to that of law or good sense, must be derived from his conscience or from God, not from society. The socially animated non-socialist is a frequently occurring amalgam who is inclined to deny his collectivist streak because of the stigma his surrounding may affix to a now frowned-upon philosophy. However, since all of us are members of groups, it is only reasonable that we should develop collectivist dispositions even withoutt abandoning basic individualistic convictions. Since this chapter is meant to be merely a sketch, I have made no attempt to make allowance for the scruples of philosophic amalgams, but have adhered to the concepts of the pure capitalist and the pure socialist for the same reasons which induce scientists to operate on the assumption of pure conditions even though they may actually never exist.

2

However, here a significant modification has to be made. As indicated at the beginning, the choice of an economic system depends in the *first* place on taste and temperament. But choice must be exercisable if it is to have any meaning. It is never a matter only of what we want, but also a matter of what alternatives are open to us. This leads to a *second* and, this time, purely objective condition determining economic systems. This is the size of the community in which we live, for only communities of a given size offer alternative possibilities.[1] As we shall see, only between certain limits of social growth is it possible for us to indulge our differences of taste and temperament, and to *choose* between correspondingly different systems. When these limits are passed at either extreme the freedom of choice begins to yield to the dictate of environment. If a community is either too small or too large, the question of socialism versus capitalism becomes irrelevant, and so does the question of our philosophic preference. In either case, the only economic system possible is socialism.

To understand this, let us visualize what would happen if a shipload of capitalist refugees from a communist country were wrecked on an uninhabited island. The smallness of their number would at once compel them to establish not a capitalist but a socialist community. No one could at first be permitted to follow his individualistic inclination and say: "I shall be the lawyer of this place," or "I shall be a landscape painter," "I, a professor of Latin." In socialist fashion, competition would have to be

---

[1] I may be forgiven if I draw again attention to the complex nature of the concept of the size of a community as comprising four elements: the number, density, integration, and velocity of population. The United States of the 19th century occupied a vast territory, but her relatively low density and velocity ranged her at best amongst the medium sized communities. On the other hand, communities of lower density may develop all the characteristic features of larger sized societies if their members as a result of modern technological advance develop high velocities, producing a social effect similar to the price-level effect of the increasing velocity of currency as expressed in the Quantity Theory of Money. However, while a large-area state may thus harbour a small community, a small-area state cannot possibly harbour a large community in the sense of this book, since physical smallness puts a relatively narrow limit to both density and velocity.

replaced by co-operation. A collective plan would have to be drawn up; property to be held in common; work be allocated on the basis of social need rather than personal desire; individuals withdrawing from the community or following the lures of private profit would be ostracized if not liquidated; the purpose of all would be the purpose of each, eliminating diversity, impeding deviation, and rendering uniform all existences. Only after the population has grown to a size enabling it to specialize, would freedom of taste, disposition, and choice become possible. Only then would the assertion of individualism in the face of collective pressure cease to be equivalent to treason. Only then would emerge the condition in which the choice of an economic system is determined by taste and temperament of the individuals concerned rather than by external circumstance.

As too small a community precludes freedom of choice, so does a community that has become too large. Even in the absence of a conscious socialist movement, socialization will set in at a given development stage quite spontaneously. With the purely quantitive growth of problems resulting from increasing numbers, the capitalistic self-balancing mechanisms operating so satisfactorily at lesser population densities begin to develop rigidities which can be dealt with only through an outside controlling agent such as the government. Freedom of enterprise or the pursuit of private profit then cease to function as reliable guiding devices and no longer lead to social welfare simply because they lead to personal welfare. At a certain stage of growth, these two forms of welfare, previously complementary, must by necessity become mutually exclusive.

This socialization process manifests itself at first in productive activities associated with national defence. As long as states are relatively small, defence requirements are easily met by drawing from established sources without thereby changing their basic character or purpose as private enterprises. Though even here a certain degree of social direction and public subordination becomes necessary, both the social effort and the time needed to terminate the problem by victory, defeat, or negotiation is by nature limited. Hence, the socialism engendered by every national crisis will automatically recede once the crisis has come to an end.

But when national powers have grown beyond a certain size, the picture changes. Having absorbed the surrounding little states, they now find themselves bordering on other political organisms of such magnitude that, like all organisms piercing the barriers set by the inexorable law of diminishing productivity, they require not only a disproportionately greater degree of social preparedness than was necessary before; the previous ephemeral need for preparedness now becomes a permanent feature, leading to the creation of a productive apparatus that can no longer be reconverted from social to private use and is, therefore, best retained under the direction of society as a whole. Finally, when the ever-present tensions between the surviving overgrown powers erupt into open conflict, the ensuing war supported by such vast resources will last so long that, after its termination, a significant reduction of the swollen socialized sector of human activities and a return to an uncontrolled economy becomes not only technically impossible and politically inadvisable; the most compelling socializing element is then that, on a purely personal level, such a return is no longer even particularly desired. Too many businessmen have adjusted themselves to the relatively riskless pleasure of gaining income through social service rather than through the private customer, to value the traditional ways of private enterprise as they did before.[1]

However, the unavoidable militarization of societies growing beyond optimum limits is not the only factor contributing to their insensible socialization. The very nature of mass societies

---

[1] Henry C. Simons, advocating the dismantlement of the great powers, those "monsters of nationalism and mercantilism," has brought out the connection between collectivism, war and large-scale social organisms with particular clarity when he writes: "War is a collectivizing process, and large-scale collectivism is inherently warlike. If not militarist by national tradition, highly centralized states must become so by the very necessity of sustaining at home an inordinate, 'unnatural' power concentration, by the threat of their governmental mobilization as felt by other nations. and by their almost inevitable transformation of commercial intercourse into organised economic warfare among great economic-political blocs." — *Economic Policy for a Free Society*. Chicago, (The University of Chicago Press, 1948, p. 21).

inflates and multiplies the normal problems of life to such dimensions that their solution outgrows eventually the possibilities of private action, creating the need for ever-increasing public control and power not only in the military but also in all other spheres of life.

To this purpose, let us see what happens, for instance, in a strictly private economy from a strictly *economic* point of view when large territorial units begin to fill up their space with increasing populations. At first, opportunities are created not only for existing productive enterprises to expand the scope of their activities but also for new enterprises to develop alongside the old, maintaining for a time on a larger scale, like the growing and multiplying stars in an expanding universe, essentially the same self-regulatory competitive balance existing at the outset of expansion. This means that enterprises may at first grow, and yet leave the harmony of proportions, so vital in a self-regulatory system, undisturbed. However, unlike the apparently continuously expanding universe, social expansion, after slowing down as it begins to press against available food supplies, reaches eventually the limits of political and even physical space. When this is accomplished, further growth of firms can, in the absence of a parallel population growth, be effected only at the expense of other firms, leading to a new phase of competition which, at first, disrupts the capitalist proportions and, in its final stage, terminates competition. And, as enterprises become fewer and bigger, a growth and consolidation development sets in also on the side of labour, producing a new and simplified form of balance not only between economic units, but also between economic classes.

While this contributes temporarily to the continuation of a certain degree of precarious capitalist equilibrium, it is no longer of the same self-regulatory nature that characterized previous periods, when balancing forces were both many in number and relatively small in power. What is the result of this? With the loss of an automatically functioning *internal* balance, occuring whenever parts of a dynamic system begin, like logs on rivers, to fuse into immobilized large aggregations, a regulatory force must be introduced from *outside*. Since only society as a whole can furnish such a force, its principal agent, the government, is recalled to the scene from which earlier forms of capitalism had once so successfully banished it, and charged to assume, in addition to its political role, also a significant economic role. This would not in itself constitute socialism since government has certain regulatory functions even in a self-balancing small-unit economy. But to be an effective regulator also in the face of giant concerns, it is not sufficient that government be merely recalled. Its powers must at the same time be increased to such an extent that none of the economic colossi surviving the competitive struggle can challenge its decisions. And this is the element which, by logic of development, must in the ultimate lead beyond mere social regulation to outright social control.

The purely economic sequence leading excessively large political units to inevitable socialism even if there were no need for their perpetual military preparedness — as would be conceivable in a world state embracing all mankind — seems thus quite clear. For, as the historic development of the world's variously sized politico-economic complexes seems to have amply demonstrated, the larger the social unit, the bigger will, as a rule, be the productive enterprises and aggregations of economic power resulting from the various consolidation processes, and the bigger the enterprises and aggregations, the bigger must be the power and role of the government. But the bigger the government, the smaller must become the area of individual freedom and the decision-making power and significance of private enterprise. Thus, as the growth of competition finally ends competition, so the growth of private enterprise, provided that a large political hinterland permits it to outgrow proportions compatible with competitive capitalism, finally ends private enterprise.

Marxian as this may sound, the conclusions of this analysis are nevertheless based on entirely different premises. While Marx thought that capitalism is destroyed by the growth of *capitalist institutions*, here it is maintained that it is destroyed by the *growth of society.* In other words, contrary to the implications of the Marxian theory, capitalism seems to lead to its own destruction only in overgrown social complexes. In smaller states, even where capitalist development has reached its most advanced phase — and only in smaller states — can this purely biological and quantitive transition of a free enterprise system into inevitable socialism be averted for the simple reason that their limitation of size will, as a rule,[1] put a limitation also to the size of private enterprise, and the limitations of private enterprise will eliminate both the possibility and the need for social power to develop to a magnitude that the free interplay of economic forces would be impeded on this ground alone. This does not mean that a mature smaller state cannot be socialist. It can. But if it is, it is so not because it must but because it wills it.

Aside from the military and economic causes driving large-scale societies into gradual socialization, there is thirdly also a purely physical cause arising from the fact that vast populations accumulating in vast societies do not remain evenly spread but draw together in communities of great density. And densely populated communities cannot permit the free pursuit of individual aims any more than societies composed of too few members (whose very smallness of numbers, by the way, causes them to strengthen their shelter by drawing together in greater protective density than would be necessary in communities of optimum size). A large city may give room to free action in periods of calm such as still exist on Sundays or at night. But during weekdays and at the height of business hours, when the already large populations are further multiplied not by their number but their velocity, and the resulting hyperdensity is increased beyond the limits up to which free movement and choice are possible, most

---

[1] The rule is broken when small states, either as a result of trade agreements or because they happen to possess in great quantities universally desired but scarce resources, become parts of large market areas, defeating thereby the limiting effect of political boundaries. This is the case, for instance, with the giant steel industry in the Grand Duchy of Luxembourg. Yet, even where free trade agreements have enlarged market areas far beyond political areas, firm growth will by nature never be so uninhibited and so lacking in cautiousness as in the unified and dependable large market areas of great political entities.

individual decisions, instead of being adjusted to *personal* desires, must give way to *social* plan, to order, direction, control — concepts characteristic not of the capitalist but the socialist way of reaching ends. Where there was freedom, there is now discipline, where there was diversity, there is now uniformity. So powerful is the all-levelling socializing pressure of great density that, when people reach the rush-hour compactness of a subway crowd, those interested in preserving a minimum of personal comfort must not only act and proceed but sometimes even breathe in unison.

Of the three principal socializing elements affecting every overgrown society — military necessity, economic opportunity, and physical density — the last, though most briefly sketched, seems by far the most important. Not only are the other two derived from it, but it is the condition which ultimately leads to a fourth, final, and the most irrevocable of all socializing elements — its own rationalization. While the other two produce socialism in fact, density leads to socialism in spirit. While the former develop collectivist *attitudes,* the latter must by necessity lead to a collectivist *philosophy;* for few people would be able to accept the mounting restrictions imposed on them by the synchronizing pressure of great multitudes if they could not be induced to transfer the meaning and sovereignty of existence from the person to the group, from their increasingly insignificant individuality to the increasingly significant social mass. Being perpetually awed and hemmed in by the swelling volume of their own numbers, it is only natural that they should as a last resort prefer to swim with the tide rather than keep struggling in futile assertion of a now impractical freedom of action against the currents of the age. And, since surrender they must, what is more rational than to find ideological joy in surrender, accepting with zeal as master what they had created as servant, and glorying in the new meaning of a community which they had previously considered a nuisance.

The final disintegration of the capitalist system in fully developed large societies is therefore not so much, and certainly not necessarily, caused by the onslaught of a successful socialist movement battering at it from without as by the insensible ideological consumption afflicting its own exponents, the businessmen, from within. Unable on pure physical grounds to impress their individualist philosophy on a surrounding that has become too tightly integrated, the only thing left for them is to adopt themselves the collectivist philosophy emanating from an increasingly irresistable life in common and generated as the indispensable social cohesive in the process of every large-scale integration. Like the indigenous collectivists before them, they too begin to move the community into the central position they had previously assigned to the individual, and to identify in reverent subordination the purposes of society with their own. Instead of accumulating fortunes in sovereign disregard of public censure, they now vie for the honour of conspicuously sacrificing their income as dollar-a-year men; instead of aspiring for pecuniary rewards, they aspire for social recognition; and instead of upholding against their socialist critics the merits of the profit motive, they become so demoralized that they are at first ashamed of it, then they deny it, and finally they abandon it. Their principal claim to distinction henceforth no longer rests on their success as businessmen or their cultivation of the customer but on their patriotism and their service to the community; not on their economic but on their social perfection.[1] And with this ends the ideoligical basis of capitalism leaving to the Kremlin the joy of

[1] The ideological communization of large-scale societies even in seemingly still capitalist countries such as the United States is well illustrated by the recent selection of a Young-Man-of-The-Year. In making its choice, the local Junior Chamber of Commerce of a typical business-town, instead of selecting as its representative hero a successful businessman or rugged individualist, conferred its honour on a young man whose principal distinction was the great number of communal activities to which he gave the major part of his devotion and time. As a little side gesture, it honoured at the same time with a certificate of merit the young man's wife for her great understanding of the fact that her husband's social service kept him from spending most of his evenings where a devoted family man should be — at home. In a reversal of ideas that could hardly occur in less collectivized societies, the husband is here shamelessly complimented for taking on a new mistress, the community, with whom he spends nearly every evening, while the community, instead of at least hiding the fact, has the tactlessness of thanking the deserted wife for her gracious acceptance of the husband's near daily adultery.

burying it. For if, under the inevitably communizing pressure of organized multitudes, even businessmen begin to subordinate individual to communal purpose, what force is there left to prevent the extinction of a system in which the community and its agent, the government, has never been a particular cause of either affection or concern?

3

To summarize: the choice of an economic system depends, first, on the taste and temperament of people and, secondly, on the physical size of the political community. For only within certain physical limits of social development is it possible to exercise the freedom of choosing between alternatives. Below or beyond these limits, if a community is either too small or too large, there can be neither freedom nor freedom of choice. The only possible system is then a system of discipline, direction, control. Economically speaking, this means socialism.

While the economic systems of too small and too large communities thus necessarily resemble each other, they differ fundamentally in their development possibilities. Both grow. But in too small a society, growth produces eventually the condition leading to the development of philosophic as well as material alternative opportunities. It has an individualizing effect. In too large a society, on the other hand. growth has a collectivizing effect. Instead of eliminating the need for social control, it emphasizes it for the reason that, beyond a certain point, social bigness begins to outgrow the limited possibilities of individual man. When this happens, one sphere after another becomes subject to social organization until, in the end, the mind itself adjusts by surrendering to the appropriate social philosophy. This means, the only way to protect the members of an overgrown community from the implications of a life in common and its rationalization in the form of a collectivist philosophy is not the preaching of an anti-collectivist philosophy but the destruction of the condition of which collectivism is nothing but a natural concomitant — excessive social size.

V. Size Cycles

1

Chickens are rather a harmless lot. Yet farmers raising them in large numbers are frequently troubled by a phenomenon usually associated with the world of man: cannibalism. When a chicken gets accidentally hurt, the heretofore peaceloving birds around it get so excited by the sight of blood that they peck at the unfortunate compatriot until it is dead.

On an Orwellian chicken farm we could well imagine what sort of proposals the various members of the flock would advance to end the shameful condition. There would be the reeducators suggesting that all that is needed is better training. There would be those attributing cannibalism to bad leadership. They would favour the extermination of the wicked. There would be some attributing it to clannish disunity. They would suggest the unification of chickenkind and the outlawing of all bloodshed. And there would be the Marxists amongst them, attributing the evil to the pecking mode of feeding. They would suggest a change in the manner by which chickens acquire their living.

But each time one of the suggested policies is put to trial, its advocates would sooner or later discover the same thing: chicken cannibalism all over again. Finally, however, some might stumble on the clue to the mystery. Puzzled by the fact that cannibalism seemed never to occur in smaller chicken societies, they would attribute it to the excessive volume of their own numbers. As a result, instead of trying different training or feeding methods, they would propose the breaking up of overgrown chicken societies into a number of smaller ones.

This is exactly what Louis Harwood, a prosperous New Jersey chicken farmer, did. Only he did not solve the problem by the physical division of his flock. This would have meant either a reduction in the number of chickens or their separation into sub-critical flocks over a wider area. Both alternatives would have been more costly than the tolerance of cannibalism. So he solved it through psychological division. He invented spectacles and later plastic eye lenses which had the effect of narrowing the vision of chickens in such a manner that they could see only a few members of their group at a time. This did not alter their innate cannibalistic lusts at the sight of blood. What it did alter was the statistical chance of bloodshed occurring within the reduced size of the small nationalities into which the magic spectacles had suddenly divided them. For within small numbers, bloodshed was not only an infinitely rarer occurrence than in the previously unified chicken empires. When it did occur, it stayed localized. It could not release a chain reaction since it remained unnoticed by most. The device proved so successful that Mr. Harwood gave up chicken farming, and ever since earns a handsome income by producing peace-insuring chicken spectacles instead.

2

The relevance of this story is that it illustrates the still largely ignored fact that group size exerts a vital influence on social behaviour not only if the society involved is one of animals but also if it is one of men. For just as the phenomenon of chicken cannibalism is less the product of lack of training, bad leadership, moral aberration, or mode of production than of the sheer physical fact that the flock has reached critical size, so a great many human miseries seem to arise not from the numerous conventional causes to which they are ascribed but from the fact that societies have reached critical proportions. Then complexities set in which are no longer the result of human failing but of the size of the society within which we live.

As I tried to show in Chapter 1 in a more general manner, this explains for example why the casualty figure produced by a given traffic volume with such predeterminable precision is proportionate not to the carelessness but to the mass of drivers which, at a given magnitude, turns the uncertainty of chance into the certainty of statistical law; why a city the size of Chicago will yield murder and rape at the rate of 15 and 30 per month respectively, irrespective of the disposition of its citizens; why at a given density a crowd of amiable citizens will be thrilled rather than shocked by an anguished fellow man jumping to his suicide from a sky-scraper, indicating that, what Gulliver says of human creatures, applies also to human masses: they become "the more savage in proportion to their bulk." It explains why peoples have usually committed their most barbarian atrocities not in their stage of barbarism when lack of integration kept their social size sub-critical, but at the pinnacle of their civilization as was the case with the Italians during the Renaissance or the French during their *grand siècle*. And it explains why at critical national size wars were caused not only by such monuments in search of a pedestal as Napoleon and Hitler, but also by Pericles, the most enlightened statesman of antiquity, or Julius II, the most urban pope of Rome. In fact, with some application, it should not be too difficult to construct an exact size-crime table correlating the schedule of all the various social sizes with a corresponding schedule of all the various crimes produced by them – starting with the size of crowds at which men begin to pinch girls in buses, proceeding with the volumes setting off in ascending order pickpocketings in churches, knifings in taverns, massacres in town squares, and ending with the critical size of nations that leads to warfare. This should enable us to read off at a glance which crime is produced at which frequency by which social mass, or which social size is critical for each crime.

Another and equally far reaching consequence of overgrowing social size has been discussed in the preceding chapter. This is the unavoidable extension of government activities beyond the limits compatible with liberal democratic laissez-faire societies. At first this extension has only social and political implications. With the rising rate of accident and crime, a greater police and judicial apparatus must be maintained. And with the rise in national power, also the military apparatus must be enlarged.

Moreover, as it is revealed by the various expenditure statistics, the enlargement of government functions affecting these two sectors will be more than proportionate to the increase in social size.[1] For the paradoxical result of social overgrowth, is that not only the needs but also the feelings of security seem to vary inversely with the magnitude of security measures.[2] Hence Saint Augustine's famous question directed at the might of Rome (*The City of God, IV, 3*): "What reason then, or what wisdom shall any man show in glorying in the largeness of empire, all their joy being but a glass, bright and brittle, and evermore in fear or danger of breaking?"

However, the process does not stop here. For once a society out-grows optimum limits, its political and military complexities are soon joined by a host of economic complexities which, at smaller social size, resolved themselves through the automatic balancing effect of competition, but now, as a result of the enlarged proportions imparted to them by overgrowth, require likewise the intervention of government. This means that the sheer physics of size must, at a given level of expansion drive the government of

---

[1] The rate of progression of government costs resulting from increasing social size is well illustrated by the following police figures from the *Municipal Yearbook* of 1951: North Plainfield, N.Y., with a population of 12,760, requires a police force of *15*. Plainfield, N.J. with a population of 42,212: *78*; Elizabeth, N.J. with a population of 112,675: *257*; Buffalo, N.Y., with a population of 577,398: *1,398*; Chicago, Ill. with a population of 3,606,439: *7,518*; and New York City, with a population of 7,835,099: *19,521*. In each case, the growth of the police force is more than proportionate to the growth of population. Read also in this connection the pertinent exposition of bureaucratic growth in C. Northcote Parkinson's: *Parkinson's Law* (London: John Murray, 1958).

[2] This is expressed by what may be called the *Saharoff exemption* from the law of diminishing utility (according to Sir Basil Saharoff, the munitions' magnate): The more armaments one has, the more one wants to have more. An anti-aircraft gun costing $10,000 in 1945, cost $275,000, or 27 times as much, in 1950 to match improvements achieved in aircraft production. But the costlier and more formidable equipment decreased rather than increased the feeling of security. The larger the hydrogen bombs, the greater the fear of the countries producing them, And the larger the countries, the disproportionately more they are driven to increase their defence costs. See E.A.G. Robinson's (*The Economic Consequences of the Size of Nations*) table comparing relative defence expenditures of the countries according to their size. The per capita figures for Italy, France, Great Britain, and USA are, in that order: 12, 37, 43, 100. (p. 237).

even the freest society into assuming also an ever increasing economic role – first as a balancing third force, and finally as a centralizing and actively socializing first force. As so many other phenomena restricting the individual's control over his environment, also socialism appears therefore as a result not of choice, conviction, indoctrination, or communist grave digging but of critical social size.

3

To complement the emphasis which the preceding chapter laid on the socializing pressures generated in mass societies by population density, military need, and the disturbing effect which growing size of enterprise exerts on the self-equilibrating mobile of a capitalist economy, the analysis of the present chapter will concentrate on a different approach, explaining likewise the size-determined transition from competitive capitalism to controlled socialism, but setting out from a different starting point. This is a still largely unidentified element affecting and changing at a given state of economic growth the nature of business cycles.

In pre-industrial periods, business fluctuations were principally due to influences which, such as wars, diseases, or sunspot activities, were external (*exogenous*) to the economy. Since the main kind of economic activity was then agricultural, however, these fluctuations were more in the nature of *farm cycles* than business cycles. The most famous of them was the biblical cycle of seven fat and seven lean years. The precision with which Joseph of Egypt predicted it was probably due to the fact that, long before Jevons, he must have been one of the first sunspot theorists, relating farm and weather cycles to storms ravaging the surface of the sun. Farm cycles disappeared not as a physical phenomenon but as a major economic problem when the industrial revolution made conservation and storage processes available, thereby neutralizing the disturbing effect of nature's fickle temperament.

But while the industrial revolution diminished the significance of farm cycles, it helped to increase along with the growing importance of business enterprise as the principal form of economic activity, the significance of *business cycles* proper. These were caused not by external but internal (*endogenous*) forces, generated by the inner working of the uncontrolled free enterprise system of capitalism itself. However, as long as market areas and business units were relatively small, the scale of fluctuations they could produce was so limited that no external stabilizer was required. For, as the various then emerging self-generating theories pointed out, each phase of the cycle – prosperity, recession, depression, recovery – created automatically the forces leading to the next phase.

However, as trading areas fused and business units grew, both competitive collisions and cyclical fluctuations, growing in intensity with the growing size of increasingly integrated market areas, began to assume such proportions that the shocks they produced could no longer be absorbed by the self-balancing mechanism of capitalism. Only three of the four phases of the cycle were now still capable of producing unaided the forces leading to the next: recovery, prosperity, and recession. Depression had become a terminal stage. Intellectually, the change was acknowledged through the formulation of *limited* self-generating theories which completely reversed the conclusions of the older unlimited self-generating theories. While the unlimited versions rationalized the *laissez-faire* ideal of freedom from government, the new versions rationalized government intervention. For who, except government, could marshal the force necessary to propel an overgrown economy, that had crushed its bones by falling into too deep a valley from too high a peak, out of the pit of depression once it had landed in it?

Of the two forms of government intervention now proposed to avert future downswings, which henceforth threatened to end not so much in depression as in collapse, one is symbolized by Marx, the other by Keynes. The assumption of both is the same: business cycles, being offsprings of an uncontrolled system, cannot occur if the economy is under control. But while the Marxian approach advocates the outright replacement of uncontrolled capitalism by fully controlled socialism, the Keynesian approach offers social control merely as a 'compensatory' emergency measure fluctuating in intensity with the free enterprise system's fluctuating need of support. In practice, however, the Keynesian approach entails a degree of socialization which may differ in purpose from the Marxian aim, but hardly in its effect. For as the preceding chapter has shown, once government is equipped with the necessary machinery to become an effective interventor in the private economy, it is clear that its enormously enlarged apparatus cannot be dismantled each time a crisis has passed. This would itself at once lead to a new crisis. Thus, even the Keynesian approach leads, in the last analysis, not to fluctuating but permanent controls which, in addition, must be the more sweeping the larger the economy and the greater the disruptive potential of its cyclical fluctuations.

The recent history of the great capitalist powers seems to confirm both the inevitability of this development and the validity of the Marxian prediction that capitalism breeds the germ leading to its own destruction. Its lack of social control produces business cycles, and business cycles produce the need for social control.

Yet, while the conclusion seem compelling, there appears to be a fundamental flaw in the premises from which they are derived. For contrary to the implications of the limited self-generating theories, the element requiring government control is not a business but a *size cycle* — a term that does not yet exist but is in pressing need of being coined. Cyclical fluctuations as such are no more harmful to the economy than breathing is to a man, and there is no more need to call for an external stabilizer on their account than there is for man to call a doctor because of the recurring contraction and expansion of his breathing mechanism. What turns them into a problem is the disruptive *scale* they are able to assume as the economics engendering them outgrow certain proportions. And scale is as external to the economy as are sunspots, taking its measure not from the system producing cycles but from the size of the society through which the cycle is able to transmit itself. Contrary to Marx, the element leading to the destruction of capitalism is thus not the inner working of a free enterprise system but *social size* which, at critical magnitude, appears once more as the principal cause turning nonproblematical phenomena into major problems.

4

The identification of size cycles as distinct from business cycles is both theoretically and practically of prime importance. Theoretically, it clears up the basic error of the limited self-generating theories whose rationalizations dealt such a mortal blow to the defensibility of capitalism. For, by separating the self-generating elements *inherent* in capitalism from the strictly *external* factor of social size, it will show that government intervention is caused by the latter, not the former, and that the self-generating forces are limited in their effectiveness not by the system-defects of capitalism but by the scale of its operation. And it will show also that, though size cycles appear at first as riding in on the back of business cycles and seem to be capable of giving added volume only to fluctuations created *within* the economy, they are actually completely separate phenomena in both origin and effect. It is the same as with waves blown up by a hurricane which are likewise completely separate phenomena from the waves produced by the inner agitation of the ocean which the storm may have amplified.

Practically, the distinction is of importance on three grounds.

It reveals the fundamental change that has in recent years affected the nature of cyclical fluctuations. It permits the precise anticipation of cycles. And it offers an infinitely more constructive solution to the problems caused by them than is possible otherwise. For as long as theory keeps on mixing externally caused size cycles with internally caused business cycles, it cannot cope with the problem of business *cycles* except through the partial or total abolition of the business *system*. It suggests relieving the patient of excessively heavy breathing by stopping his breathing. But once it is realized that the true problem is not the business but the size cycle, entering the scene at a critical social magnitude from the outside, the damaging intruder can be eliminated without at the same time eliminating the system it has invaded. All that is then needed is not the introduction of social controls but the reduction of social size to proportions within which fluctuations can do no harm because the market area through which they can transmit themselves is simply not large enough to permit dangerous amplifications.

To realize this is the more important as the government controls offered as panacea by present theory, while eliminating basically harmless business cycles, are paradoxically the very element aggravating the danger of size cycles. True, the impact effect of controls is that, by making business cycles impossible, they eliminate at first also the size cycles riding them. However the undisturbed calm and purposeful direction that usually follow the introduction of a planned economy invariably leads to renewed political and economic growth, but this time on a scale that, what previously was out of control because of uncontrolled capitalism, now outgrows control because of excessive social size. This is when, to the surprise of so many theorists in economic planning, size cycles reappear. But this time they do so no longer as mere amplifiers of business cycles. They enter the stage as wholly independent phenomena having their own wave length, following their own laws of periodicity and bedevilling the economy in their own right, irrespective whether the system is controlled or uncontrolled, capitalist or socialist.[1]

An excellent example of this, to which I have briefly referred in Chapter I, has been provided by Soviet Russia whose tightly controlled economy seemed to have eliminated fluctuations forever. Yet in 1933, as in an old fashioned capitalist depression, "mines, steel works and plants in the light and food industries were chocked up with unshipped output . . . The railroads could not even deal with shipments of rails, fastenings, or pipe, the needs of transport itself." By the end of 1934, the situation had deteriorated to such a point that there were more than 3 million tons of timber awaiting rail shipment, along with 2 million tons of coal and almost 1 million tons of ore. A total of 15 million tons of cargo, altogether, awaited shipment at that time. Heavy industry alone had 80,000 freight cars piled up awaiting transportation."[2]

What caused this? Capitalism? It did not exist. Communism? Of course not, since the same things happened in the capitalist

---

[1] How ineffectual controls have become in the face of uncontrollable scale was dramatically illustrated in early June 1965 by Federal Reserve Bank Chairman William McChesney Martin, himself one of the central control agents of the American economy. Noting that there were "disquieting similarities" between the prosperity of the 1960s and the boom preceding the great depression in the 1920s, he was horrified at the realization that he had thereby triggered off a giant shock wave on the stockmarket that resulted in a loss of more than $3.5 billion. Actually, the most disquieting feature of the 1960s was not a similarity but dissimilarity with the booming 1920s. In the 1920s, the economy, overgrown as it already was, was still of a scale that permitted the subsequently instituted government controls to counteract with a measure of success the ravages of history's first major size cycle. In the 1960s, as the very result of the earlier successful government intervention, economic volume and, with it, economic problems had reached such a degree of integrated, chainreaction-producing expansion that only chance, but no longer intelligent direction could prevent fluctuations from assuming catastrophic magnitudes. It was not only Mr. Martin who experienced that under these conditions disaster can be caused by a mere word of caution; in March 1976, a nearly identical sequence of events was triggered off when a widely publicized warning by a group of Cambridge economists that the pound's preceding unprecedented slide downward was merely a prelude of worse things to come, was promptly followed a few days later by the prediction leading to its own cataclysmic accomplishment. And even this was mild compared to the almost mortal wound inflicted on the battered pound on 'Black Monday,' October 24, 1976, by a reckless article published in the prestigious London paper, *The Sunday Times*, barely 24 hours earlier, on October 23.

[2] Harry Schwartz, *Russia's Soviet Economy*. New York: Prentice Hall 1950, p. 337.

depression ravaging the United States and the rest of the world at the same time. Mismanagement? Hardly, since the Soviet manager knows that this failure, unlike in capitalist countries, might mean not only loss of his job but of his freedom and life as well. Absence of experience and technical knowhow? Unlikely, since their uncontested possession in capitalist countries could not prevent *their* depressions either. Trotzkyite-Bukharin treason or bourgeois nationalistic deviationism? None of these. It was the plain unadulterated inability of man to cope with the problems of societies that have outgrown his limitations.

5

If the preceding pages have tried to show that most contemporary social problems are problems of national or group size, this does not mean that problems such as brutality, socialist domination of individual existence, or cyclical fluctuations, may not also be caused by personal disposition, ideological zeal, or economic system. They may. And to the extent that they are, they can be solved at their own level, through the repression of the brutal, the conversion of socialists, or the socialization of the unconverted. But what really concerns our age is no longer so much the particular nature of problems as their scale. And their scale, as we have seen, is a function not of education, philosophy, or system, but of the size of the community which they affect.

Thus, what the preceding pages as well as all other discouses of this volume submit, is an essentially new interpretation of history in which the chief influence on historic change, which Marx assigns to changes in the mode of production, is assigned to changes in social size. Within optimum limits, these are of minor significance. In fact one of the characteristic features of optimum size is that the dominant influence is exerted by man, not size. But beyond it, a Malthusian gap begins to develop. From then on, the problems of size continue to multiply at a geometric ratio while the human ability to cope with them can be increased only at an arithmetic ratio – and even this only up to a point. No doctorate, no university education, no pattern of organization, no economic system can then compensate for the pace with which the problems of size out-distance man's effort to catch up with them. Nor can any measure of human control, whether suggested by Marx or Keynes, offer a solution for problems which have arisen precisely because the organism of which they are part has outgrown all human control.

The principal contemporary problem thus being one of scale, we are always driven to the same conclusion: that salvation must lie in the opposite direction from the now fashionable trend towards bigness. It must lie in scale-reduction and the restoration of optimum social size. Instead of advancing further on the road of economic integration and political unification which, along with the size of the world's already overgrown social units, also magnifies rather than diminishes their problems, we must retrace our steps. Not *Union Now* but *Disunion Now* holds the key to a future of manageable proportions. And proportions are manageable only as long as society is adjusted to man, not man to society. For man, not society, is the measure of all things.

The only questions that must be answered if the theory is to be applied to reality, are: What exactly is optimum size? And: How can societies, once overgrown, be returned to optimum proportions?

As chapter II has dealt with the first question in detail, a brief restatement of the idea will be sufficient at this juncture. A society can be said to reach optimum size when it becomes large enough to provide its members with the convivial, economic, political, and cultural amenities necessary for the good life – Aristotle's *summum bonum*. As history has proved, groups numbering as few as 20,000 individuals begin to fulfil this function to perfection. This represents the lower limit of optimum size. The upper limit is represented by the maximum number of people which can be held together under a single roof by means of the three size-extending factors (education, integration, and technological advance) without having to sacrifice the fullness of the good life. Taking into account the latest in administrative and technological devices, this limit seems to lie in the neighbourhood of populations numbering from 12 to 15 millions.[1]

This does not mean that societies cannot become larger. But optimum size now turns into critical size, a concept that is characterized by our instruments of social control developing defects which neither the physical nor the social sciences, neither education, nor technology, nor integration can surmount. It represents the magnitude at which we come face to face with the instability inherent in everything that has outgrown its function. It means that we have passed the *point of compulsory socialization* at which business cycles turn into size cycles, and the power of government rather than the welfare of man must be increased in a futile attempt to check the uncheckable problems of scale. It signifies that we have passed the *point of diminishing living standards* at which an increasing share of the national product must be diverted from individual to social consumption to assist society in its effort to protect its members from the double danger of external attack and internal collapse which social oversize has imposed on them as perpetual companions. It implies having reached the *point of spontaneously erupting war,* at which societies, unified and integrated by the organizing effort of their governments, assume such critical compactness that, like uranium reaching critical mass, they blow up by themselves, irrespective of whether they are led by sinners or saints, Republicans or Democrats, fascists or communists, women or men, Blacks or Whites, Moslems or Jews.

[1] In non-technological ages, when the boost provided by size-extending factors was by nature highly restricted, the lower, function-determined, limit tended to coincide with the upper limit of optimum size which, in the words of Aristotle could "be easily ascertained by experience. For both governors and government have duties to perform. The special functions of a governor are to command and to judge. But if the citizens of a state are to judge and to distribute offices according to merit, then they must know each other's character: where they do not possess this knowledge, both the election to offices and the decision of lawsuits will go wrong. When the population is very large, they are manifestly settled at haphazard, which clearly ought not to be. Besides, in an overpopulous state, foreigners and metics will readily acquire the rights of citizens, for who will find them out? Clearly then the best limit of the population of a state is the largest number which suffices for the purposes of life, and can be taken in at a single view." (*Politica*, VII, 3).

But what about the second and more important of the two questions? How could a reduction to optimum sub-critical dimensions of overgrown social units such as the world's great powers be accomplished in practical terms?

Unfortunately men are not as easily handled as chickens. Otherwise the problem could be solved with the same psychological trick through which Mr. Harwood ended the problem of chicken cannibalism: through spectacles limiting our vision. For once we could be made to believe that we constitute nations of only sub-critical size, we would neither indulge in group violence nor in the building up of firms and markets of such dimensions that they cannot be co-ordinated except by large-scale, complicated and therefore relatively inefficient social planning. But since psychological division cannot be applied to human societies, the only method of reducing them is by physical division or, in the terms of Henry C. Simons, through the dismantlement of those "monsters of nationalism and mercantilism" whose existence has proved such an obstacle to healthy relationships between men and nations.

Though the idea of division seems highly unrealistic in an age glorying in the greatness of bigness, it is the only sound principle of social organization. In fact, as I have already pointed out in Chapter I, the most successful organizers in history have always been not the unifiers but the dividers. The device keeping the empire of the Persians intact was the division of their conquests into manageable small *satrapies*. The Roman empire was based not on the power of its legions but on the weakness of its dismembered national groups, the *provinces*. Great Britain divided her unruly, unequally large and ever-feuding English, Scottish, Welsh, and Irish nations, uniting instead a host of nondescript counties. And even the organizational success of the United States is due to the fact that she is actually a Disunited States. The flourishing enterprise of 50 pliable small states would obviously be impossible to handle if it included in United Nations fashion 4 or 5 veto yielding great powers. As Mr. Gorham of Massachusetts stressed during the Constitutional Convention of

1787: "The strength of the general Government will lie not in the largeness, but in the smallness of the States."[1]

Thus, far from being impractical, division is such a fundamental principle of organization that even unifiers must apply it if they are to succeed. However, the purpose of my argument is not to suggest division for the sake of union, but division for the sake of division. And it is this aspect which seems to remove the device as a useful instrument for restoring optimum size to societies most in need of it: the great powers. For, whatever its merit, you cannot turn back the clock.

Yet division can be applied even here, just as the clock can, of course, be turned back, perhaps not by statesmen, but by everyone owning a clock. And the device is the more realistic as it need not be applied in the extreme sense of entailing the actual dismemberment of great powers. It is sufficient if it is applied in the less radical and more acceptable form of devolution or decentralization. In fact, in this mellower variation it commands a considerable degree of emotional support even within the great powers themselves. Economically, this is illustrated in two ways. One is the restoration to practice of the principle that business, like the medieval manor, can profitably be divided into a number of smaller estates without affecting the unity of ownership, and

[1] How consciously this problem weighed on the shapers of the American constitution, emerges from the following notes of Madison on the Constitutional Convention of 1787. On *July 6, 1787*, he writes (1 Farrand, *Records of Federal Convention* 540) that Mr. Gorham of Massachusetts "hoped to see all the states made small by proper divisions, instead of their becoming formidable as was apprehended, to Small States. He conceived that let the Genl. Government be modified as it might, there would be a constant tendency in the State Governments, to encroach upon it: it was of importance therefore that the extent of the States should be reduced as much and as fast as possible. The stronger the Government shall be made in the first instance the more easily will these divisions be effected; as it will be of less consequence in the opinion of the States whether they be of great or small extent." (Madisons's notes of debates). – *July 23:* "Mr. Gorham preferred two to three members. ... Kentucky, Vermont, the province of Mayne & Franklin will probably soon be added to the present number. He presumed also that some of the largest States would be divided. The strength of the general Government will lie not in the largeness, but in the smallness of the States." (2 Farrand, *Record of Federal Convention*, 94).

without, therefore, requiring huge, centralized territorial hinterlands as a condition of their prosperity. The other is the renewed awareness that smaller business units are actually more capitalist in character, individually often more profitable, socially always more satisfying and, above all, cyclically more resistant than large centralized enterprises.[1] And politically, it is illustrated by such popular movements as state-rightism in the United States, or the many regional nationalisms in Great Britain, France, Germany, Italy, Spain, or Russia, flourishing to this day inspite of the unifying pressures of centuries.

The carving out of social units of optimum size seems therefore to require hardly more than the strengthening of local autonomies

[1] This statement is well supported by a unmber of studies such as: Louis D. Brandeis, *The Curse of Bigness*, New York: The Viking Press, 1935; Temporary National Economic Committee, *Competition and Monopoly in American Industry*, Monograph No. 21. Washington, Government Printing Office, 1940; and *Relative Efficiency of Large, Medium-sized, and Small Business*, Monograph No. 13; David Gushman Coyle, *Day of Judgement*, New York: Harper & Brothers, 1949; and E. A. C. Robinson, *The Economic Consequences of the Size of Nations*, London: Macmillan, 1960. In the last named, see in particular the essay *Size and Efficiency in Switzerland* by professors W. A. Jöhr and F. Kneschaurek, which emphasizes both the superior cyclical stability of the Swiss economy as well as its underlying small plant structure, 82% of all Swiss industrial plants employing less than 50 workers; Professor L. Tarshis' essay *The Size of the Economy and its Relation to Stability and Steady Progress* ("The greatest instability was found in the largest economies and vice versa," p. 190); and Professor J. Jewkes' brilliant essay *Are The Economics of Scale Unlimited?* where he points out that "if size, automatically and without qualification, were an advantage - as weight in a boxer - there would be many fewer cases in history where large industrial units, particularly those which have come into existence fully grown or have attained their size swiftly, find that the very magnitude of their operations, far from being an unmixed blessing, is the source of their sharpest and most persistent anxieties." p. 95. A similar point was made by the U.K. Department of Employment whose figures present a striking picture of the deterioration of industrial relations in British industry with increasing plant size. As THE TIMES (London) reports in an editorial entitled SMALL IS HARMONIOUS (February 26, 1976): "Measured in terms of working days lost in a year per thousand employees, the detericration seems to be from about fifteen in plants employing fifteen people to about 1,000 in plants employing 1,000." The figures are taken from the February 25, 1976, issue of the Department of Employment *Gazette* (London). The list of worst industrial records is topped by the biggest enterprises: coal mining, docks, motor vehicle manufacturing. The larger they are, the worse their performance - a conclusion drawn a good seven years earlier by the ever iconoclastic Duke of Edinburgh.

by federalizing the structure of the increasingly centralized great powers along the ancient but still existing boundaries of their component historic regions. This accomplished, the worst of our contemporary social problems could once more be brought within the reach of solution by the translation of their national into a local scale. But in addition, the return of social power to the local scene from which the unifiers have purloined it, could satisfy indirectly even those glorying somewhat irrationally in the vision of still greater union. For, to quote Professor Simons once more: "A great virtue of extreme federalism or decentralization in great nations is that it facilitates their extension toward world organization or their easy absorption into still larger federations. If central governments were, as they should be, largely repositories of unexercised powers, held simply to prevent their exercise by constituent units of extragovernmental organizations, then supranational organization would be easy if not almost gratuitous. Indeed such great-nation decentralization or deorganization is both end and means of international organization."[1]

Utilizing the grassroot popularity of the idea of regional autonomy, the obstacles in the way of a reduction of overgrown social units to optimum size seems thus neither theoretically, nor practically, nor ideologically insurmountable. Even Soviet Russia has abandoned her original ideal of total centralization after, at last, it dawned on her leaders that her biggest problem was not 'anti-party activities', Trotzkyite treason or capitalist intrigue, but *gigantomania*. This is why the Kremlin has dismantled her monolithic unity in the very field in which unification had previously expected the greatest rewards: the field of economic organization.

But gigantomania still attaches to Russia's *political* concepts. And not only to Russia's. For like aggressiveness, size cycles, or socialism, also gigantomania is an example of the many unwelcome, though *spontaneously* created, by-products of social

---

[1] Henry C. Simons, *Economic Policy for a Free Society*, University of Chicago Press, p. 21.

overgrowth.[1] But if it cannot be cured, it is not because division or decentralization of the overgrown is such a reactionary or fantastic idea. It is because so many statesmen seem to be committed to the myth that you cannot turn back the clock. Yet, as I have suggested, few things are easier than exactly this. Have you tried?

---

[1] It was the ever-fascinating Nikita Khrushchev who, when still Chairman-Czar of all the Russians, provided the most delightful illustration for the connection between gigantomania, megalomania, and other irrationalisms on the one hand, and size and power on the other, when he reported in a rumbustious speech at a Soviet-Rumanian rally on August 11, 1961, on a conversation with Mr. Macmillan during the Paris summit meeting following the U-2 spy-plane incident, in which the British Prime Minister said: "Understand, Mr. Khrushchev, they (the U.S.) are a great country – they cannot apologize." To which Mr. Khrushchev replied with the peace-shattering logic befitting powerful equals: "Excuse me, we are also a great country and we demand an apology . . . *You* try to understand. You (England shorn of her imperial size) are in the same position as an old grandfather, or daddy, or mummy, when the little son no longer wears shorts, and the little daughter begins to curl her hair. But she is still regarded, so to speak, as little Verochka, or little Katyusha, and Katyusha has pretensions that she should be treated as a grown-up in line with her increased size. But they still want, so to speak, if it is necessary, to pull her plaits or even shake her by the ear. Well, to some extent, we are also being measured with the same measure. They still want to teach us. Do not do that, this is not allowed, if you do that we shall pull your ears, we shall apply our hand to another part of your anatomy too." And no apology of course. And to make his point clearer still, Khrushchev said of his demands on Germany: "This is a question of the fight for recognition of our majesty, for the recognition that *His Majesty the working-class of the Soviet Union* has assumed power and created a State with which you, imperialists and colonisers, must reckon." At last, he had pronounced the gigantomaniacal word that permits no apology, no sense, no reason when it is backed by bottom-spanking and empire-creating social size: *His Majesty*. Size had made Russia divine. – Quotations are from *The Daily Express* (London), August 12, 1961.

78 THE OVERDEVELOPED NATIONS

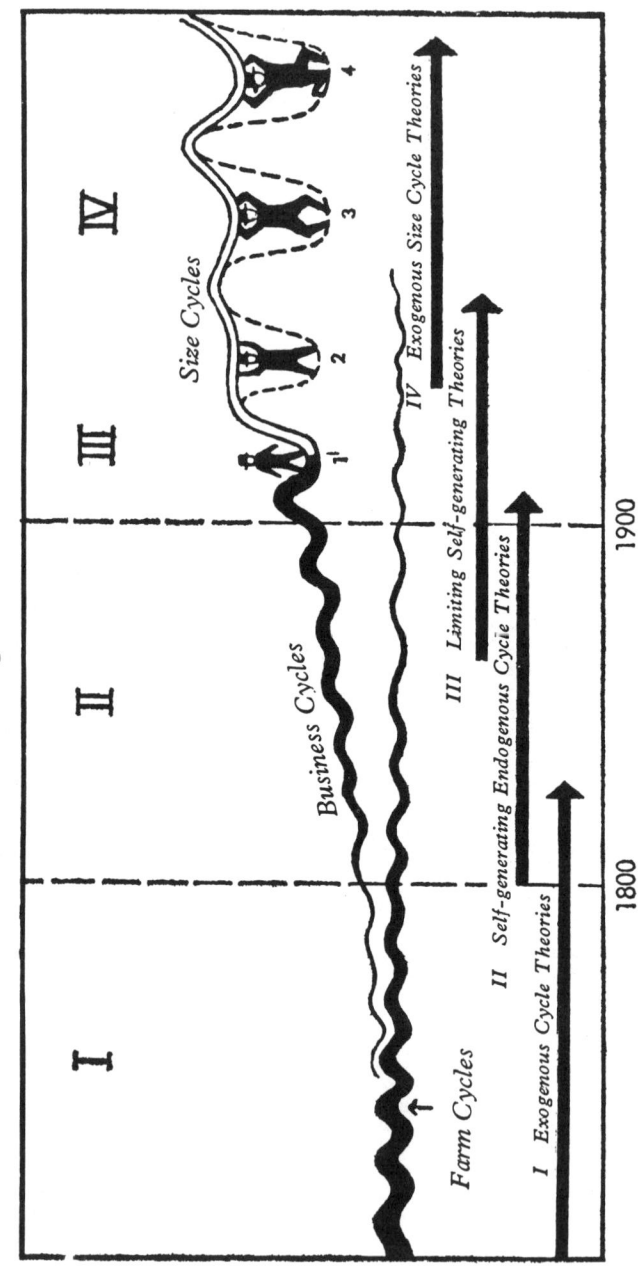

Diagram I

Caption to Diagram I

THE CHANGING NATURE OF CYCLICAL FLUCTUATIONS

Diagram I illustrates the gradual change of the nature and problem of cyclical fluctuations and the corresponding change in cycle theories in the course of four distinct historic development stages.

STAGE I. The pre-industrial age was dominated by what may be called agricultural or farm cycles developing in response to weather and war conditions. The problem of economic fluctuations could therefore often be foreseen but rarely solved. Exogenous cycle theories explained everything requiring explanation satisfactorily. Farm cycles diminished in importance and ultimately petered out (lower wave) as technological progress began to furnish efficient conservation processes, permitting storage of surplusses from fat to lean years.

STAGE II. With the growth of capitalism, business cycles proper developed, first on top and then in the place of farm cycles (upper wave). But as long as business units and market areas were of moderate size, so were the fluctuations they produced. The inner resiliency of capitalism was therefore sufficient to propel the economy out of its shallow valleys without the need of an external stabilizer — a condition well rationalized by contemporary self-generating cycle theories.

STAGE III. But now a new difficulty set in, erroneously attributed to capitalism but actually caused by the increasing size of social units through which cycles could transmit themselves. The gap between prosperity and depression became now so large, and the descent from the one into the other so steep, that the economy tended to land at the bottom with its bones crushed. This led theoretically to *limited* self-generating cycle theories, and practically to the introduction of government into the economy (1). The impact effect of government intervention (2) seemed to bear out the new theories since fluctuations resulting from lack of central control could obviously no longer occur.

STAGE IV. But while government control eliminated business cycles, its very effectiveness tended to produce the basis for a new category of fluctuations originating, like farm cycles, not within but outside the economy. Depending in magnitude as well as in origin no longer on the nature of an economic system but on the size of the social unit served by it, these fluctuations may be called *size cycles* (double-lined wave). Instead of being eliminated by control, they may paradoxically *result* from it for the following reason. As government direction becomes more effective, a new growth process enables a now highly integrated economy to expand to such an extent that, on sheer physical grounds, control becomes at first more complex (3), and ultimately altogether impossible as a result of man's creation having outrun his talent to encompass it with his limited vision. When this stage is reached, the solution is not further control or socialism, but the reduction of overgrown social units to controllable dimensions. The answer is not joining Common Markets but dividing National Markets; not integration but devolution.

The diagram tries to illustrate why the principal problem of our time is not: How to grow? but: How to stop growing? — The development phases I, II, III, IV, are somewhat distorted, I representing the period from antiquity to the 19th century, and IV approximately the last quarter of a century.

Diagram II

("G" stands for the magnitude of government control; different shadings for the limits to which it can be extended in states of various size: 1, 2, 3, 4).

1

2

3

Here, fluctuations constitute no problem. Taking their magnitude from the size of the body of which they are part, they are held down to insignificant proportions by the small size of the social unit

As society grows, so grows the amplitude of cycles. Proportions becoming disruptive, uncontrolled economic activities begin to fail generating their own stabilizers.

Up to a given social size, government control both eliminates cycles and permits further economic growth.

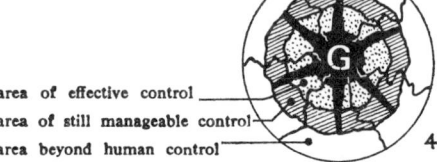

area of effective control
area of still manageable control
area beyond human control

4

But further growth ultimately outgrows the human talent for control. In the margin unfolding beyond man's intellectual horizon, new waves set in: scale cycles, pounding at the fringes of controllability until their cumulative effect undermines its very center, collapsing the entire economy.

THE PHYSICS OF ECONOMICS

Cyclical fluctuations of business activities are natural to all self-regularity economic systems. But, as diagram II indicates, taking their measure from the social unit through which they transmit themselves, they cannot constitute a major problem as long as the social unit is relatively small (1). The real problem sets in when fluctuations are amplified as a result not of the internal growth of a system such as capitalism, but of the external growth of the social unit of which they are part (2). As long as the social unit is not too large, the problem of business cycles can be solved through the replacement of a free with a government directed economy which, along with the self-regulatory business *system,* eliminates also business *cycles* (3). But, if in the calm of a cycle-less economy the social unit experiences further growth through integration and expansion, the now geometrically multiplying problems of size may ultimately outstrip the controlling power of government which even at its best seems capable of only arithmetic extension. When this happens (4), size cycles originating in the widening margins beyond the reach of control will gradually erode not only the outskirts of government control but the fabric of the entire society. Government control can therefore effectively counteract cyclical disruptions only in societies of relatively small size.

VI. Budget Diagnosis

Eye diagnosticians are persons who do not examine the human body in order to discover diseases. They do not measure your temperature, nor do they take your pulse. All they do to find what is wrong with you is to take a deep look into your eyes. When I first heard of them I thought they were frauds. I thought so until one of them looked into my own eyes, and gave me with minute precision a detailed account of all the diseases I had, the vaccinations I had been given, and the names of most of the medicines I had used during my life. It sounded like magic. But the fact was that the eye is indeed, as the poets say, the mirror of man. Each different substance absorbed by us registers in the eye by subtly changing the pattern of its colors.

It is somewhat similar with the budget. In a way, it is to society what the eye is to the human body. It registers a nation's ideology, its primitive or advanced stage of development, its cultural and technological aspirations, its economic structure, the honesty of its government officials, its political power, its aggressiveness, its history. In fact, there is almost nothing under the sun influencing a nation's life that does not find its reflex in the budget. As a result, the sciences of budgeting, taxation (which is interwoven with it), and public finance (which unites them both), are subjects of infinitely greater fascination than is generally assumed. They permeate everything, though few people may be aware of the width of their scope.

To understand the implication of this statement, let us analyze as a random example a concept dear to most of us but rarely associated with such seemingly dehydrated problems as those involving the allocation of public funds – the concept of freedom. If we look closely at it we shall find that freedom is not only intimately connected with questions of state finance, but that the entire history of freedom is fundamentally nothing but the history of budgeting. Our first act as members of a group does not, as many suppose, consist in the composition of flamboyant declarations of independence, but in the drawing up of a dry document specifying the functions of our communal agents and the methods of allocating funds for their execution (the functions' that is, not the agents'). The famous *Magna Charta* of the British is not a document of freedom but a document of Public Finance from which certain freedoms flow as a result of public revenue and expenditure provisions. Similarly, the history of American independence is not the history of spontaneously developing urges for freedom, but the history of tax irritations. It started with tax revolts and ended with a constitution whose basic text is so uninspiring a public finance document that few citizens ever manage to read it. That is why they keep on seeing romance in it. Only in the first ten *amendments*, added as if by afterthought, do they find what many think is contained in the constitution itself, a charter of freedoms.

To gain a proper insight into these seemingly strange relationships between budgetary provisions and even our most exalted concepts such as freedom or sovereignty, it is not sufficient merely to state them. We must trace them to their beginning. For, as Aristotle said, "he who considers things in their first growth and origin, whether a state or anything else, will obtain the clearest view of them." However, since the origin of both freedom and budgeting coincides with the development of man's first societies the starting point of this meditation is what at first sight must appear a digression: a theory of the origin of the state. But it should soon become evident that the way in which first societies were formed will shed considerable light on the problems which are the subject of this chapter.

1

The chief difficulty is that no one knows for certain how exactly the first state came into existence. The social contract theorists think it was formed on the basis of a solemn agreement amongst free individuals for the purpose of introducing peace and justice into previously lawless relationships. The force theorists – that it came about as a result of an act of conquest. Some economists attribute it to the integrating effect of increasing commercial intercourse. Anthropologists – to the extension of families. But, though the theories are numerous and useful in many respects, none of them has been elaborated in a manner useful for budget analysis.

This, however, should not deter us. Rather it should be an incentive to do the same thing many others have done: formulate our own theory to explain what requires explanation. This in fact is the very purpose of all theorizing. However, the theory presented in what follows is not entirely our own. Its substance comes from Aristotle who, to my mind, has given the most *sensible* account of the motives leading to the establishment of our first societies. The reason for his greater lucidity seems simple. Unlike most, he operated on the assumption that primeval man was *also* man, and was therefore in no need of subtle theorizing. All that was needed to understand his actions and motivations was to study our neighbours, or ourselves, for that matter. If we can visualize what *we* would do under primeval conditions, the mystery of early social events will soon resolve itself. For primeval man in all likelihood did the same things.

Working from this premise, Aristotle thought the motive leading men to the creation of the original state was not their desire to secure justice, peace, and defence – functions which to this day have remained the source of our principal social expenditures – but the desire to secure for themselves the benefits of a good life, the *summum bonum*. Accordingly he thought the state creating impulse could not have been the generally accepted motive of love of peace. This would have required the assumption that primeval man was essentially a fighting man. But why should men living in uncrowded dispersion with their families and early tribes fight? It seemed much more reasonable to assume that primeval man, as we are still today, was essentially a lonely man, a social man entering society for the sake of companionship, for the good life. This is why we might call Aristotle's theory, in contrast to the solemn social-contract, force, anthropological, or economic theories, a convivial theory of state origin.

But here Aristotle gives out. After all, his famous works were primarily lecture notes elaborated for his students, not necessarily for posterity. As a result, it is here where our own theorizing must set in. If Aristotle gives us a clear picture of the motivation of state creation – a vital element in the understanding of the purpose of government – he leaves us in the dark when it comes to the practical steps leading to the creation of the original state. As a result, these we have to furnish ourselves, for it lies in these first practical steps from which the interrelationship between social purpose and budgeting arises with particular clarity. Only with respect to its technical elaborations can the following extension of Aristotle's theoretical speculations therefore be considered as new, and be ranged into the category of what German political scientists like to call a *Staatsroman* – a piece of political fiction illuminating a piece of political reality.

So let us for a brief moment transport ourselves back to the beginnings of social existence. Assuming that we lived a lonely life and longed for a closer companionship with our fellowmen, our first social enterprise took in all likelihood the form of ephemeral gatherings during which isolated individuals, families, and groups decided to interrupt their chase of food in order to relax for a few days at some convenient time such as the summer solstice or the end of harvesting. These first gatherings were stateless societies, without agent, leader, or government, dissolving after each occasion into the realm of individual existence from which they had sprung. Companionship and conviviality, however, soon made a certain degree of fixity and regularity necessary. Hence, a second step towards social organization followed which consisted in all likelihood in the erection of a communal structure, a hall of feasts, in which gatherings could take place safe from the uncertainties of weather. And from here on social history can be told in terms of public finance.[1]

For the erection of the first fixed structure leading to the creation of our first social property compels us to draw up our first budget. Entrusting our newly formed society with a function, we must also finance it. As a result, our first social contract does not take the form of a charter of freedom but of the stipulation of a public expenditure balanced by a matching amount of public revenue. In fact, at this early stage, just as people and government are still one and the same thing, so are expenditure, symbolizing the social purpose, and revenue, symbolizing the individual contribution. The revenue is our work, and the expenditure item, the fruit of our work – the communal hall. And this hall being essentially a hall of feasts, it follows that our first society fulfills essentially the functions of what in later periods we have come to call an *inn*.

This is quite a different picture from that painted by traditional social contract and other theorists who like to talk only in the most exalted terms when thinking of social institutions. But this should not discourage us. For, as Samuel Johnson has said. "there is nothing which has yet been contrived by man by which so much happiness is produced as by a good tavern." Indeed, so important has been the role played by taverns and inns in the life of the public, that innkeepers are still called *publicans*, and inns have been historically amongst the first enterprises classified as *business affected with a public interest*. And to this day, one

[1] This convivial need for fixity and regularity explains why one of the first sciences was that of the calendar. This is usually attributed to the farmer's need for anticipating sowing and harvesting seasons, or the arrival of the Nile floods. However, farmers farm when nature is ready, not when the calender tells them. But when it comes to the question of attending or missing the precious gayeties of an annual solstice party, then knowledge of calender and precise dates become imperative. An event occurring as late as the 1950's is telling proof of the convivial origin of the calender. At that time, the then Prime Minister Diem of Viet Nam discovered on an inspection trip that "the mountain tribes of Annam have no calender, simply use the planting of the new rice crop to mark the new year. Diem decided it was a shame, picked February 22 for the inauguration of an annual mountain New Year's party that will last for three days. The tribesmen will stage sword-fighting contests, race on elephants. Diplomats flown up from Saigon will hunt tigers and wild buffalo." (*Time*, February 11, 1957).

of the principal state functions performed by kings and presidents on behalf of their peoples is the social host's, the innkeeper's function of hospitality,[1] from a budgetary point of view reflected in expense accounts.

But if our first social enterprise may be conceived as having been an inn, the question arises: How did those governmental functions develop which are customarily associated with modern political life – peace, justice, and defence? And how did government itself arise from an as yet stateless society united by nothing but the joint use of a piece of communal property which, as we have seen, was in all likelihood a public house, a pub, a tavern?

Continuing the fiction of the *inn-state*, the answer is not too difficult. Once we have common property, we must choose an administrator to maintain it. Our first joint official is therefore not a president or king but an innkeeper. Since the latter cannot tend our property and at the same time engage in the pursuits necessary for his own material survival, we must draw up a new social contract amongst ourselves defining the functions of our first servant, and regulating the methods of providing him with the means of his subsistence out of our own resources. At this juncture expenditures and revenues are no longer one and the same as they were when we built our first social structure. They have begun to drift apart, the expenditures henceforth being dependent on the administrator's activities, and the revenues on the members of the social group. And this division has remained to this day, although under tyrannies both aspects, though functionally separate, are under the direction of the administrator. And the document stipulating both administrative functions and the appropriation and allocation of funds is our first constitution – a budget document pure and simple.

As always when men live together, quarrels begin to develop,

---

[1] Queen Elizabeth II charmingly gave expression to the idea of the inn-state in her Christmas message of 1956, when she spoke compassionately of persons "driven from their own lands by war and violence." "We call them refugees, let us give them a true refuge," she said: "Let us see that for them and their children there is room in the inn."

and there are few places where fights seem to arise more spontaneously than in the dense and crowded atmosphere of a social gathering place such as an inn. As a result, the innkeeper must soon be charged with the function of dispensing Justice. This gives order to our enterprise. But now that it prospers and our larders are full, as yet innless neighbouring societies will sooner or later attack us. Hence the innkeeper, already the administrator of our social property and our chief police executive, must be charged with the last of the three original functions of government – the function which, if added to the two others, produces moreover the attribute of sovereignty – defence.

I do not know whether this briefly sketched theory of state evolution, based on Aristotle's theory of social motivation, approximates actual development. But, being founded on the natural tendency of man to feel lonely if unassociated, it seems more realistic than the other, more respectful theories, which talk much of freedom or justice, but little of their relation to such lowly things as their financial cost. If it had no other significance, the theory would seem to serve at least a philosophic purpose by emphasizing the clearly individualistic intent which induce men to create states and governments as instruments dedicated to the fullness of their own good life, not as self-centred structures turning men into loyalty-neurotics and political tools subservient to their own creation, as is increasingly maintained nowadays.

But it does have another significance for the purposes of this presentation. From a purely public finance point of view, it illustrates how every stage of constitutional development, from the stateless society, to the non-sovereign and, finally, to the sovereign state, from the small to the great power, from the underdeveloped to the developed society, is faithfully reflected in budgetary allocations. For, every time we extend the field of action of the agents of society, we must at the same time furnish the necessary funds. And the furnishing of funds, restricts the freedoms of those having to furnish them. This is why, strange as it may at first have appeared, even our greatest ideals such as justice or freedom are nothing but reciprocals of government expenditures as laid down in the budget, and why the great charters of sovereignty and freedom are necessarily always budget documents, the drier, the better.

2

Up till now, I have followed the simile of the human eye. But unlike the human eye, whose colours reflect the most minute changes of the body's conditions without, however, being able to influence them, the nature of budgetary allocations not only reflects the status of human conditions such as freedom but also influences them. Hence the effort of political parties to preserve individual freedoms by means of curtailing the expenditures of government. And hence the insistence of democratic reformers – whatever the majesty of governments and kings – to keep the revenue and expenditure side of the budgetary process in the hands of parliament and peoples.

And also up till now, I have emphasized the significance of budget considerations with respect to problems of freedom. But though this is an often neglected angle, it represents only one of many aspects upon which the subject touches. The economic implications which the budget both reflects and influences are no less sweeping. The nature of allocations thus reveals whether a country constitutes an agricultural or industrial society; whether it is in transition from the one to the other; whether it tends to establish an internally balanced economy or one dependent on external trade; whether it is capitalist or socialist; whether it intends to raise itself with foreign aid or by its boot straps. And it reveals the cultural, political, and moral aspirations of a people.

If one glances at the budget of Liechtenstein, for example, (which the Princely Government kindly sends me every year), one sees at once that this little state of 17 thousand inhabitants is a principality since a small sum is assigned to keeping the Prince's coat of arms polished. One sees that it has no army, since there are no defence expenditures. One sees that the rate of crime is extremely low, since the maintenance of the prison guards costs more than that of the prisoners. One sees that its traffic problems are on the rise, since the expenditures for police functions have increased so as to provide for a force of 13 instead of 9 police men without evidence of a corresponding population or crime increase. And one sees that it is capitalist from the absence of expenditure items assigned to economic controls.

But, on the other hand, one sees that it has also a small socialist sector as is evidenced by budget items assigned to a few ancient state monopolies such as the sale of playing cards or the production and sale of salt. One sees that it is a philatelist's paradise since a disproportionate amount of allocations is made for the almost constant issuance of new postage stamps, forcing stamp lovers all over the world to be perpetually up to date on Liechtenstein while at the same time returning a sizeable public revenue to the government. And one sees that one of the principal government problems is checking the power of the wild mountain streams, turning the production of electricity logically into a field of state rather than private development. From the absence of expenditures on customs services and the use of Swiss currency one realizes that the principality is united in a customs and monetary union with Switzerland. From the allocation of funds for a single foreign embassy – in Bern – one can deduce that Switzerland is charged also with Liechtenstein's external representation. From the absence of funds set aside for an Un-Liechtensteinian Activities Committee one sees that problems of subversion, anxiety, and hysteria, so common in larger powers, are non-existent; and that, as a result, the mood of the country is placid and serene.

From items dedicated to the study of new industries one discerns both the trend towards limited industrialization as well as the cautiously slow pace at which it is to be effected. From educational items one sees that elementary and vocational training, as well as the first half of highschool education is a state concern, while, by an apparently strange contrast, no allocations are made for advanced highschool or university education. But, there is a great deal of wisdom in this. As the Prime Minister told me, to make it appropriately difficult, higher education must be taken at the student's own initiative and expense abroad – in Austria or Switzerland – on the healthy assumption that too much education would damage the easy balance of the principality since its small dimensions could not possibly accomodate more than 8 to 10 lawyers, the same number of dentists, and perhaps twice the number of doctors. As a result, a state-supported higher education, instead of enriching people, would merely frustrate them since even as Ph.D.'s they could do nothing but farm or emigrate. And aside from that, a small country's problems are so translucent, that it needs no college education to grasp them. The Prime Minister himself was an elementary school teacher and prides himself on being the son of a stable boy. Yet unaided by doctors of law, economics, or political science, he prepares a budget whose excellence is such that I find it more useful for classroom study with my students than the vast documents of large powers whose problems differ from those of Liechtenstein not by their nature but by their unmanageability. Hence, as a European wit once said to an American friend in pre-Hitler days: "We have Liberty, you have the Statue," so tiny Liechtenstein may say to the prestigious academic institutions of the great powers such as Oxbridge and Haryale: "We have the sound economy, you have the great professors."

And lastly, one can see from Liechtenstein's budget allocations dealing with personnel expenditures that the Prince must be a rich man since no funds are set aside for either his public or his private functions; that the only public official working full time is the Prime Minister; that Catholicism is the state religion; and that the honesty of public servants is great. For one of the minor revenue items of one of its recent budgets consists in a refund for unused travel allowances from an unnamed land surveyor.

But through it all, it must always be emphasized that the budget is not only the mirror of a country's condition. It is also the tool through which this condition can be subtly or abruptly changed. It is the lever of political and economic life. This is why it is no coincidence that both the political and the economic sciences have their origin in the field of public finance.

And it must be emphasized that what is true of little Liechtenstein, is also true of giant Russia, and that what is true of the overdeveloped economy of the United States is true also of the underdeveloped economy of Puerto Rico. Russia has expressed her development policy and priority scale particularly succinctly in the various mottos given to her succession of five-year budget plans: *Transportation, Industrialization, Collectivization, Victory in War, Reconstruction,* and *Surpass the United States.* But all, whether they be Russia, the United States, Liechtenstein, or Puerto Rico, proceed on similar roads. All expand their economies by a careful balancing of budgetary allocations expressing the importance and urgency of their projects, and the methods by which they try to turn underdevelopment into development through an elaborate order of priorities for their projects and a meticulous determination of the desired pace for completing them. Allocations granted to immediate capital construction on a large scale in preference to educational projects may lead to waste and ruin, not to wealth. Too fast a de-slumming pace made possible by excessive allocations under the pressure of social and political needs or in response to a magnanimous philosophy, may lead to worse slums in the future. For slums breed not only in the social condition of over crowding but in the architectural condition of uniformity. They are at least in part the results of the socialization of taste and uniformity of architectural style which speed, made possible by misdirected priority allocations, nowadays so often imposes on the social planner.

3

In the past few pages I have chosen as illustration for the relationship between the seemingly dry and narrow field of budgeting and the width and depth of political, economic, and human problems, primarily the small state of Liechtenstein. As mentioned, the reason for this is that its problems differ from those of larger complexes such as Puerto Rico, or large powers such as the United States, only in proportion, not in kind. As a result, they can just as well be studied there as anywhere or, for that matter, even better since, the smaller the dimensions of political bodies, the more easily surveyable are their problems.

Now, however, it becomes necessary to make a few modifications. For, as the preceding chapters have by now amply demonstrated, the size of society is not altogether insignificant in the analysis of social problems. True, the scope of government activities is reflected with equal precision in the budget of large countries such as Germany or the United States as it is in small countries such as Liechtenstein or Puerto Rico. But if we compare the budgets of large countries on the one hand, and of small countries on the other, over a succession of years, we shall find that, aside from reflecting momentary historic situations in both, successive budgets reveal a process of evolution which varies considerably with the size of the country. In smaller countries, this evolution depends exclusively on the varying social philosophies prevailing in them and, accordingly, may take a different course in each. In larger countries, on the other hand, it is intimately associated not with philosophy but with their size and rate of growth, forcing them at given levels into identical courses irrespective whether their social philosophy differs or not, whether their inclination is collectivist or individualist, or whether the state in question is the Soviet Union, Great Britain, or the United States.

This requires a qualification of what this chapter has maintained so far: namely that the budget not only reflects the scope and nature of government activities but can also determine them. For this seems true only up to a certain degree of social growth. When a society exceeds this degree, when it becomes too large, the budget continues to reflect its structure as well as its purpose, but it can no longer alter what it reflects. Fully now like the human eye, it becomes a passive mirror. It is no longer determined by the conscious will of parliament or government but by the purely physical circumstances of the social mass of its society. Up to the limit of critical size, the normal tendency of individualistic and freedom-loving men seems to be to restrict government functions to the minimum necessary for the bare maintenance of the social machinery in order to keep a maximum of freedom for themselves. But once their number grows beyond it, their swelling multitudes become so unmanageable that, instead of impeding the increase of government functions, they themselves, not governments, begin to clamor for their extension.

This means that at a given social size, further growth will trigger off the spontaneously erupting socialization process which has been pictured in the the two preceding chapters and which, as a rule, will run through the following now familiar stages. At first, the original functions of government – justice, internal peace, defence – will increase with growth, but as the comparison of police and defence figures have shown, they will increase at a faster rate than the growth of society. Then, the functions, having already increased in magnitude, will now increase also in number, turning previously private activities into spheres of public interest. Finally, the requirements of modern monster societies will become such that governmental direction can no longer be restricted to mere *sections* of personal and economic life; it must be extended to every aspect of existence. An increasing number of constantly overgrowing tottering private industries must be swallowed up; and a uniform and, therefore, collectivist system of education must be established if for no other reason than to train the citizen in the ability to understand in the briefest terms the directives of the great co-ordinating Big Brother as George Orwell calls the phenomenon, or the government as the rest of us call it.

This is why one of the important features reflected in the budget of large countries is that, as I have pointed out before, the United States, for instance, ranks inspite of her capitalist heritage or individualist ideology today second only to China, the countries of the Soviet empire, and Great Britain in her advanced degree of socialization. It explains why even such an arch-conservative succession of British prime ministers as Sir Winston Churchill, Sir Anthony Eden, Sir Alec Douglas Home, Harold Macmillan, or Edward Heath could during their tenure do little with England except gracefully preside over what had become qualitatively if not quantitatively a socialist state. And it is the reason why the largest countries, while helping others to develop, seem themselves paradoxically bound for a type of overdevelopment, which amounts both practically and psychologically to the same thing as underdevelopment.

If they did not feel so over-underdeveloped already, why on earth should they be engaged in such a desparate struggle to push their growth rates still further? This in spite of the fact that, as I have tried to demonstrate again and again: the larger their social and economic size, the greater are their problems. And the greater their problems, the less their ability to catch up with them. For though human talent can be somewhat stretched through such control-extending factors as education, technology, or organization, as Justice Brandeis was so tireless in stressing: there is a limit to which even this can be achieved.

Thus, a look into the unromantic, cold, and dry pages of budgets often gives us an insight gained elsewhere only with difficulty. Schools and textbooks may continue to treat students to splendid visions of liberty. And newspapers may spray us with comforting illusions. But it is in budgets where we find the unadorned facts telling us that freedom as our ancestors knew it, or as the citizens of smaller countries still know it, can not be maintained in modern large powers if they continue to grow at rates which seem to enchant no one but statisticians and chambers of commerce. Unless the sorcerer returns in time to stop their continuing galloping growth, unleashed by a host of eager apprentices who learned the lesson without digesting it; or better still, unless Professor Henry C. Simons' monsters of mercantilism, breeding nothing but collectivism and militarism, are dismantled, an era of world embracing totalitarianism will be in store for us. But fortunately, as few read constitutions, still fewer read budgets. As a result, illusions can for a time continue to be maintained, the more so as, at the present state of growth, our freedoms, though rapidly shrinking, are after all still considerable. But what about 1984, when many of us will still be around?

4

There is a last point to which reference should be made. Budget history is dominated by the ideal of balance. A balanced budget has since time immemorial been considered a sign of a healthy household, while deficit spending has been considered as a sign of dangerous instability. If the limited frame of this chapter would permit, much could be said on this subject. But so much has already been said, that it seemed preferable to deal with neglected aspects and speculations such as the *Convivial Theory of State Origin*, rather than add to a discussion which has gone on for a long time and is becoming a little stale. But one brief comment may still be made.

Like many minor details, the overall fact whether a budget is balanced or not, reveals a story, though it is doubtful whether the story is significant. Balanced budgets have prevailed in two stages of social development. They prevailed in eras characterized by the prolonged existence of a social still-life resulting from the fact that development processes had come to an end. Deficit budgets, on the other hand, have been characteristic of stages of movement, such as is on the one hand caused by conditions of poverty or war and, on the other, by periods of transition, social expansion, and development.

At best, the idea of a balanced budget, towards which a similar emotion is frequently displayed as the one that gloried in the mercantilist ideal of a favourable balance of trade, is therefore a very relative proposition. It may be a sign of health as well as a sign of stagnation. Yet, unlike the favourable balance of trade, a balanced budget is still today considered by many as such an unadulterated virtue – which, indeed it would be in times of normalcy, levelled-off conditions of social growth, and at a level of living standards so high that it would render further development unnecessary – that numerous other considerations and policies have been subordinated to its realization.

Thus, under the arch-conservative administration of President Eisenhower, Washington declared with undisguised relish that, after years of democratic squandering, balance had at last once again been achieved during the year 1956 – an election year at that. But what was at the time ignored in the exultation, was that the *level* at which balance had been achieved was higher than at any other period in history. In other words, under the anti-socialist presidency of Eisenhower, the socialist sector of the American economy had assumed greater proportions in a time of relative normalcy than under any other President. Thus, if President Truman was a socialist, as he was so often accused by his successor, President Eisenhower will, by comparison, have to be classed a Communist. And so will all who came after him. Which only demonstrates once more the degree to which not man nor philosophy, but social size, determines at given levels everything, including the direction of budget policies. For the last one to lead us *voluntarily* along the road of socialism would have been Dwight Eisenhower.

All this seems to bear out the prediction which Eisenhower's sparkling antagonist Nikita Khrushchev addressed in his hay day to his capitalist hosts when he said during an animated cocktail party: "We shall bury you." Communism will indeed bury capitalism. But contrary to Khrushchev's Marxist interpretation, it will not be the communism of the Soviet Union or China that will do the job. The actual gravedigger will be the communism engendered by the cancer of excessive national size which is so perversely cherished by the overgrown capitalist nations afflicted with it that they would give up anything rather than the cause of their own undoing.

VII. Velocity Theory of Population

1

According to the Quantity Theory of Money, primitively expressed, the total supply of money (M) exchanges for the total supply of goods offered in Trade (T). For the only market function of money is to operate as a medium of exchange. If the supply of money doubles or is halved without a corresponding increase or decrease in the supply of commodities offered in trade, the price level (P) must also double or be halved since at all times all the money, having no other than an exchange function, is needed to purchase all the goods offered in exchange. As a result, the primitive Quantity Theory is expressed by the formula $P = \frac{M}{T}$.

There is however a slight snag to it. For a dollar bill does not only purchase a dollar's worth of commodities offered in trade. It purchases a dollar's worth of commodities each time it changes hands. The person receiving it can buy something else with the same bill; and so can the next, and the next. If in a closed community a million dollars worth of goods are offered in trade, a million dollars in money are needed if each bill or coin changes hands once. But if they change hands twice, that is if their velocity (V) doubles, only $500,000 are needed to effect a million dollars worth of transactions, and only $10,000 if the velocity is 10.

In other words, a change in the velocity of money has the same effect as if the quantity of money had changed. As an inflation may thus be caused quantitatively, by an increase in the supply of money, it may also be caused qualitatively, by an increase in the money's velocity. When this happens, as for instance in the case of panic, a tightening of the supply of money would have no restraining effect whatever on the price level. Only the administration of a mass tranquilizer slowing down the velocity of monetary circulation would in this case be capable of producing results. Because of the quantitative effect of velocity, the adjusted theory reads: $P = \frac{MV}{T}$. There are other refinements, but these are not needed for the purposes of this analysis.

2

The interesting thing about the Quantity Theory is that, as has already been briefly mentioned in some preceding chapters, its underlying principle applies also to population problems. For just as the price level changes in response not only to monetary quantity but also to velocity changes, so the 'mass' of a population may change not only as a result of a change in its physical size but also because of a change in its pace, of the velocity of its movement.

In anology to the Quantity Theory of Money, we may therefore formulate a Quantity Theory of Population. Primitively expressed, it states once more the obvious: that the mass of population (D) is determined by the size or number of a population (P) in relation to available living space (L). Its formula, similar to the primitive monetary formula, reads therefore: $D = \frac{P}{L}$. This means that if a rise in the population figure increases its mass to the point of overpopulation, two solutions are possible. One is to reduce P through either birth control or emigration (if Malthus' positive checks – war, famine, disease – fail to do their macabre job). The other: to enlarge L through either conquest (extensively) or through the mobilization of technology (intensively). Since the population theory has never been pushed beyond its primitive formulation, no other solution could so far have been offered beyond these two.

But as in the case of its monetary cousin, here too a modification becomes necessary if the formula is to take into account all forces exerting pressure on mass. For, as I have suggested in the first two chapters, the quantity of a population may increase not only as a result of an influx of more people, but also as a result of an increase in the pace, the velocity, with which people move. This explains, for instance, why theatres must have emergency exits, though ordinary exits are amply sufficient for audiences moving at ordinary pace. But if the velocity of movement doubles under the impact of apprehension or quadruples as a result of panic, the effect is the same as if the audience itself had doubled, quadrupled, or multiplied by some other coefficient. Dealing with the problem quantitatively, theatres furnish a greater number of exits than are normally needed. But, were it not for the brevity of time available in an emergency, they could deal with it also qualitatively, as indeed they always try when they exhort their audiences that, in case of fire, they should keep their pace slow: *Walk! Do Not Run!*

As a result, according to the adjusted theory, which because of its emphasis on the volume increasing effect of pace may be called the *Velocity Theory of Population,* mass is determined not by population number alone, but by the number of a population times its velocity in relation to available living space. Its full formula should therefore read: $D = \frac{PV}{L}$.

3

This indicates that there exists a largely ignored third solution of overpopulation problems, aside from the first two which are derived from the primitive formulation of the population theory. This lies in a reduction of the velocity with which people move. This third alternative is the more significant, as the two older solutions seem to have reached the limit of usefulness; the one – territorial expansion – because, even in the age of space ships, the supply of *Lebensraum* capable of absorbing excess populations is nearly exhausted; the other – technological progress – because, whatever may be added in means of subsistence through more intensive exploitation of existing resources, tends to be lost because of progress' concommittant side effect of increasing man's velocity. Thus, instead of solving the problem of overpopulation, technological advance merely changes its character from one involving the quantity of particles to one involving their speed. Moreover, since accellerating velocity must ultimately have the effect of increasing the mass of a population at a faster rate than the rate at which progress can come forth with appropriate solutions, technological advance has the tendency beyond a certain point not only of changing overpopulation problems but actually of aggravating them.

This is why remedial measures, such as are now universally applied in all modern urban areas, seem invariably to create more problems than they solve. The most common of these, and the most symbolic of contemporary overpopulation problems, is the traffic glut, attributed by most planners to the fact that too many people have come to live together in too narrow a space. Interpreting and, therefore, attacking the problem quantitatively, they try to solve it through more and better highways, one-way streets, unobstructed over and underpasses, ampler parking facilities, and so forth. The result? Worse traffic gluts after every improvement than before.

For to stress once more, gluts are the product not only of too many people in a given area but, like the gluts of logs floating down rivers, also of the pace with which people move. And pace is, of course, not reduced but increased by the construction of new traffic facilities which, while likely to *shift* the location of the problem, are unlikely to *diminish* it (unless all terminal points such as cities were to be eliminated and all people kept moving in the flow of traffic all their lives).

Numerically, the population of New York is about eight million. But multiplied by its daytime velocity, its mass, depending on the hour, is in effect that of a population of twenty to fifty million with the result that the same city, which is amply adequate at the near zero velocity prevailing at night or the low velocities of late evenings, is hopelessly inadequate at the high and increasing velocities of the day. Ancient Rome, with two million inhabitants but a velocity that was very slow even at daytime, produced few accounts indicating that it suffered greatly from overpopulation problems. Nor did the beehive populations of medieval cities. Twentieth-century New Brunswick, New Jersey, on the other hand, with a mere 40,000 inhabitants but a daytime velocity that multiplies its mass perhaps tenfold, is glutted from morning to night, day in, day out, not in spite but because of the effort of modern municipal governments to speed traffic by every means including, if necessary, through the gradual erasure of their cities.

Thus, technological improvement, far from correcting crowd conditions, actually worsens them because of the effect it has on the increasing pace of life. Another factor responsible for intensifying overpopulation problems as a result of its accelerating influence on velocity lies in the improvement achieved in techniques of administration which, spurred on by technological improvements, permitted in turn a high degree of social and economic integration. Previously, remote and largely autonomous districts discouraged large-scale movement since they hardly ever required contact with their distant central government. This changed when technical advance brought them closer to administrative centres and they could be assigned special as well as specialized roles in the integrated pattern of their national societies. For with increasing integration came increasing contacts; with increasing contacts, increasing communication; with increasing communication, increasing velocity; and with increasing velocity, an increase not in the number but in the *effective* mass of the people. A provincial, who used to visit his capital or other cities perhaps once in a life time, for pleasure, must now visit it with increasing frequency, on business, to straighten out things which got entangled in the process of centralization. And while it looks to him, and 9,999 others of his kind, as if he were visiting London or Washington only ten times a year, the collective entry in his capital's statistical surveys recording the same data lists not 10,000 but 100,000 visitors – 10,000 actual visitors times their velocity. And the corresponding accommodations must, of course, be adjusted to a crowd not of 10,000 but 100,000.

4

The modern problem of overpopulation thus being so largely a problem of velocity rather than of actual population number or living space, it follows that it can be successfully attacked only if remedial measures are directed not at the population or space but at the velocity factor. But how can this be reduced in an age whose every invention and policy seems to speed it up?

The answer is not too difficult once we find what makes people move at the mass and density-increasing pace of our day. Is it cars? Indeed! But cars are primarily a means, not a cause, of movement. The principal cause of the acceleration of modern movement is the necessity of spanning what may be called *technological* distances, that is distances imposed not by the needs but the tools of social existence. Amongst these may be ranged the growing distance between home and work made possible through high-speed commuting facilities; the growing distance between factories of parts and factories of wholes resulting from increasing specialization; the growing distance between producer and consumer; between residence and administrative centre; between home and market, home and school, home and theatre, home and inn. The wider these become, the greater becomes social speed, the more so as most persons are normally involved in the task of spanning not one but several of these distances every day, thereby increasing glut, crowd, accident, and overpopulation problems at a geometric ratio with every arithmetic increase in the distances to be negotiated.

This being the case, the answer to the modern in contrast to the older problem of overpopulation lies paradoxically, not in expansion but contraction. While expansion, such as we witness in the widening urban sprawls, reduces *physical density* by spreading a given population (P) over a wider living space (L), this very process increases more than proportionately *velocity density* by permeating the wider L with greater V. This is why, after a given point, communal expansion produces more burdens than gains. Contraction, on the other hand, while adding to the physical density of communal centers through the narrowing of L, diminishes the aggregate density (D) through the more than proportionate reducing effect it has on velocity density. Theoretically, velocity could of course also be reduced by legal speed limits which would ultimately draw populations also physically more tightly together simply because at low speeds they cannot afford to live too far apart. But practically the only reliable method seems not the *control* of speed but the elimination of the *motive* of speed through the elimination of technological distances.

5

The solution of overpopulation problems offered by the Velocity Theory is therefore the very opposite from the one tried during the first three quarters of the Twentieth Century on the basis of the more primitive Quantity Theory of Population. Instead of increasing the growing sprawls of undefinable, cancerous suburban galaxies, it suggests that cities become cities again, that is: metropolitan centres of smaller area, larger populations, and yet lesser aggregate mass and densities resulting from the restoration of a largely pedestrian mode of life.

To bring this about, one must above all deprive people of the motive of commuter travel by persuading them that, instead of maintaining expensive suburban prestige dormitories, it is both more sensible and more elegant to LIVE WHERE YOU WORK and WORK WHERE YOU LIVE. Once this is understood, the most wasteful of technological distances accounting for perhaps 60% of all traffic and road gluts will have disappeared. But commuting is only one of the motives of movement responsible for modern superdensities. Other things besides one's working place must be brought back to within walking distance too, such as operas, museums, universities, sidewalk cafés, and all those amenities of social existence which can now be reached only with expensive high-velocity means of travel. This is why so few of them exist: not because interest in them is lacking or admission cannot be afforded but, servicing 20 or 30 million people spread over thousands of square miles, the cost of getting there is too high. But once every town of perhaps 30,000 inhabitants offers these institutions in urban arrangements free of technological distances, its citizens, when invited to travel to Paris or Milan, will soon ask: "What for? What can we find there that we cannot find at less cost in our own town?" The effect will at once be a significant lessening of crowd conditions; seats in the opera will again be available without the need of half a year's prior reservation, and leisurely visits to museums and galleries will be uninterrupted by the barbarian shocktroup invasions of contemporary tourist hordes.

The only question is: Could smaller cities afford the sums needed for maintaining theatres or universities of a calibre that would effectively diminish the motive of travel? The answer is: Of course not, as long as their citizens have to spend the sort of sums now needed for the maintenance of highways, cars, and other instruments of integrated long-distance and vast-area living. But once velocity expenditures resulting from purely technological travel are reduced to nearly zero, the savings would be such that, as the far less endowed Italian and German city states of earlier ages have shown, even relatively small towns could afford not only first rate theatres, universities and galleries, but many other things besides, such as splendid cathedrals, parking places and streets laid out in marble, fountains, swimming pools for horses, and what not. The slow moving medieval cities afforded all this.

The reduction of social movement to purposes of commerce, holidays, and adventure, would thus have not only a social, but also an unexpected cultural consequence. In the first place, it would lead to a significant diminution of the *effective* (aggregate) mass of populations, thereby relieving the pressure of one of the worst problems of our time. And secondly, it would restore to the city its original mission of being a centre of leisure, thought, elegance, and culture. To turn the Velocity Theory into a tool of policy, however, more is needed than its mere statement. Its variables must be expressed with precision by mathematicians, and movements such as those motivated by commuting, entertainment, cultural, and commercial reasons must be measured statistically before plans can be worked out on the basis of its principles. But this would exceed the purpose of this sketch which was to identify the problem, not to solve it.[1]

---

[1] The urban implications of the Velocity Theory have been elaborated by the author in *The City of Man*. University of Puerto Rico Press, 1976.

VIII. Sky-Scraper Economics

When nearly 80,000 Welshmen voted in the British General Elections of 1959 for *Plaid Cymru*, a party advocating the establishment of a separate Welsh state within the British Commonwealth, they gave new vigour to an old Celtic ambition. But coming as it did at the very time when the newly created European Economic Community seemed to produce the first dazzling figures showing the advantage of large-scale association, it also instilled new life into old doubts about the economic soundness of the dream. For even if one grants that a separate Welsh state would show greater concern for its two and a half million Celts than a British Government which, after all, must also and primarily attend to the needs of fifty million Englishmen, would a contraction into its own narrow confines not result in severe economic disruptions? Cut off from the British market, would this not lead to a loss in the savings of mass production, to lower living standards, higher unemployment, more severe depressions? It is therefore not without reason that even the partisans of Welsh home rule who, in the October elections of 1974 sent three Members of Parliament to the House of Commons, should ask themselves what economics has to say to this? Would Wales not be too small to be viable?[1]

Actually, as the preceding chapters have tried to establish, economics provides not the weakest but one of the strongest sets of arguments for the separate existence of small states, be they Wales, Denmark, Iceland, or Switzerland - the seeming miracle of the European Common Market notwithstanding. The riches of the Italian peninsula are the product not of a united Italian economy which all but dissipated them in a series of sterile wars, but of the unaffiliated small city states to whose divisionist competition and manageable proportions we owe the matchless splendour of Florence, Venice, Siena, Genoa, Verona, Parma,

---

[1] I have tried to answer this question at length in *Is Wales Viable?* (Swansea Christopher Davies, 1971.)

Perugia, and what not. The richest German regions are to this day those which until not so long ago were the small sovereign states of Hamburg, Bremen, Frankfort, Hesse, Wurtemberg, Bavaria, Saxony rather than the large power of Prussia. Historically smallness, even in the absence of natural resources, can thus hardly be considered an obstacle preventing countries from getting rich. On the contrary.

1

One of the numerous reasons for this, and one I have not yet dealt with in this book, is that the size of the market on which a country's economic life depends has nothing whatever to do with the size of the country. The market accounting for the wealth of Great Britain is not Great Britain but the world. Without the latter, Great Britain in its present organization would collapse tomorrow. But to enjoy a global market, no British economist would suggest that Great Britain must on that ground be united with the rest of the world also politically. By the same token, to have access to the market of England, there is no need to be united with her also politically, quite apart from the fact that, just as in the case of England, the Welsh market would not be England but the world. As the American colonies realized at an early date – and, for that matter, all the host of countries ranging from Canada to Iceland, from Norway to Austria, from Ghana to Israel, whose withdrawal from larger communities constituted not the end but the beginning of their dramatic rise – separation *never* entails loss of markets. Indeed, generally the very opposite is true. A national market becomes an international one. Even for those who consider smallness an economic prison, foreign trade – as the 32 eminent participants of the 1957 Lisbon Conference of the International Economic Association have concluded with such rare unanimity – is always an 'escape' from it.

Another and infinitely more important cause enabling small countries to rival large ones in riches and high personal living standards is, however, of a quite different kind. As I have suggested earlier, this is the absence of those geometrically multiplying problems of scale which affect overgrowing societies in the same manner as costs affect the profitability of sky-scrapers (or toilet space the comfort standards of jumbo jets) once they begin to exceed a certain size. For above the height of 50 or 60 floors, the cost space of sky-scrapers increases faster than pay space. This goes on until, as I have mentioned in Chapter III, at the height of 400 floors, the sheer problem of servicing the structure would assume such proportions that the entire sky-scraper would have to consist of nothing but lifts necessary to transport the people who would have room in it if the space needed for transporting them would not have deprived them of all space needed for housing them. In spite of its splendour and phenomenal beehive productivity, all the giant structure could offer us, is employment as lift boys.

By the same reasoning, the admittedly superior productivity of overgrown states can do little to benefit the economic welfare of the individual citizen. For it is more than compensated by the geometrically rising costs of maintaining a government large enough to cope with problems whose swollen scale continuously threatens to outpace the resources of even the richest powers. As the data and detail arguments of the table and diagram accompanying Chapter III indicate, this means that high living standards must at last be recognized to depend not only simply on high productivity (or, as socialists tend to stress, on just distribution), but above all on the ability of a country to keep the cost of its social machinery down to proportions which permit the fruit of high productivity to be justly distributed in the first place, rather than having to be retained by the fear-and-problem ridden state. Only a relatively small state with its proportionately diminished problems of administration and co-ordination has been shown to afford this opportunity, even as only a smaller sky-scraper leaves enough space to contain also flats – not just an impressive array of lifts.

But what about the famous savings of mass production in which large states take such inordinate pride? In the first place, as we have just seen: to the extent that mass production depends on the size of markets rather than of countries, they are available also to smaller states. Think of the industries of Iceland, Denmark,

Sweden, or Luxemburg (even before the latter's absorption in Benelux and Common Market). It is this that has enabled Switzerland to develop an export intensity of industry that puts her at the top of all countries in the world in this category. Secondly: since the conditions of mass production vary with the nature of the product from hair pins to cars, the domestic market of moderately sized countries will often be large enough to permit optimum plant development and its accompanying savings in unit costs even in the absence of foreign trade. Only the heaviest of equipment, sputniks, hydrogen bombs, or the long distance marches of Barbara Moore seem to require larger areas than those at the disposal of smaller nations, and in their case the question is whether they are really that much needed for a good life. Thirdly, as Egypt, Laos, Marocco, Ghana, Jugoslavia, Afghanistan, and many others have demonstrated, small countries enjoy paradoxically such an enormous bargaining and blackmailing advantage in the tug of war raging between the jealous great powers trembling for their support,[1] that they have little difficulty in extorting sizeable chunks of the latters' low-cost production and diverting them into their own economies at savings considerably greater than those of their efficient and abused suppliers. And lastly, where small countries do fall short in exploiting the economies of large scale to the fullest, they may bask in the knowledge of benefitting from the no less significant economies of *small* scale.

These often prove so great that Switzerland, for example, followed closely by such other small countries as Sweden and Belgium rank again far ahead of such great powers as Great Britain, West Germany, Italy, and France in 'economic potential, productivity and welfare,' being second only to the United States in this respect. In degree of industrialization, she ranks first with 53.6%, followed by Belgium with 51%, Germany with 49%, the United Kingdom with 47.5%, Sweden with 40.5%, and trailed by the United States with 40%, Italy with 36.3%, and France with 35%. As far as gross investment is concerned, which represents 20% of her gross social production, she is likewise

---

[1] See Annette Baker Fox. *The Power of Small Nations*. London: Cambridge University Press, 1960.

ahead of all other countries in this important area. And most significantly perhaps, considering that 80% of her industries employ fewer than 50 workers, Switzerland more than compensates through industrial peace what others might gain through greater technological productivity. Thus, while the United States loses through strikes 530 working days annually per 1,000 persons employed, and France 410, Japan 280, and Germany 100, the Swiss rate is 18. This is not because Swiss workers are more modest in their wage claims. It is because the human scale of small industrial units permits, like the bloodless 'manœuvre' wars of the Middle Ages, both the faster comprehension and the swifter settlement of disputes without the need of more forceful means of persuasion.[1]

2

Nevertheless the fact remains that the 'discontinuities' represented by narrow political boundaries do have a discouraging effect on the full utilization of potentially available world markets and, as a result, on unlimited expansion, so that some of the most significant savings achieved by large-scale business in large-scale powers may indeed be lost in small ones. But even this is not necessarily a drawback. For what do the savings of scale mainly consist in? Man-power! Which means that in their bulk these technological savings are economically and socially no savings at all! They are waste! To the extent that smaller countries,

---

[1] These figures, as all figures must, have somewhat shifted since I prepared them for the 1962 German edition of this volume, but the relationships underlying them have not been affected, as has been shown by the more recent figures of the U.K. Department of Employment from the year 1976 to which I referred in a footnote on p. 75, and on which *The Times* of London based its leading editorial entitled *Small is Harmonious* (26 February, 1976). So I trust I shall be forgiven for not producing a new set of ephemeral figures for illustrating relationships of permanence. This would be important only if the relationships illustrated would be ephemeral too, in which case I would not have written this book in the first place. – For further details illustrating the permanent, see the excellently documented paper by Professors W. A. Jöhr and F. Kneschaurek of the St. Gallen Institute of Commerce. "The Study of Efficiency of a Small Nation – Switzerland," in Austin Robinson's *The Economic Consequences of the Size of Nations*. London: Macmillan, 1960, p. 54 g.

adjusting their industrial horizons in the main to the more easily surveyable and controllable limits of their political boundaries, enjoy fewer of the doubtful excess savings of mass production, they benefit socially more by their correspondingly greater economic ability to absorb man power. This is precisely because of their inability to absorb at their more modest scale of activities labour-saving machinery with such abandon that the process becomes self-defeating. And as the scale of their economy is smaller so, as has been shown in Chapter V, are the waves of depressions which contrary to the main stream of current theory affect countries more deeply not the smaller but the bigger they are. For this reason small states — like small firms, always provided (as must be emphasized) that they are no longer underdeveloped but have reached optimum expansion and organization — not only offer invariably greater benefits in proportion to their size than integrated large ones; but as again Iceland, Switzerland, and other *fully* developed[1] small nations have proved, they are also better equipped to ride out the storms of cyclical fluctuations. For the amplitude of such fluctuations is as automatically checked by small national size as waves are in the shelter of a harbour (or

---

[1] The failure to stress the development stage of small countries in appraising their resistance to cyclical disruptions is responsible for a great deal of confusion that has arisen in this question. Thus in his paper "The size of the Economy and its Relation to Stability and Steady Progress" (Robinson, op.cit, p. 190 ff.), Professor L. Tarshis produces a table which, all too short as it is, bears out his initial contention that "the greatest instability was found in the largest economies; and vice versa." Yet, in the end he cautiously returns to the conventional interpretation by reassuringly concluding that the opposite is true of what the table seems to prove: the greater vulnerability, instability, and insecurity of smaller economies. Now which is which? The contradiction would have been resolved by distinguishing between the various stages of small economies. For while it is true that *under*developed small countries suffer more from cyclical instability than developed large ones, *developed* small ones, as his fellow participants in the Lisbon Conference of 1957 (discussing the Economic Consequence of the Size of Nations), Professors Jöhr and Kneschaurek, have shown in such excellent detail, may be considerably better off than developed *large* ones. What actually disrupts raw-material exporting underdeveloped small countries is not their smallness but their underdevelopment which turns them into helpless appendices of *large* economies, making them subject to the latters' notoriously severer cyclical fluctuations on *that* ground, not because they are small. The introduction of wave mechanics which would have attributed the amplitude of fluctuations to the size of the body they transmit rather than to systems of organization, might have made the understanding of the problem easier.

as the danger of spilling water in an ice tray is checked by the insertion of a cube partitioner).

However, in fairness one must admit that large states are not only capable of saving costs through mass production; through government intervention, they are also in a position to re-absorb those whom the efficiency of mass production has made unemployed. Granted! But re-absorb where? In *economic* production? If this were possible, government intervention would not be necessary in the first place since the private sector of the economy would never have ejected them for long enough to give government the task of scooping them up.

If government assistance is nevertheless required, it can only mean that neither the private *nor* the public sector is able to absorb them *economically*. This is particularly true in those countries whose size-fostered overdevelopment has brought them to the threshold of the millenium: the age of automation which is characterized by the fact that its innovations, unlike those leading to earlier forms of technological unemployment, deprive people of work not temporarily but permanently. Hence the consternation with which American and British economists have suddenly discovered that employment is no longer rising but declining with productivity, and that unemployment has become as acute a problem in prosperity as it used to be in depression, or even worse. For there is no super-prosperity conceivable that could solve the depressing effect of automated prosperity in the sense that prosperity used to be able to solve the problems of a conventional recession.

The only way in which government can therefore re-employ the *economically* unemployable in the enormous numbers released daily by efficiency and progress (which it must both foster and dread), is by enlarging its always available *political* areas of employment. In less sophisticated times, these would have included more clearly nonsensical and, on that account, more directly functional work-creating projects such as those of the French Revolution which provided for the alternative digging and filling in of holes in the parks of Paris. However, since featherbedding of this sort is no longer compatible with the concepts of human dignity espoused by the more rational labour unions of the present time, the government of a modern industrial great power has no choice but to fall back on its two *principal* reserve pools of political employment – the bureaucracy and the army. These not only ensure a more dignified employment; they have also the advantage that their combined absorptive capacity is practically infinite.

As a result, one part of the unemployables of large countries is nowadays turned into bureaucratic supervisors (there being no room for additional *primary* officials doing the real work); the others – into soldiers. Economically, the gain is nil, as was well illustrated by the late Chairman Krushchev's complaint that production in the Soviet Union, which has always boasted of its full employment, was constantly obstructed by too many supervisors supervising supervisors. What he did not say was that this was one of the very causes of communism's vaunted full employment. However, since by far the greater part of unemployables is turned into soldiers – who, like the Paris hole diggers, are interminably kept busy with doing, undoing, doing; stretching, bending, stretching; assembling, dispersing, assembling; coming to attention, relaxing, coming to attention – we must once more arrive at the conclusion that it is *large* power rather than, as Marx suggested, *capitalist* power, that is inherently militarist. For an army, so carefully prepared and sollicitously kept busy – whatever the nature of its original and relatively uncostly makework purpose[1] – is ultimately bound to be put to exercise if for no other reason than that its members might otherwise lose their self-respect by realizing that they are nothing but society's hole diggers and gap fillers.

What we really find in efficient large powers is therefore not full employment but hidden unemployment, its size being proportionate to the size of their armies plus that part of their bureaucracy that owes its existence to the operation of Parkinson's

---

[1] This can be recognised by the fact that the pay of the common soldier is still adjusted to the rate of doles rather than of prevailing productivity wages.

Law.¹ Even their vaunted mass production efficiency is therefore largely an illusionary or, better perhaps, a self-liquidating asset. For whatever large powers may economize through technological efficiency and automation, is swallowed up on the one hand by their scale of cyclical disruption, industrial strife, and the difficulties arising from their excessive need of co-ordination, and on the other, by the sterile cost of their military establishment² and

[1] As Sir Leon Bagrit said in his fifth Reith Lecture on Automation (*The Listener*, December 10, 1964): many knowledgable economists doubt this. They feel that the increased efficiency of automation is itself sufficiently powerful to generate its own corrective forces in the sense that new jobs arise as old ones disappear." And the 1964 *Manpower Report* of the American Bureau of Labour Statistics seems to bear them out. Though automation has severely reduced agricultural employment, it shows that between 1957 and 1963 there was a growth in non-farming employment of more than 4,000,000 persons. This would indeed seem to indicate "that increased productivity brings increased employment with it and so there is nothing to worry about." But is this increased employment caused by the increased productivity of automation? Or is it not rather the result of an increase in non-productivity jobs created by government? Bearing out my contention that labour released by automation ("when perhaps no more than 20 or 30 per cent of the population can provide everything necessary for the 100 per cent") can be absorbed only through sterile, non-economic, government-connected employment, Sir Leon shows in a breakdown of the *Manpower-Report's* figures that only a minuscule 5 per cent of the more than 4 million new job opportunities were created by industry itself. "Direct employment by federal, state, and local governments accounted for 45 per cent of this extra employment, government purchasing for nearly 20 per cent, and other non-profit making, non-economic institutions for a further 16 per cent." In other words, at a time "when perhaps no more than 20 or 30 per cent of the population can provide everything necessary for the 100 per cent," 95 per cent of the 4,000,000 newly employed would have been condemned to idleness had the governments not opened its gates to them. – One additional advantage of government created employment of both the military and the bureaucratic variety is that the more sterile and high-faluting it is, the greater are its educational requirements, so that one may say that education is rapidly emerging as a third receptacle for swallowing unemployment partly through the increasing armies of teachers and partly through the longer time needed for higher education.

[2] Even if one disregards the economics of unemployment which looms behind the maintenance of large armies, and concentrates on the more conventional economics of defence, the scales will still not tip in favour of great powers. True, Professor Austin Robinson (op. cit., p. 223 ff.), whose concept of ideal size, as that of most of us, seems somewhat influenced by the size of his own country, England, comes in his paper on *The Size of the Nation and the Cost of Administration*, read before the aforementioned 1957 Lisbon Conference, to the conclusion that, in matters of military defence, it is small and not large national size that is at a disadvantage. Since the burden of defence is determined by the length of

Footnote continued overleaf

the man-hungry inefficiency of a bureaucracy whose performance, beyond a certain point, varies inversely with its size. Thus, while technological unemployment has historically tended to function as an automatic regulator, transferring resources from inefficient to efficient uses as long as countries stay small or economies are not yet fully developed, in large overdeveloped countries it has the opposite effect. It transfers them from efficient to inefficient and, indeed, dangerous uses. For it produces the man-power for those immense floating armies whose cover-up function for modern technological unemployment forbids their diminution except through either their mutual annhilation, setting in spontaneously when their mass reaches critical magnitude; or what would seem more sensible were it not so contrary to accepted dogma: through the reduction of the overgrown size of overdeveloped national complexes to proportions that would once more permit the re-absorption of the bulk of military personnel into old-fashioned economic employ.

3

There is thus little reason to assume that the political separation of Wales from England would lead to economic decay. It did not in the case of the separation of the American colonies, nor of

---

the frontier (another panel member relates it to the population number of a country's enemies), and the length of the frontier increases at an arithmetic ratio with the growth of a country while area and population contained by it increases at a geometric ratio, Professor Robinson reasons that defence costs per head will therefore be larger and more burdensome in smaller than in bigger countries. Yet the accompanying table, listing the per capita defence costs for the United States, Great Britain, France, and Italy as 100, 46, 37, and 12 in that order, indicates exactly the opposite. And so does historic experience, considering that in their strictly military aspects defence costs seem neither related to the length of a frontier nor the size of an enemy population but to fear, to *Angst*. And *Angst* has shown a tendency not to diminish but to increase with the size of a nation. The souvenir shops of tiny Liechtenstein sell a postcard of the principality's last soldier – dismissed more than fifty years ago – because it is lacking not in boundaries but in fear. By contrast, already Saint Augustine doubted the superior defence value of large nations when he asked the Romans the same question quoted earlier in this volume, which might today be asked of Russians, Chinese, and Americans: "What wisdom should any man show in glorying in the largeness of empire, all their joy but a glass, bright and brittle, and evermore in fear and danger of breaking?"

Canada, Australia, New Zealand, or Ghana. Nor was decay the consequence of similar separations of Austria from post-war Germany, Iceland from Denmark, Norway from Sweden, Egypt from Turkey, Belgium from France. On the contrary! In each case it set an end to stagnation. In spite of the gloomy predictions of established schools of interpretation, they proved in each case to be the opportunity, the great innovation that, far from interfering with economic progress, was the very cause of their spectacular rise.[1] Maybe that, if our scale economists and unionists are right, all these countries would be better off today had they remained filially united. Maybe! Yet those who seceded feel rather positive that they could never have had it better, and never had it so good. And this is true not only with regard to their own condition. For the energy released by their dramatic ascent (particularly during their early years when their alien, 'other-directed' economy became self-centered and 'innerdirected') boosted along with their own development also that of their motherlands simply because these too could not but benefit from the lifting power gained from the reduction of their size and their loss of excess weight. Also France, Germany, Sweden, Denmark, Great Britain, or Turkey became therefore richer than ever after amputations which so many of their aggrieved

[1] Lest my selection be considered unfair, reference must be made to the continued stagnation long after independence of a small nation such as Ireland. Does this contradict my argument? My answer is, give her a chance. Even amongst small countries, some proceed faster, some more slowly. In the case of Ireland, her dragging sluggish backwardness was in the first place caused not by her independent existence as a small state but by her obviously highly unprofitable centuries-long union with a completely disinterested large England whose far flung world involvement was so great that she could hardly be expected to concern herself with a region so small, though it was at her door step. The response of the Irish was to launch that crippling mass emigration that filled the manpower needs of America from domestic service and the New York police force all the way up to the presidency, while it depopulated their own country as dangerously as the policy of the communist regime of the East Germans depopulated theirs. This lasted so long that, like a conditioned-reflex, emigration continued even after independence had put a stop to the conditioner. And it is this, not lack of resources, or the 'handicap' of small size that is responsible for Ireland having started her development so slowly and so late. Now that she has at last begun moving, she will soon bless herself for having only the area of Ireland and not of India on which to bestow her talent and her resources.

citizens thought could not be survived.[1] From a strictly economic point of view, rather than object to a Welsh state on the ground that it would be too small, it would actually be more sensible to go a step further and, along the lines pioneered in 1957 by the Kremlin,[2] create regional autonomies also on the soil of other Celtic nations of Great Britain such as Scotland and Cornwall and, for good measure loosen up and federalize even England herself.[3]

4

However, there is a last question that must still be answered. For whatever facts and arguments I have marshalled in favour of the economic soundness and, indeed, the superior overall efficiency

---

[1] Compare in this connection John Strachey's pamphlet: *The Great Awakening* (1961), in which the author explains from a Marxist and Keynsian frame of reference, why the former colonies need not fear a revival of imperialism. During earlier periods, the search for surplus value forced capitalist businessmen to secure foreign markets through political domination because of the domestic unprofitability of monopoly capitalism. However, since the loss of empire the rise of living standards has raised the purchasing power of the workers of capitalist countries to such an extent that domestic markets are no longer unprofitable, and militarily secured foreign markets therefore no longer needed. As Mr. Strachey points out, metropolitan countries are now wealthier than ever while imperialism, far from being profitable, has become a costly extravagance depressing no longer the exploited but the 'exploiters'. True, Mr. Strachey attributes the rise in living standards of workers primarily to the Keynsian revolution rather than to the loss of empire. But what stimulus did this revolution get from imperial disintegration and territorial contraction without which it could neither have been afforded, nor would it have been needed or, for that matter, been tolerated.

[2] In 1957, Khrushchev's Government divided the Soviet Union into 105 districts which were later regrouped into 17 regions with populations ranging from 8 to 14 million. These fall neatly within the optimum limits suggested in Chapter II. The Russian Soviet Republic alone was divided into 10, the Ukrainian into 3, such regions. Only the Moscow region comprised a population of 25 million. The declared purpose was not only to make the individual regions so self-sufficient that in case of war the loss of one would not affect the rest any more than a torpedo, crashing into one of the numerous sealed compartments of a modern battleship, affects its sea worthiness; through regional competition and the management of small scale they are specifically designed to contribute to the more rapid development of the Soviet Union's vast still underdeveloped areas.

[3] Today in 1976, twenty years after parts of this chapter were first published, it is of course no longer necessary to suggest Britain should follow the example of Soviet regionalism. Devolution does precisely this.

in human terms of the small state and of *Kleinstaaterei* as against the wastes of modern sky-scraper and Tower-of-Babel unifications, there is one snag. And a big one at that. What about the spectacular and unprecedented economic advance achieved in Europe after six[1] of her war ravaged nations had come to the conclusion to scrap their discords, join forces and, though three of them were already highly integrated great powers in their own right, to merge their destiny in a still larger union: the European Economic Community.

Yes, what about it? Certainly the success of the European Economic Community has been dramatic. In fact so much so, that it has not only inspired imitators in all corners of the world, reaching from Africa to Latin America; it has at last managed to break the resistance of even its greatest antagonist, Great Britain who, viewing the new colossus across the Channel at first with disdain, then with humour, and finally with apprehension, became suddenly obsessed with such a dwarf complex that, in an attack of panic, she renounced her ancient aloofness, applied for admission, and is now a full member herself.

But this is about all that can be said in the community's favour. As far as its unprecedented development is concerned, it is neither unprecedented nor due to the union. The advance of the small Icelandic republic on the Arctic Circle was as spectacular. And so was that of tropical Puerto Rico, a small island state with a population of less than two and a half million. In the case of the latter, it is often suggested that the cause of her dramatic rise is the fact that she forms part of the tremendous common market of the United States. But it has been part of that market since 1898. Yet nothing happened to disturb her sommolence until 1942, and not much until 1952 when the great energy-releasing event occurred: her transformation from part to whole; from a distant outpost of a giant United States into a tense, small, self-centred and self-governing near-sovereign *Commonwealth*. Suddenly, what could not be done by the Americans, so famous for their

---

[1] Actually, the Common Market originally comprised not six but eight members. Monaco, united with France in a customs union since 1865, and San Marino with Italy since 1862, should not have been omitted from the count merely because they are small. They are as sovereign as the rest.

efficiency and know-how, in half a century, could be done by Puerto Ricans, so famous for their tropical indolence,[1] in barely ten years, during which they designed and executed that blueprint for rapid development that has become known as *Operation Bootstrap*.

But if the success of the European Common Market is not due to the union of its members, what else is responsible for it? There are a variety of causes.

The first is the 'miracle' of German recovery. This set in long before the Treaty of Rome of 1957 established the Common Market, and was due to the coincidence of two factors which would have provided the boost for an economic revival in a highly industrialized society singly. Jointly they acted like a space rocket. One was the total ruination of the German economy as a result of the greatest war destruction and post-war reparation dismantlement ever inflicted on a nation. The other: the Allied prohibition of German re-militarization. This gave the country both the tremendous opportunity for new economic action and the man-power needed to undertake the task of reconstruction at a pace so rapid that it created the illusion of a miracle being performed. Yet, the situation was fundamentally not much different from that of ancient Thebes whose frequent destruction at the hand of invading armies was responsible for the fact that, as Pausanias tells us: to the surprise of travellers Thebes alone amongst the ageing cities of Greece looked always modern, gleaming and lively – the last in fashion. In the case of Germany, the twin ravages of destruction and dismantlement were moreover distributed throughout the country so evenly that local and private initiative could spring up everywhere at the same time without requiring co-ordinaton and direction from a central authority which, even if it had been attempted, could hardly have encompassed the magnitude of the task. This in turn accounted for the little understood temporary resurrection and success of a vigorously competitive free enterprise system such as the saturated stage of overdevelopment existing in the less war-damaged

[1] If the term disturbes national sensitivities, please see footnote on p. 126.

integrated victorious large powers had long made impossible.[1]

The second cause of European revival originated likewise in conditions that preceded the establishment of the Common Market. This was the energy-releasing effect of national contraction experienced by all the major members of the subsequent European Economic Community as a result of the loss of empire in the case of France, Italy, the Netherlands, and Belgium, and the loss of half of her national territory in the case of Germany. Able to apply their undiminished talent and industrial strength to a reduced scale, the inevitable advance in productive efficiency soon showed itself in two ways: the unexpected speed with which particularly the smaller countries freed themselves of their dependence on American aid; and in daring new projects such as the resumption of land reclamation from the Dutch seas on a scale that would have been impossible as long as national energies were consumed in the administration of distant empires.[2]

If less attention was paid to this, it was because of the emotional shock that for a long time beclouded the mind of nations after it dawned on them that the war they had thought they had won was lost by them as much as by the defeated. How little the loss of empire can, however, have meant except in terms of national

[1] A precedent for this can be found in NEP, the New Economic Policy, instituted in 1921, through which the Soviet government encouraged the temporary return of capitalist business before eliminating it anew in 1928.

[2] Also the welfare-state aspects improved dramatically with the loss of empire, as was shown for example, in Great Britain. In 1899, when the power and glory of empire was at it its greatest, Joseph Rowntree recorded that 27.84% of the citizens of his native York (30.7% in the case of London), or 43% in terms of only the working class, were in a state of destitution. According to the same author, this figure stood still at a shocking 31% in 1936, when the empire was no longer quite so impressive but still in command of the enormous area of India. Only by 1951, when the empire was at last all but liquidated, and the British economy had begun to serve the United Kingdom rather than the world, did the figure of working class destitution show a dramatic change, shrivelling in the space of a few years to a mere 3%. And this was due no longer to low wages but to old age. The more Britain shrank, the easier it became to divert her resources from the power to the welfare state, and turn destitution ino affluence. The welfare state itself was thus a consequence not so much of legislation and redistribution but of territorial contraction without which the two former could never have been effected. For this reason, the immense Soviet Union may forever stay a *communist* state, but will never be a *welfare* state.

vanity becomes obvious when one realizes that, for instance, the vast Belgian colonial holdings were, according to Professor Duquesne de la Vinelle of the University of Louvain, "as unimportant as tourism in Switzerland in raising *per capita* income. Income from capital invested in Belgium's overseas territories made up only 1 to 2 per cent of national income, though the income from trade with overseas territories represented 5 or 6 per cent,"[1] a figure which was as bound to increase after these territories gained their independence as British trade income was bound to increase after the independence of her American colonies.

The third cause had for once actually a connection with the establishment of an economic union. Entering into a partnership with a Germany still galloping ahead at full speed for the reasons mentioned,[2] it was only natural that the new associates should for a while have been carried along by the momentum and benefitted from the spread across their former economic boundaries of the opportunities, the élan, and the action generated in the devastation of German defeat. Though the spectacle of victorious powers joining the vanquished in order to escape the bankruptcy of victory must have seemed a baffling paradox, it was not more paradoxical than Bismark's declaration after the Franco-Prussian War that the next time he won a victory he would demand of the defeated country not that it pay reparations *to* Germany but that it accept reparations *from* Germany. For the result of the record payment extracted on that occasion from France was that, while the defeated nation modernized its

[1] Austin Robinson, op. cit., p. 257. One could ask why, if empire was really such an economic advantage for its heart lands, capital cities of empireless countries such as Stockholm, Prague, Munich, Dresden, Florence, Berne, can hardly be said to be less splendid and prosperous than London, Paris, Madrid, or Brussels.

[2] One may ask why the same causes – destruction, contraction, etc., – did not produce the same kind of prosperity also in East Germany. The reason for this is that unlike the Western European countries – whose own advanced industrialization, lack of excessive war destruction, and availability of man-power resulting from imperial contraction could absorb only that much from West-Germany – the underdeveloped condition of the immense Soviet block with which East-Germany became linked has continued to act to this day as a sponge of practically unlimited absorptive capacity for what otherwise might have been retained by the latter. This has long overshadowed the fact that East Germany, though not benefitting from it, has actually become the sixth largest industrial producer in the world after the USA, USSR, West Germany, Great Britain and France.

industrial equipment and worked itself into a flourishing prosperity in order to rid itself of its obligations as fast as possible, its enthusiastic deliveries were one of the main reasons that pushed victorious Germany into obsolescence and depression.[1] What the members of the Common Market have therefore belatedly done was to adopt Bismark's wise counsel, and even carry it one step further. They joined the defeated.

This means that even where union did produce benefits, they were not of the kind usually implied by the defenders of scale and 'sky-scraper' economies. In fact, as the *Monthly Review* of the Federal Reserve Bank of New York pointed out in its April issue of 1959 with respect to one of the main arguments for union: in the case of the majority of enterprises, the domestic markets of most member-states of the European Economic Community were in all likelihood alone sufficiently large to convey the full advantages of mass production even without their unification.

The mere increase in market size could therefore have added little in benefits not already enjoyed and, had it not been for the establishment of an Investment Bank for developing its backward areas, would probably have worsened rather than improved the latter's conditions. This was the more likely since, as Professor Robinson noted, the retarded territories were characteristically parts not of the smaller but "mostly" of the larger countries of the union.[2] Why Southern Italy, for example, should henceforth

---

[1] This is why America, after World War 1, caused a number of her debtor nations to default not because they could not pay, but because America would not accept their deliveries. The sole exception was in the case of Finland which, glorying in the role of the only honest debtor, was permitted in an often photographed ceremony to hand over year after year her annual instalment because her debt was so insignificant that her repayment could hardly add to the poverty of a creditor suffering from *embarras de richesse*.

[2] Austin Robinson, op. cit., pp. 424-452. – I have formulated the relationship between large national size and the underdevelopment of outlying regions in a *Law of Increasing Peripheral Neglect* which suggests that, as gravitational pull diminishes with the square of the distance, so does the power and concern of central government. The only way of avoiding this inevitable consequence is to turn the peripheral regions of overgrown communities into central regions of their own, with their governments, capitals, and autonomies all close by. – See: *Is Wales Viable*, and *Development Without Aid* (Swansea: Christopher Davies, 1971 and 1974 respectively.).

be less neglected in a still larger European economic complex than it was within its own overextended motherland, would therefore be difficult to understand were it not for the fact that the new Investment Bank was specifically designed for relieving its largest members of the shameful consequences and incapabilities inherent in their excessive size. But there is of course no reason why such an investment bank could not just as easily have been organized nationally or outside the Common Market. Nor is there any reason to believe that the grant of political autonomy to Southern Italy within a federation of small Italian states would not have achieved the same results, and faster, through the mere stimulation of local ambition that follows every acquisition of a significant share of local sovereignty.

Finally, there is a fourth cause that contributed to the initial success of the Common Market. This was the passionate *conviction* amongst the nations concerned that their union would usher in a new age of prosperity. As a result, an infective psychology of action arose, similar to the surging optimism that helps bring about a revival at the end of a depression when an increasing number of businessmen become agitated by the conviction that stagnation has lasted so long that a change for the better cannot be far away. Actually, what businessmen never realize is that it is not the expected change that causes their conviction, but their conviction that causes the change. By the same token, what caused the success of the Common Market was not the Common Market but the conviction that it would be a success. But *any* conviction maintained with similar action-producing enthusiasm would have led to similar results. It would have made no difference had the aim involved been the abolition or the dismemberment of nations; their socialization or their return to capitalism; the introduction of authoritarian or of democratic methods; colonization or de-colonization; communism or fascism; centralization or devolution, sense or nonsense – anything as long as it led to movement. It is the same with the force that instills into people, taken on a march after the languor of a long wait, the exhileration that comes from marching, even though the direction be the abyss – as young Pliny discovered when, unhappily yielding to the demand for leadership in the midst of the blackout caused by the eruption of Vesuvius, he started marching the relieved evacuees under his care right towards the centre of the disaster zone. All that was needed to restore courage was that someone in whom they had trust gave the signal for moving. As Pliny records: luckily, the smoke dispersed before it was too late.

5

As a result, though the honeymoon success of the European Economic Community cannot be disputed, it rested on a set of circumstances so exceptional and passing that there is no reason to assume that it should last;[1] that it should become another *Zollverein* from whose example, though set under entirely different conditions, it has taken so much encouragement,[2] or that it should be better equipped than other similarly size-plagued social organisms to withstand the pressures of scale building up as integration proceeds. Even though it still continues growing – this is precisely it! For growth in the mature is as doubtful a blessing as the continued swelling of a balloon. When

[1] I wrote this word of caution in 1960 in preparation of the German edition of this book. The only thing that can be added in preparation for the English edition 17 years later in 1976, is that the events since then are ample proof of the ever-mounting difficulties of scale as the Common Market continues to grow in membership and interdependence. Even its very riches have become a problem. There is now more butter, milk, eggs, beef, and wine than ever. But like boils and sores on the skin, their very abundance in the form of butter *mountains* and wine *lakes* is a sign not of health but of a disease of such malignancy that by 1976 it produced its first violence and deaths in a "wine war" waged not between have's and have-not's but between the EEC's own two most convivial have's. But the trend in this direction was discerned by the leaders of the Common Market itself as early as 1959 when Konrad Adenauer warned that the enterprise might become too unwieldy, or twelve years later when Charles de Gaulle confided to the British Ambassador that Britain should give up trying to get into the Common Market because, between him and the Ambassador, it was on the verge of collapsing anyway – the Common Market that was, not Britain as yet.
[2] The *Zollverein* was successful because it was organized at a development stage and time that permitted a last extension of optimum size as a result of the new conditions produced by the industrial revolution. Though the economic small-state world preceding it was by no means a stagnant pool – considering that its splendid city-state civilization had made it so rich in music, poetry, art, and architectural achievements that its ancient villages and towns have remained to this day a principal
Footnote continued overleaf

it is largest and seems proudest, it explodes. As I have tried to show in Chapter IV, this is the pathetic difference between growth problems affecting the too small and those affecting the too big; between the problems of the underdeveloped and those of the overdeveloped nations. Outwardly, they are so similar that the afflicted often mistake their senility for adolescence. Elated by the last amorous flare-up of the flickering spirit of life, they are always prone to interpret as a sign of returning youth what is but nature's gently mocking way of reminding us that our days are counted.

Even the initial success of the Common Market is thus hardly a compelling argument against the idea that the logical solution of the scale problems of our age must lie in the opposite direction: in the *reduction* of our overgrown societies, not in their further amalgamation.[1]

> income-yielding asset for their industrialized large-state modern successors – it did not provide the hinterland for the general industrialization then setting in. Once this had been embraced, the larger market secured by the *Zollverein,* coupled with the simultaneous guarantees for unchanged small-state political sovereignty insuring a continued scope to local initiative, proved indeed a great boon to productive efficiency. Yet even here it is doubtful whether the *Zollverein's* main achievement was not in the construction of more 'lifts' to meet the requirements of its new 'sky-scraper' economics, than of more opera houses or universities such as the preceding economies were able to afford. But as long as its members stayed politically sovereign, the pool of unemployment resulting from the success of technology could at least to a large extent still be absorbed by the multitude of harmlessly competing regional bureaucracies, in contrast to the immense armies needed for sponging it up when the economic union of the *Zollverein* was turned into the political union of the *German Reich.*
>
> The main difference between the pre-Reich *Zollverein* and the Common Market set up in Rome 125 years later is that the latter started with the post-optimal size conditions with which the former ended. Because of this the contemporary or automation stage of the industrial revolution is achieving such stupendous self-defeating increases in productivity that products on the one side and unemployment on the other threaten to become so excessive that the only alternative to scale reduction is to use the excess products for atom bombs and the automation-unemployed for armies and then release each against the other so that neither should feel hurt by the awareness of having been created to no purpose. Though this solution is not pleasant, the simplicity of its arithmetic must, it seems, have won over most of the union-struck statesmen of our time, as it may have done with those three million years ago, of whose existence we have, appropriately, no record.
>
> 1 Actually as far back as 1961, barely four years after the signing of the Treaty of Rome, the Commission of the European Economic Community began a campaign under the leadership of M. Margolin, its then Vice-

Returning to the starting point of this Chapter this means two things: first that a nation such as Wales is certainly not too small to be economically viable. This is no more true than it is of Catalonia, Corsica, Britanny, Burgundy, Wurtemberg, Denmark, Iceland, Switzerland, or any region of similar size. And secondly, that for the great powers such as Great Britain, France, Germany, or Italy, the most sensible course to follow in their attempt to escape the cancerous clutches of their overgrowth is not to enlarge the ship of their Common Market which is continually on the verge of sinking not because it is fragile but because it is already overloaded with too many heavy-weights; the most sensible course is to decentralize, devolve, and dissolve themselves into the lifeboat structure of a loosely linked free-trading system based not on common but regional markets composed of easily manageable and even self-manageable small units. All that is needed to bring this about is for the great powers to restore statehood to their ancient nations: France to Britanny, Burgundy, Savoy, Corsica, etc., Italy to Lombardy, Sardinia, Calabria, Sicily, etc., and Britain not only to Wales, Scotland and its other Celtic nations, but also to the kingdoms of England's own ancient *heptarchy* (Wessex, Sussex, Essex, Kent, East Anglia, Mercia, and Northumberland).[1]

President, to persuade the member states to split themselves up into uniformly small regions of from 3 to 5 million inhabitants, as it would be easier to deal with them than with the unwieldy big powers. This indicated that, after years of obsession with the economics of *growth,* at least the practitioners if not yet the theorists are beginning to feel that what really matters in our time is the economics of size, of shape, of *form.*

[1] I should mention in conclusion that once political units are reduced to optimum size there is no reason why in areas of joint interest they should not be loosely linked in customs unions, or limited international product and service unions such as coal, steel, dining and sleeping car, or postal unions. Like the electricity, heating, and lift unions of apartment houses, such unions unite, where union has sense, in certain economic respects, and keep separate where separation has sense, in political, cultural and social matters. However, to be successful, none of the members of such unions must be of such disproportionate size that it can disrupt the union by wielding excessive power. See in this connection the author's: *Customs Union – A Tool for Peace.* (Washington: Foundation for Foreign Affairs, 1949); his *History of the Common Market* (Journal of Economic History, September, 1960). J. P. Mackintosh's *Devolution of Power* (Penguin, 1968), and the *Regional Manifesto* by Alexander Thynne, The Viscount Weymouth (Longleat House, 1976).

IX. Is Reason Treason

Economic Development Versus National Identity

I

Many of the formerly imperialist countries must feel with Ovid that "it is annoying to be virtuous to no purpose." Here they pour advice, funds, machinery, know-how into their former colonies and other underdeveloped regions, and what do they get in return? Suspician, censure, contempt for their institutions, sympathy for the Soviet Union which barely lifts a finger, and a hatred for themselves that increases in proportion to the economic assistance they offer. Could anything be more unreasonable.

The trouble is that there are situations in which the unreasonable is reasonable and, conversely, in which reason becomes treason. It is not for nothing that these two words are so similar. Thus, it is certainly reasonable that retarded countries should wish to develop. But what do they mean by economic development? The patriotic preservation of the Cuban, Puerto Rican, Ghanaian, Laotian way of life with its engaging emphasis on musing, dozing, praying, feasting, dancing? This is precisely what retarded them. What they mean by development is the treasonable opposite: to stop living like indolent[1] Cubans, Puerto Ricans, Ghanaians, Laotians, and begin living like energetic Westerners. Instead of somnolent churches they want buzzing steel mills (the new objects of tribal worship, as Colin Clark has called them); instead of wind-cooled tropical bamboo huts, air-conditioned concrete pneumonia traps; instead of mules, cars from Detroit; instead of siestas, American efficiency. In other words, what they mean by

[1] Lest my Puerto Rican friends misunderstand, let me stress that the term 'indolent' is not to be intrepreted in the dictionary sense as 'habitually lazy, slothful,' but in the sense of easy-going, musing, unacquisitively serene, peaceful of soul, and generous of heart (which, true enough, to those many harrassed contemporaries striving for rapid worldly improvement may mean habitually lazy, slothful). Here it is used in the sense of Keats' *Ode on Indolence* in which the poet places 'honied' indolence high above Love, Ambition, and even Poesie, the demons haunting him.

economic development is Westernization or, considering the technological leadership of the United States, Americanization – at first perhaps only in form, but ultimately also in content.

Thus, whatever the new nations are gaining in development, they seem to be losing in identity. The first to experience the full impact of this unexpected by-product of progress was Puerto Rico for the simple reason that, as a result of her justly famous *Operation Bootstrap*, she was also the first of the underdeveloped countries able to declare by 1960 that she had reached the threshold of development. But at the same time she had suddenly become so alarmed by the magnitude of the psychological damage caused by her rapid progress that her Governor, Luis Muñoz Marin, lost no time in arranging that priority must henceforth be assigned to what he hopefully christened *Operation Serenity* – an emergency program devoted to the preservation of the national image which the very success of *Operation Bootstrap* had so visibly undermined.[1]

[1] The Americanization effect of all economic development can be observed in Puerto Rico particularly well during elections. On these occasions, the slum sections invariably display a forest of the graceful standards and flags of the ruling party (reminiscent of a medieval tent city before a tournament), indicating their passionate devotion to the Puertoricanness of their beloved Governor. This in spite of the fact that the benefits of *Operation Bootstrap* and other blessings of economic development have obviously not yet come their way. The *new* housing developments, on the other hand, containing the rapidly increasing number of fortunate Puerto Ricans who have already been de-slummed into an almost middle-class kind of life as a result of the conspicuous success of the Government's development program, display a mysteriously increasing number of oppositionist 'statehood' flags, indicating their preference not for an autonomous Puerto Rican destiny but for absorption as the 51st state of the United States. People thus show that, as their living standard rises, they become not more but less Puerto Rican. Having come closer to the American mode of life, they want to reach it altogether. Instead of giving thanks to their government for having raised them above their former native standards, they begin to oppose it because even these considerably higher standards are still far below those of the United States. Hence the paradoxical result: the greater the economic and social success of the government, the smaller becomes the political base from which it draws its strength, and the greater becomes the voting power of the opposition whose muscles the government's success is unwittingly nourishing. This is not unlike the fate that has befallen the British Labour Party which has contributed so much to the affluence of the common man, only to discover that the affluent man votes not Labour but Conservative. And so does the developed man vote not native but American – a consequence which, in the eyes of so many modern nation builders, can be effectively combatted only by propagating ideological *aversion* to what is materially *desired*.

Thus, while economic development is undoubtedly altogether reasonable, it threatens at the same time to wipe out the identity of the very nations who have fought so hard for the freedom to cultivate their own personality. To ensure their national survival, the leaders of the new countries have therefore no alternative but to balance the rational, which helps their economy, with the irrational, which helps their identity; to ask for assistance from the former colonial powers and, when they receive it, accuse them of neo-imperialist aspirations and treat them with scorn. For in contrast to the building blocks of sound economic structures, the material from which nations are formed is not reason but emotion; not mind but feeling, not the rational but the irrational; not the sensible but the romantic.

In a way, the new nations are in a position in which Germany found herself at the beginning of the 19th century, when the *Age of Reason* radiated from England and France its detached universalist message of the likeness of all human beings, the universal character of their inherent rights, the wisdom of the natural order, the horse sense of economic man, the soundness of laissez-faire, the beneficence of free trade. But while these concepts served wonderfully the further advance of France and, particularly, of Great Britain which by then had long consolidated her national image and was already far ahead of everyone else in economic progress, they did little for a retarded and nationally still shapeless Germany (or the then similarly underdeveloped United States) except make her still more retarded. For what interest should a rationally acting German businessman, bent on maximizing his gain through the free importation of inexpensive machine-produced British goods, have had, for example, in the enforcement of trade impediments such as tariff walls? Though these would have enabled his country to develop its own industry, they would at the same time have severely cut into his profits. As a result, all the enlightened principles of the *Age of Reason* could, under the circumstances, have achieved, would have been to demonstrate the validity of the pungent Roman no-nonsense phrase of *ubi bene, ibi patria,* my country is which ensures me the best material life, and turn the world as British as a similar no-nonsense rationalism is now threatening to turn it American.

To avert this consequence which, from a denationalized one-world point of view would have been highly commendable, protectionist schools of thought developed in both Germany and the United States in reaction against the (for them) damaging rationalist free-enterprise and free-trade doctrine of the English classical economists. The members of these schools might have been called *Economic Irrationalists*. Actually, they have become known under the name of *Neo-Mercantilists, Nationalists* or, in the case of those whose work is perhaps the most significant for the understanding of contemporary development problems, *Romantics*. The outstanding representative of the *Romantic School* was the German economist Adam Müller (1779-1829) whose romanticism consisted mainly in his insistence that economic considerations must play a *secondary* role in nations which, such as his own, have not yet reached maturity. No wonder that his profession has not taken kindly to him. The center of the stage, he thought, ought to be held by questions concerned with national identity; by policies designed to strengthen community feeling; by the formation and cultivation of the national mind or, as he called it, the *Volksseele*. Instead of embracing the atomistic idea of self-interest, however enlightened, he therefore stressed the community value of mystic collective experience such as is engendered by the shared hardship and comradeship of war. This is another doctrine rationalist economists have found hard to forgive him though no less a rationalist than Sir Francis Bacon had, when England was in similar circumstances, come to a similar conclusion when he wrote that "nobody can be healthful without exercise, neither natural body nor politic, and certainly to a kingdom or state, a just and honourable war is the true exercise".[1]

Modern nation builders such as Nehru or Sukarno demonstrated that they were more appreciative of the concepts of the romantic German economist's ideas than either his or their critics. And so have leaders like Fidel Castro or the late Dr. Nkrumah who, unable to indulge in actual warfare, tried to strengthen the

---

[1] Francis Bacon. *Essays*. New York: Walter Black, 1942, p. 121.

national identity of their peoples by falling back on the next best thing – psychological warfare. Wherever this device is resorted to, the exhilarating experience of collective action is replaced by the equally exhilarating experience of collective hatred – hatred of Americans, hatred of the English, hatred of capitalists, the white race, of anything as long as it is zestful enough to close the ranks of the haters and make them emotionally distinguishable from those of the hated. This is the whole mystery behind the spectacle of new countries raving even at those who assist them, and having to rave at them the more the the greater the benefits they receive. For the spontaneous, human, and rational response in such a case would be love. But love brings peoples together, creates bonds, forms unions, inter-nationalizes and denationalizes them – the very consequence which in the eyes of nation builders, bent on separating peoples, prying them loose from existing unions, and endowing them with distinguishing features and differences that do not exist, does not spell reason but treason.

That is why the Romans had to burn the Christians whose doctrine of the universality of human brotherhood threatened to deprive them not only of their national distinction but also of their collective *raison d'être*. They also felt they had to dispatch Cicero, though not exactly on this formal ground. But how must he have sapped their national strength when, instead of confirming their uniqueness, he had the tactlessness of telling them that "no single thing is like another, so exactly its counterpart, as all of us are to one another"; and "however we may define man, a single definition will apply to all. This is sufficient proof that there is no difference between man and man, for if there were, a single definition could not be applicable to all men" (*Laws*, 1, 10). Unreasonable thoughts? No! But of what use could they be to the Romans? On what grounds could they have continued to insist that all other tribes should bow to their rule? And for the same reason, by what logic could Ghanaians, in search of a national image, be convinced they should live apart from the British, or the Cubans from the Americans, if they are told that the definition of Fidel Castro defines also Richard Nixon, or that no single thing was so exactly its counterpart as Dr. Nkrumah was to Lord Beaverbrook?

They cannot. Hence the unhappy need of underdeveloped countries to supplement their *Operations Bootstrap* with *Operations Hatred* rather than *Serenity or Gratitude*. The only other way of gaining an identity that would make them distinguishable from other peoples would be developing their economies the hard way. Not with American, British, Russian, capitalist, or anybody's help but, as I have suggested in *Development Without Aid*,[1] slowly, obstinately, painfully through trial and error, and within the limits of their own resources. This is the method by which not only all the nations of Europe, but also, within the nations, all their countless principalities and city states, have achieved their much admired identity and scintillating difference.[2] And, as the young United States of the 19th century has demonstrated, the physical struggle connected with a defiantly independent economic development is quite as effective in creating the institutions, shared heroes, folklore, poetry, and national romance necessary for fusing peoples into strong communities as

[1] Swansea: Christopher Davies, 1974.

[2] The proud way was, of course, also the way in which the Soviet Union (so often cited as an easy alternative source of development funds) built herself up from a peasant to a sputnik economy. This is why the West need not be afraid of the constant threat that the present underdeveloped nations might do things the communist way, if they do not get enough help from the capitalist countries. Let them! For the communist way, as Cambodia has so shockingly demonstrated, is to do things not through corrupting foreign but through native resources; not with the help of Russian or Chinese savings but of those extracted at whatever deprivation at home. However, most developing countries would not wish to make use of the threatened communist alternative in the first place since, in spite of sputniks which cannot be served for dinner, they consider Soviet living standard aspirations inferior to those they associate with the West and, in particular, with the United States. This is, incidentally why they can continue to sport their vexing affection for the Soviet Union (or China for that matter), whose image is unable to threaten their identity for the simple reason that they do not want to duplicate it. There is also another reason why the West should not be disturbed if underdeveloped countries threaten to turn to communism. The combined efforts of the vast Soviet block are hardly enough to help Cuba. If suddenly a swarm of newly converted countries would knock at Moscow's or Peking's gates with equal requests for assistance, the result would not be delight but embarrassment. All Moscow and Peking could do would be to give them a Marxist castigation for having come over too early, and refer them back to the capitalist West. This might not only cure them for a long time of their illusions; the cost of the cure would have to be borne by the Soviet world, not by the harassed ingratiators, propagandists, and tax-payers of a perpetually intimidated West.

the hardship of war or the intoxication of hatred. Moreover, this would leave them with pride and self reliance, not an inferiority complex engendering still more hatred. But to set out on a program of this nature at a time when results can be had so much more quickly by frightening the strong and blackmailing the rich would, of course, again be nothing but a piece of irrational and romantic nonsense.

In view of the increasing degree with which problems of national identity are beginning to overshadow those of economic development, Adam Müller's much despised romanticism may yet offer better guidance to the understanding of the puzzling actions and responses of underdeveloped countries than the austere mathematical rationalism of contemporary experts, teaching the leaders of formless steaming pre-capitalist tropical lands the economics picked up in the long cooled environments of post-capitalist centres of learning such as Haryale or Oxbridge. They offer fur coats in Havana because they have proved useful in Boston. A study of Müller, on the other hand, might prove the more rewarding as he himself is not a befuddled romantic but an analyst who, rather than advocate war or similar irrational devices in group building, merely stressed in clinical fashion that such things are good for the body politic, the *Volksseele*. Nor did his conclusions indicate that he had no appreciation for the *Age of Reason*, the British, or their luminous classical economists – not any more than the late Dr. Nkrumah's anti-imperialist exhortations meant that he did not appreciate the Queen. On the contrary! Just as Dr. Nkrumah was the most enthusiastic admirer of British royalty and, in spite of his inflammatory actions as a nation builder, a man of such engaging personal dispositions that he was able to charm the most antagonistic birds out of their trees, so Adam Müller had boundless admiration for the glories of reason, the English people, and in particular in an almost embarassing degree, as Sir Alexander Gray put it, for the soundness of the philosophic and economic doctrines of Adam Smith. He thought them all unexceptionable. But what he also thought was that giving the heady wine of reason to the too young raises not rationalists but alcoholics – an idea which, though also quite reasonable, has only rarely appealed to the sellers of wine.

2

So far, I have attempted to explain the role of hatred and war as potent emotional antidotes to the enescapably denationalizing effect of contemporary economic development. As group builders they have always proved invaluable. They are however by no means the only exercises in irrationality on which nations thrive. *Anything* that is irrational qualifies as a tool for strengthening the social fabric. Moreover, while unquestionably the most effective, hatred and war are actually the last of the nation building devices to be brought into play, being themselves but the final offsprings of a long string of prior though considerably less ferocious catalysts.

The earlier ones are those relatively harmless community moulds by means of which an as yet unorganized number of people in search of a collective identity make their first attempt to develop features that will make them distinguishable from all other human groups. But if we agree with Cicero that there is nothing in the nature of man as a social animal permitting this sort of differentiation, it follows that none of the features created in this manner can be of a *natural* order. They are worn, not born, and must therefore be grafted on artificially. This does not yet render them unreasonable, not any more than a hat is deprived of its sense when it is put on one's head. The irrationality sets in when, in order to make the distinguishing features stick, their wearers are induced to believe that the resulting mechanical *collage* leads also to their organic fusion into a new cohesive superstructure of which no one but they themselves can form a part. Once this belief has taken root, the *Volksseele* is born - a mystic romantic new divinity filling its communicants with an eery lifting power that simultaneously raises and unites them in the secret knowledge that they are the only ones able to see profundity and sense in what to the uniniated outsider seems nonsense.

Amongst the most common as well as the most useful of these relatively mild irrational first building moulds of nations are communal emblems. To fulfil their function of creating differences where none exist with greatest effect, their best specimens must be so outlandish, weird, and so beyond human reason that only a meta-human common ancestor could have thought them up. This enables them to produce the same delightfully thrilling sense of annointed tribal uniqueness which children derive from their private spooks, or carnival crowds from their fantastic masks. Dragons, unicorns, double-headed eagles, and other similarly uncannily irrational objects, having no counterpart in the physical universe, have therefore always proved particularly felicitous in their group building effect. Even where natural creatures are chosen, the reason is invariably an irrational or singular association as, for instance, in the case of the black bull of Salzburg. Though not unique in himself, this fierce heraldic animal commemorates a reputedly unique historic event – the effort of a group of patriotic citizens to wash a black bull white with soap so that he could be entered in a competition of white bulls. To this day, the Salzburgers identify themselves with befitting pride as 'Bull-washers', though the only thing that is singular about the incident is the unrivalled degree of its folly. Still it has made them so unique that there is none amongst them who would not rather boast of this than of the slightly less distinguishing fact that Salzburg is also the birthplace of Mozart. After all, there are unfortunately other places that have produced great composers, too.

As with emblems, so it is with group costumes. Though often endowed with a secondary rational function, as community builders they are likewise the better, the more ridiculous they make you look, and the less they can be suspected of rational usefulness. We only need to think of such garments as the aprons of Free Masons (which man of sound mind cares to be seen in an apron?), or the mitres, staffs, ecclesiastical collars, and the marvellously embroidered pregnancy gowns worn by the male dignitaries of various church hierarches. Into the same category belong the capes of scholars, wigs of lawyers, skirts of Scotsmen, the unfunctional halfstockings from above the ankles to below the knees of Bavarians; the effeminately cut, adorned, and frilly uniforms of the virile military; the feathers of the Indians;

the elongated necks, the squeezed foreheads, the nose rings of savages.[1] To make doubly sure of their apartness, ancient tribes attributed for good measure to others even such inborn anatomical differences as foreheads with either one or three eyes, human bodies topped by birds' heads, human heads endowed with birds' beaks, or webfeet which their single-legged possessors could, when sitting down, bend conveniently over their head for use as umbrella or parasol. Though Heredotus would in his conscientious way of recording history not vouch for their existence, "not having seen such peoples himself," peculiarities of this sort must have convinced even the more sophisticated of sceptics of the reassuring differences separating nation from nation.[2]

Other important group builders are language and accents. Similar to costumes, these have likewise a rational use on the side. They may facilitate communication. But in their capacity as identity shapers they are used to opposite ends. Instead of assisting communication, they limit it, until even the insiders are united in the subterranean layers of emotion rather than on the surface of rational comprehension. What Harold Nicolson says of the poets, that "they elevate, they produce ecstacy in us, especially when they are not sure what they are talking about" (and *we* still less so), applies also to them. Thus, if the Catholic Church, in contrast to her Protestant offsprings, retained such a tremendous mystic appeal, it was because she did consistently the seemingly irrational: speaking to her countless flocks of ignorant

---

[1] Much of this was displayed when "in a short ceremony watched by some of the greatest in the land, and recorded for posterity by the busy pencils of his fellow trade unionists, the Earl of Snowdon took his oath of allegiance and his seat in the House of Lords". Having learned "of the Queen's determination to enoble him 'by girding him with a sword and putting a cap of honour and a coronet of gold upon his head'", Norman Shrapnel delightfully describes the ceremony in The Guardian (March 1, 1962) as a "curious mixture of the sedate and the gaudy. Great officers of state – the Earl Marshal, Garter King-of-Arms, the Lord Great Chamberlain – perambulate the Chamber like fabulous walking birds of brilliant plumage, at a pace which seems to symbolize the timelessness of it all. Their footfall, you might say, is the metronome of the centuries."

[2] Amongst the many strange peoples singled out in Herodotus' *Histories* we find the one-eyed Arimaspi (III, 116); a tribe with feet like goats; a race of men who sleep during one half of the year (IV, 25); and the Neureans, everyone of whom "once a year becomes a wolf for a few days, at the end of which time he is restored to his proper shape" (IV, 105).

worshippers in Latin rather than the vernacular. Since all understood the latter, this would have been much less likely to elevate, or produce communal ecstacy in us.[1] Similarly, if the British have shown strength in staying united in the diaspora of empire and in the face of the gravitational pull exerted by their more numerous American cousins from across the Atlantic, it is not because of the English language. This is nowadays so universally spoken that it has long ceased to confer distinction. It is because of the Oxford accent which is almost as forbidding to the majority of Englishmen, and therefore mystically as appealing, as Latin was to Catholics. Mispronouncing the vernacular until "shower" sounds like "shah", or "golf" like "guff", and releasing it all as if through a tunnel of mufflers invented by Kingsley Amis until little is left except the national pitch, it imparts an exalted feeling of unrivalled exclusiveness not only to the few who practice it but also to the multitudes who feel diplomatically represented by it. At least the English can say to their American co-linguists with proud emphasis: "Here we have something in which we differ; something you'll never understand."

And they can say the same thing of such other irrationalities as the Crown, the duodecimal system, or cricket. They all confer distinction because of their ritualistic power of baffling the outsider. No one except the British seems able to grasp their sense, their value, their humour. And even in their case, the unifying effect is based less on understanding than on the *pretence* at understanding, similar to the pretence of people sitting enraptured through a Latin mass as if they were listening to a gossip columnist. This is why swiftly moving sports such as football or tennis are of relatively little community building value (if one leaves aside the warlike sentiments, maniacal partisanships, and vandalism which joy of victory or distress at defeat often inspire as unsporting by-products). They are so visibly exciting that even the non-initiated are able to derive the insider's instantaneous pleasure from watching them, and thus become part and parcel of the group. It is quite different in the case of slow moving and,

---

[1] This was written before the Church, giving in to her rationalists, abandoned the Latin mass. Now that everyone understands what his priest says, he may soon wonder why he should need a priest at all.

therefore, inherently ritualistic games such as cricket or baseball. Leaving the outsider with a hopeless stare of non-comprehending consternation (such as was made famous by the expressive face of Fernandel when he was asked how he liked the American national sport), they fulfil their nation building function to perfection. Their ceremonial irrationality causes at once the ranks of the insiders to close in the heart-warming awareness that they are alone in the fun. This closeness is further strengthened by the fact that, even in their own case, the ability to extract fun from such games has not been come by easily. It is the result of years of indoctrination on those famous playing fields where the nation's future battles are won. It is the product of a preparation so long and Spartan that the consummation of a true national game is in the end more than a mere act of enjoyment. Like a religious service, it becomes an act of sacrifice. And there is nothing that could enhance the value of a communal activity more than when it is imbued with a sacrificial character. This explains also the passion with which such hotly contested tribal communities as the sophisticated lovers of modern art, of modern music, or modern Greece rally so determinedly around such unclassically forbidding standards as the soulless geometry of abstraction, the frozen landscape of atonality, or the bitter medicinal taste of *Retsina* wine. It requires determination and sacrifice to enjoy them – a price of admission so few people are ready to pay that the groups in question have no difficulty in retaining their elemental strength behind the impenetrable walls of their demanding sophistication.[1]

[1] Another excellent illustration of the community cementing effect of sacrificial rituals is furnished by the trials of both nonsense and pain imposed as the price of initiation by student fraternities and sororities. *TIME* (January 13, 1947) contains an account of one of these: "The high-school girls . . . . were dressed for a tea party, but they carried long bundles containing paddles, and pails for vomiting. In the corner of the room one girl was mixing a drink out of castor oil, cold cooking grease, coffee grounds, raw oysters and mackerel's eyes. The first girl to be invited was brought in, wearing a bathing suit and blindfold. She was pale, trembling, and sweating. They made her lie on the floor, face up. Then one of the girls poured the concoction into her mouth. She choked and retched. Two girls held her shoulders. They told her if she vomited, she would have to drink it back . . . Then they made her take a crawling position, and took turns burning her with lighted cigarettes – not deep, just enough to leave

Footnote continued overleaf

The greatest group value derived from these and similarly irrational first building blocks of nations lies however not so much in their mild impact effect as in the sequence of fierce secondary emotions they produce. The impact effect of group identity tags such as rings drawn through pierced noses in the case of solemn savages, or of wigs worn on top of a natural shock of hair in the case of solemn British judges, consists in no more than the creation of conspicuous membership certificates. But being so obviously nonsensical, these tags also make those displaying them look utterly ridiculous in the eyes of outsiders viewing them from the cold distance of reason such as we all are wont to do when casting our eyes beyond the limits of our own congregations. To escape this ridicule, two ways are open to the exposed group member. One is to abandon the coveted membership certificate and appear reasonable once more. This would regain him the esteem of the outsider, with whom he has but few contacts, particularly if he adopts at the same time the latter's own tribal follies. But it would lose him the more cherished affection of the community of his accustomed neighbours. So he will as a rule choose the second alternative. Instead of feeling ridiculous in his irrational outfit, he will, with the solid backing of his group, declare the unreasonable super-reasonable.

As a result the savage nose ring or the English wig will henceforth not only be displayed; they will be displayed with the dignity and pride that comes from the conviction that the outsider's lack of appreciation is not a sign of his greater reason but of his rank stupidity. One of the most significant secondary effects of the identity creating process is thus the transformation of an at first inoffensive belief in national difference into an aggressive conviction of national superiority.

---

blisters . . . . Then they spun her around until she was dizzy and started to vomit, but the girls grabbed hold of her nose and mouth so she couldn't. Next, they told her to assume the angle-kneeling with her head down on her arms, which were flat on the floor. Her buttocks were up and her legs apart. They seemed to know where it hurt most. They did not hit her horizontally, but between her legs, towards her sexual organs . . . The next day I asked my young friend whether she had had any fun last night. 'Not exactly', she said, but it was one of those things that has to be done. You have to, to join a sorority. Otherwise you can't go to dances and everything'."

The outsider, on the other hand, noticing now not only the ring through the nose or the wig on the head but also the indescribably aloof dignity with which each is worn, finds the spectacle still more ridiculous. This now leads in turn to the creation of the two ultimate moulds in which the group image becomes solidified. One consists in a formidable outer containing ring, a nonsense-strengthened wall of ridicule, a belt of contempt, preventing escape, and compressing all identically tagged individuals into a superheated single mass. The other is an inner ring of interlacing nerves, secreted by the captive mass in defense against the pressure from the externally imposed ring of contempt, and generating as its terminal product a nuclear force of hatred and counter-contempt of such intensity that it is able to hold the compressed individuals together as a now also internally integrated single group even after the external wall of ridicule has vaporized into a deferential cloud or respect in awe at the unforeseen power it has released.

So we are back at hatred as one of the principal community building tools. But this is not the end. Rising from the need to defend our group follies, hatred, when put to exercise, soon leads to the emergence of the second of the most effective identity shaping devices – war. And with this, the process is brought to its culminating point. For there is nothing quite so convincing in establishing the reality of national difference than the tonic evidence of national superiority supplied by the indisputable fact of having proved able to beat up one's neighbours. Even if one lands unexpectedly on the receiving end of the beating, there is always the consoling thought of another encounter. Then one will yet be on the side dishing it out, as is inevitable in the long course of history. War will thus ultimately entitle all nations to graduate into the ranks of those able to prove to themselves, if not to their treasonable philosophers, that they are fundamentally different from, and superior to, all others.

However, though war is the culminating offshoot of the most irrational of all identity building devices, in the old-fashioned romantic sense of Bacon, Müller, or Churchill for that matter, there is a redeeming feature to it. Instead of further aggravating irrationality, it begins to mellow it. Disinhibiting as well as purifying the body politic through the 'healthful' exercise it entails, it produces in the end a decompression in which its ugly original hatreds are not only overshadowed by gentler attitudes. They are to a large extent actually replaced by the infinitely more rational and more human considerations of chivalry arising from the compassionate awareness amongst the belligerents that each is as plagued by the same miserable irrational needs of group existence as any other. From a therepeutic point of view, there is therefore very much more to old fashioned romantic warfare – curing as it does the degrading neurosis of hatred – than rationalist theorists are willing to concede.[1]

Moreover, once war has produced its assortment of deeds and heroes necessary to fire the popular imagination, it may itself be superseded as the principal tool of identity building by the folklore and poetry besinging it. Indeed, the true architects of the *Volksseele* have always been the historians, the propagandists, the artists and, particularly, the poets – who have provided the substance that endured; the national archetype outside the cave – not the political or military leaders who put up the perishable scaffolding.

Thus, while the shared experience of the Trojan wars was indispensable as the framework within which the identity of Greece could be developed, the content of this identity, its character and features, the *image* of Greece, was fashioned by Homer. To this day, the abiding sense of Greek unity rests not on the Achilles or Ulysses of history. They may have been a couple of bums or Hell's Angels. It rests on the Achilles and Ulysses of the Iliad and the Odyssey. A similar relationship emerges in the case of Rome. When Augustus thought the public image of the Imperial City was still in need of enrichment in spite of two centuries of solid military triumphs, he did not commission his generals to deliver a new series of crowd pleasing victories by means of the sword. He commissioned a poet to invent a more gloriously imaginative past by means of his pen. The result was Virgil's *Aeneid* in which the author not only

---

[1] Romantic, nation-building warfare must not be confused with dehumanized, centralized, modern mass warfare in defence of which nothing can be said that makes either sense or reason.

supplied the Romans with a long stretch of appropriate new 'ancient' history that was never had but at last paralleled the much envied exploits of the Greeks; he also produced for their benefit a thrilling genealogy that gave a new sense of uniqueness to the softening race of urban circus goers by tracing their ancestry right back to the lap of the gods. Similarly the Icelandic personality was fashioned not by the Vikings but by what the Sagas wrote of them; the personality of Imperial Britain, not by Queen Victoria or Disraeli but Rudyard Kipling; of the United States, not by Lincoln or the frontiersmen but Carl Sandburg and Hollywood; of Nazi Germany, not by Hitler but Goebbels – the Mahatma Propagandhi, as he was called. And the same will be true of the future identity of the nascent nations of our own day. It will not be the product of their Maos, Castros, Kenyattas, or Idi Amins. They supply the horsepower. Their real identity will be shaped by the authors scribbling in sidewalk cafés or pounding away at their typewriters until the features are born and the mask is determined which, in the last analysis, they themselves, not Mao, Castro, Kenyatta, or Amin, consider best for the public to wear.

The only question still to be answered is this: If war in the romantic (never in the scientific dehumanized modern) sense acts as a decompression chamber in which the nasty hate aspects of the irrational community-building process are first materially mellowed, and then sublimized into a no less irrational but a considerably less destructive body of patriotic music and verse, why should so many contemporary nation builders continue to use the furious whip of hatred?

The reason for this is that a considerable proportion of underdeveloped countries groping for a pleasingly heroic image are either too weak to indulge in the therapy of a 'just' Baconian war; too lacking in history to make up for the deficiency by feeding on the poetic glorification of past deeds; or as yet too unsophisticated to commission a Virgilian agency to invent a properly inspiring national record through poetic imagination. True, some of them have by now accumulated a short history of patriotic violence, goal, and even revolution through which they have hastened their liberation from colonial rule. However, while this may ultimately supply the future national image with a number of its traits, colonial rule has in many instances passed too quickly to have produced a sufficiently impressive folklore out of the struggle for freedom.[1] And it is this that caused the leaders of a number of nations, which have found their freedom too fast, to fall back on hatred as the most efficient community builder within their reach, creating the appropriate targets either by reviving the ghost of the colonial past, or by accusing the reformed masters of that past of continued neo-imperialistic evil intentions for the future.

One of the few contemporary nation builders trying to prove that the identity of people can also be built through moderation and reason rather than the usual string of fiery irrationalities, was Julius Nyerere of Tanganyika. As a reward for his level-headed realism, he obtained national independence faster than most other colonial leaders. And, once free, he secured not only a maximum of technical and financial assistance but also the most affectionate respect – from the West. Yet, all his example showed was that there is no exception to the rule. Barely three weeks after liberation, the liberator resigned from his office of Prime Minister, forced out not by communists, not by neo-imperialists, not by the white settlers, but by his own native supporters (even though they were subsequently impelled to restore him to power). As Tom Stacey pointed out in a penetrating analysis ("Freedom Was Not Enough", *The Sunday Times*, January 28, 1962):

[1] It was different in the case of the long-lasting Algerian war, on the end of which *TIME* (March 16, 1962) wrote the following significant comment: "As they stood on the threshold of independence, Algeria's Moslems could feel like men who had broken through a time barrier. The F.L.N.'s first Premier and grand old man Ferhat Abbas wrote despairingly in 1934: 'If I had discovered an Algerian nation I would be a nationalist. Men who die for a patriotic ideal are honoured and respected. But I would not die for an Algerian fatherland because such a fatherland does not exist. I cannot find it. I questioned history. I questioned the living and the dead. I searched through the cemeteries. Nobody could speak to me of it. You cannot build on air.' But last week, most of Algeria's Moslems felt that they had built their own fatherland in seven years of life-and-death struggle. Said an F.L.N. Leader: 'We now have a history, a nation, even our own myths, our songs and our legendary heroes.'"

"Nyerere's very success was his liability. For just as intensely as these supporters needed independence and all it implied, they also needed to demand it, and struggle for it, and suffer for it [even though they had already won it]."

"However illogical, this is a fundamental truth. It applies to all of emerging Africa, and will continue to apply. The passion to feel equal in the world of nations and individuals insists upon a pretext for having felt inferior as nations and individuals. If that pretext escapes – through the liberality of the colonial regime or the benign co-operation of the settlers – it must be manufactured."

Thus, we should not be surprised by the apparent paradox of personable and intelligent men such as Dr. Castro or even Idi Amin spouting maniacal hatred whenever they involve their peoples in community-building exercises.[1] They proved that they are reasonable enough when they won their promotions and degrees. But this does not relieve them of the witchcraft irrationalities demanded of anyone serving as midwife to the delivery of the national archetype. In this latter capacity, their function is not to charm, but to battle the villain. And if none exists, they must see to it that he is created. As nation builders they are rather like the German student from a famous old *Simplizissimus* cartoon. Searching desperately for a pretext for fighting one of the annual duels which membership in his fraternity required, the anxious student barks out at a member of a rival fraternity while both stand in front of the marbled urinal wall of a Munich beer garden: "*Herr Kollege,*" he shouts, "you are staring at me! I challenge you to a duel! Your card please!" The other however, looking all the time straight ahead at the wall, stays unmoved. "I do not dream of staring at you," he says. "Then I am a liar," answers the

[1] This is what accounts for their strength, in contrast to the so-called Monrovia states (mostly former French colonies), which, "carrying the label of being 'moderate' and crippled by the stigma of too much praise from the west" (*Times,* London February 2, 1962), have so far proved considerably less effective in re-enforcing their image. It also explains the seemingly insane insistence of Rhodesia's guerilla leaders to continue in 1976 an identity war for majority rule which they can have peacefully with infinitely less struggle and sucering by 1978. But peace has never proved of any value as a shaper of a nation's image.

first. "Herr Kollege, your card please!" Like the well meaning West, the umbelicose companion never had a chance.

3

An examination of the group-building process will thus always reveal the same basic method: the protective application of a succession of bandages of manifestly irrational rituals, symbols, practices, gestures, costumes, sports, modes of behaviour and speech, to a fiercely irrational elemental nucleus – the conviction that membership in one's own group is the main source of human dignity, difference, and superiority.

If there is no need for similar irrationalities in the process of *individual* identity building, it is simply because, except in the case of certain kinds of twins or triplets, we possess enough differences in character as well as in our physical, emotional, and intellectual endowment to be readily distinguishable from one another without having to resort to artificial tagging. Only in our Ciceronian humanity, as species, as a social entity, as Germans, Ghanains, English, Americans, Greeks, Puerto Ricans, are we indistinguishable. Only in this latter capacity are we completely interchangeable. This is why any German entering the English group orbit such as the Battenbergs or the Saxe-Cobourg-Gothas became at once as English as the Baldwins or the Disraelis; or why any Englisman entering the national orbit of the United States becomes at once as American as the Roosevelts, the Wagners, the Du Ponts, the Tannenbaums, the Kubishtas, or the Kennedys without the need to sacrifice even a fraction of his personal identity or individuality. Were it otherwise, Siegmund Freud could hardly have distilled from the observation of a handful of Viennese patients those famous psychoanalytical devices that have proved as effective with schoolmarms from Minneapolis as with princes from Arabia, artists from Kabul, Viscounts from Yorkshire, students from Toronto, gangsters from Sicily, or millionaires from Manhattan. Only as groups and nations do assemblies of unlike individuals become so alike that they require an artificial set of distinguishing features, a password, a mask, an identity founded on neither nature nor reason, if they are to remain recognizably different, not in their person, but in their affiliation.

However, at this point a number of gradations must be introduced to give the theory of national unreason its proper range. For while all groups are held together by their bandages of irrationality, the *intensity* of their required irrationality is far from uniform. It fluctuates in response to four factors. These are: the age of the group; its similarity with neighbouring groups; the rational enlightenment of its individual citizens; and the size of the group. In other words: 1. the younger or, beyond a certain age, the older a group; 2. the greater the external affinity with its neighbours; 3. the more enlightened its members; and 4. the larger its physical size, the greater must be the irrationality of the collective beliefs and practices needed to counteract the disruptive contrifugal force generated by the rationality and commonsense of its self-centered individuals.

Thus, young nations, as they are now trying to form in a number of underdeveloped countries in Africa, require everything from magic rods, fly-whisks, blood oaths, male or female circumcision, titles, orders of the garter or other undergarment, private divinities, public deification, to oriental pomp, proletarian anti-pomp pomp, republican personality cult, ritualistic trials, firing squads, balcony speeches, national mass communion exercises, hatred, war. And the same applies to very old societies attempting rejuvenation, as we can see in the case of a number of ancient nations, both small and large, in contemporary Asia, or in the long lasting empires of the past such as the Persian, the Roman, the Holy Roman, the Ottoman, the Austrian, or the British.

Not quite so much irrationality, but still enough to make each squirm at the incomprehensible follies of the other, is needed in the case of neighbouring tribes sharing the same identification tag such as a common language. Unable to use this simplest of all tools of group differentiation, such neighbours will invariably draw on their common tongue not for bridging but for deepening the gulf between them. As Bernard Shaw said, the reason for the continued verbal hostility between America and Britain is that both speak the same language. Each understands the other. And neither likes what the other is saying. This accounts also for much of the antagonism the Canadians 'verbalize' for the benefit of their American brethren, though this is paradoxically not true the other way round. For the Americans, drowned as they are in the vastness of their own numbers, are either only half conscious of the existence of English-speaking Canada as a separate national entity, or have the vague feeling that she is a part, or at least like a part, of the United States already – all of which contributes only to making Canadians still more insistent on emphasizing their separate identity.

An even greater 'verbalized' antagonism has long characterized the relations between Bavarians and Prussians, both German speaking, within Germany or, to a lesser extent, between Bavarians and Austrians across the boundary. I myself remember happily how, as small school boys in the Austrian border village of Oberndorf, we used to shout our coarse local dialect across the river Salzach in a wonderfully envigorating daily group-building exercise to the not less outspoken school boys of the small Bavarian town of Laufen:

Boarische Dompfnudln	Bavarian dumplings
Bleibts a weng stehn!	Won't you stop?
Losts eng a weng beidln!	Let's pull out your hair!
Kennts glei wieda gehn!	And on you may hop!

This in the village that gave the world the peaceful song of "Silent Night"! Later, we felt we had to defend our local identity as proud citizens of the formerly sovereign Archbishopric of Salzburg not only against the alien Bavarians on the other side of the border but also in the face of our neighbouring tribes in Austria herself such as the unsufferable Tyrolese or the dim-witted Upper Austrians. We did this by frequently singing with great verve our archiepiscopal anthem which, unlike the American, German, or British anthems, had as its theme not the contented result, but the lusty process, of nation building. Establishing our difference in the most indisputable manner by claiming superiority in the art of beating everyone else up, the song ran like this:

Soizburger samma,	We are men of Salzburg!
Do loss ma uns nix sogn!	There is no mistake!
Viere, fimfe fiacht ma net,	Never feared of taking on
Sexe, sieme ah net!	Five, six, seven, or eight!
Ochte ham ma ah scho ghaut!	How they marvelled here and then
Buama, do hams gschaut!	When we singly beat up ten!

Thirdly, the more enlightened the citizens of a community – that is the more they are animated by a Ciceronian attitude of individual reason or a Christian attitude of individual love – the more they tend to weaken the magnetic force radiating from the group's indispensable belief in its singularity. But the weaker this magnetic force becomes, the more will the community feel compelled to compensate for the subversive wisdom of its members by an all the fiercer insistence on an all the more fanciful tribal mythology. Thus the Jews, whose system of thought had turned them already in antiquity into the most rational of men,[1] required a more irrational central article of collective faith than most other groups: the conviction that they had been tapped into the private fraternity of the most abstract of all lords by God in person. This was enough to hold them together through thousands of years of persecution as a tightly knit national unit in spite of their dispersion over the surface of the entire globe. But the article had to be upheld with such rigour that when Jesus, the greatest of their many great, gave it a universalist rather than nationalist interpretation, he had to be nailed to the cross for failing to submit to the nuclear irrationality without which their community could not have survived.

And as the Jews were sustained by their direct connection with the Lord, so were the Greeks; only that in their case the deity was not an unpronounceable abstraction but a passionate army of thundering, hammering, feasting, fighting, love-making Super-Greeks, all of whose irrationalities were needed to neutralize the

---

[1] And they are still so rational that, as Anton Kuh once said, "in the Salzkammergut, the natives think Doctor is a Jewish first name".

national corrupting effect of a no less imposing dispassionate army of wise Greeks. Had the city states produced fewer of the latter, Socrates, who said: "I am neither an Athenian, nor a Greek, I am a citizen of the world," could have been tolerated as an amiable crack-pot. As things stood, he had to be executed for withholding due reverence from the celestial monstrosities venerated by the state. If, a little earlier, Protagoras and Anaxagoras escaped a similar fate, it was only because the one drowned during his attempt in 415 B.C. to reach the safety of distant Sicily before the Un-Athenian Activities Committee could convict him of religious desecration (asébeia), while the other managed to flee to Lampsakos (432 B.C.) after having been warned by his great friend Pericles, whose brilliant defence had barely secured the acquittal of his mistress Aspasia, that he had little chance of escaping the death penalty. Both Aspasia, famous for her hospitality towards philosophers, and Anaxagoras had likewise been accused of asébeia.[1] So afflicted was the glorious city of Athens with its plethora of wise men still by the year 306 B.C., that the patriotic orator Demochares considered it his McCarthian duty not only to warn his compatriots that all philosophers were "notoriously bad citizens", but also, quite understandably, to insist that "the state will benefit if we drive out Plato's brood and at the same time destroy the peripathetic nest of traitors".[2] And if we are to believe Diogenese Laertius in his life of Heraclitus, Ephesus went so far on the occasion of the banishment of Hermodorus, the best among her own citizens, as to announce: "Let no one of us be preeminently good; and if there is such a person, let him go to another city and another people" (*Diog. Leart.*, IX, 2).

[1] See Wilhelm Nestle. *Griechische Geistesgeschichts*. Stuttgart: Kroner, 1944, pp. 154, 217-218.
[2] See Willian Scott Ferguson. *Hellenistic Athens*. London: Macmillan, 1911, pp. 103-107. The occasion of Demochares' outburst was the repeal of a law of 307 B.C., banishing the philosophers, amongst them Theophrastus, from Athens. Diogenes Laertius writes of this incident in his life of Theophrastus: "... he went away for a short time, both he and all the rest of the philosophers, in consequence of Sophocles, the son of Amphiclides, having brought forward and carried a law that not one of the philosophers should preside over a school unless the council and the people had passed a resolution to sanction their doing so. If they did, death was to be the penalty" (*Diog. Leart.*, V, 38).

To this day, little has changed in the validity of this appraisal in respect of countries and societies which suffer from an excess of intellectuals,[1] philosophers, wise men, or even mere 'egg-heads', or 'squill-heads' as the Attic poets would have called them.[2] One needs only to cite the periodic witch and egghead hunts in the United States; the massive repressions and expulsions of intellectuals by modern France, Italy, Germany, or Spain each time their Napoleons, Hitlers, Mussolinis, Francos tried to reshape an erratic and sagging national image through the infusion of a new dose of inspiring irrationality; or the repeated gaoling of perhaps the most eminent philosopher of our time, Bertrand Russell, by his native England, which is certainly not one of the darker spots on earth. His crime? The enactment of his Socratic Christian philosophy which, compressed into a single sentence, states nothing more vicious than that "Love is wise, and hatred foolish." True, he was gaoled not because of his philosophy but because he violated the laws of the land by putting it to unilateral practice. But the point is that wisdom is often in itself a violation of the laws of the land. Individual reason is often in itself social treason. The only kind of society in which it can be tolerated with impunity is therefore one in which neither the reasonable nor the wise exist in critical abundance.

Lastly, the body of irrationalities must be the larger the greater the physical size of a country. For the larger a country, the more

[1] According to Victor Brombert (*The Intellectual Hero*, London, Faber, 1962), the very word 'intellectual' was characteristically coined as an expression of doubtful compliment for those suspect professors, teachers, writers, and scientists in France who took up the unpopular cause of coming to the defence of Alfred Dreyfus, whose conviction for treason was such a tonic for the patriots. Yet, as Philip Toynbee comments (*The Observer*, May 6, 1962), instead of giving praise to the defenders of justice and truth, "in France – and as we all know, in England, too – the term 'intellectual' has been one of constant hatred and contempt." To Barrés, the "aristocrats of the mind," were nothing but a "bunch of people crazy with pride." As Toynbee notes further, "they were regarded as the subverters and corroders of patriotic ideals whose mean analytical minds bored like woodworms into the old and notable structures of accepted faith."
[2] To judge from Plutarch's *Lives* (Bohn's Standard Library), the first real egg, squill, or sea-onion head seems to have been Pericles. For "his body was symmetrical, but his head was long out of proportion, for which reason in nearly all his statues he is represented wearing a helmet, as the sculptors did not wish, I suppose, to reproach him with this blemish. The attic poets call him squill-head" (I, p. 254).

complex becomes its administration; and the more difficult its far-flung administration, the more imperative is its need to bind its drifting populations together with a network of persuasive conceits of the most lapidary simplicity. The irrational claims to national distinction on the part of large nations must therefore be even more extravagant than those of the usual kind. Moreover, unlike those of smaller communities, they are as a rule swallowed even by the bulk of their intellectuals.[1] Like mother's cooking, everything

---

[1] Even so radical an intellectual as the charming Alexander Herzen could not fend off the conviction of the mystic difference of his great Russian fatherland, or of the existence of innate national qualities of a kind by which most of us recognize foreigners until we discover that someone is describing ourselves. Though doubly tolerant towards the many countries in which Herzen lived as an exile, Russia always seems to come off best, the tyranny of Czar Nicholas notwithstanding. Of America he thought she was next to Switzerland the only country where one could "escape from serfdom into being a free tiller of the soil. . . .I believe that she is destined to a great future . . .; but American life is distasteful to me. . . .Moreover, America, as Garibaldi said, is the 'land for forgetting home'; let those who have no faith in their fatherland go there – they ought to get away from their graveyards. It was quite contrary to me: the more I lost hope of a Latin-German Europe, the more my belief in Russia revived again; but to dream of returning home while Nicholas was Tsar would have been madness." – With regard to the Austrians, who like to think of themselves as one of the more comfort-loving, musical, and softer races, he seemed to share the feelings of the Italian who shouted at them "E brutissimi, brutissimi", and thought their accent in German "loathsome". Of the typical Frenchman he was convinced that he "is innately a soldier; he loves discipline, command, the uniform; he loves to inspire terror". Could he have had the Germans in mind? The Italian, on the other hand, "if it comes to that, is rather a bandit than a soldier, and by that I do not mean anything at all to his discredit". As so many, he was in love with Italy. Of the English, he notes their "coarseness in street mockery, this lack of delicacy and tact in common people", which "helps to explain how it is that women are nowhere beaten so often and so badly as in England, how is it that an English father is ready to cast dishonour on his own daughter and a husband on his wife by taking legal proceedings against them". Could he have confused them with Corsicans? "The rude manners of the English streets are a great offence at first to the French and Italians. The German, on the other hand, receives them with laughter and answers with similar rudeness; an interchange of abuse is kept up, and he is very well pleased with it. They both take it as a civility, a pleasant joke. 'Bloody dog!' the proud Britain shouts at him, grunting like a pig. 'Beastly John Bull!' answers the German, and each goes his way." – But all is forgiven. For the nations cannot help it, and Herzen, the Russian, is a great liberal. Thus, though "the Anglo-Germanic race is far coarser than the Franco-Roman", he tolerantly concludes that "there is no help for that: it is its physical characteristic; it is absurd to be angry with it. The time has come to accept once for all that the different races of mankind, like the different species of animals, have their

footnote continued over leaf

large nations cherish, they consider on wholly dispassionate grounds cooly, and in all modesty, to be the world's best, greatest, biggest, tallest, heaviest, highest, richest, profoundest, deepest, even silliest, as long as it beats everyone else. The ability to beat all comers emerges always as the seemingly most important argument in the claim to national superiority, preferably in the physical meaning of the term. If this is out of the question, the claim to victory in cultural, technological, educational, economic, or even merely moral respects will serve as a satisfactory substitute.

Thus the British, no longer able to administer sound military beatings, are gradually convincing themselves that they are beating the world in political wisdom and moral leadership. Yet, anyone with political wisdom knows that no country on earth has ever taken the slightest notice of anybody's claim to moral leadership unless there was indisputable evidence that the claimant could beat it up also physically. As the Indian sage told Alexander who inquired "What a man should do to be exceedingly beloved." "He must be very powerful," was the answer, "without making himself too much feared."[1] Similarly Malenkov argued when insisting on maintaining the full strength of Soviet power after World War II: "The weak are not respected, and it has often been shown that the weak have been beaten. It is no secret that friends respect us because we are strong, and it follows that friends respect us only as long as we are strong";[2] or as Stalin

---

different characteristics and are not to blame for them." This distinguishes him from such lesser liberals as Lord Beaverbrook or the *New Statesman*, who could hardly be included when he says: "no one is angry with the bull for not having the beauty of the horse or the swiftness of the stag; no one reproaches the horse because its flesh is not so good to eat as that of the ox: all that we can ask of them in the name of animal brotherhood is to graze peaceably in the same field without kicking or goring each other. In nature everything attains to whatever it is capable of attaining to, is formed as chance determines, and so takes its generic *pli*: training goes some distance, corrects one thing and develops another, but to expect beefsteaks from horses, or horses' paces from bulls, is nevertheless absurd." Unfortunately Herzen does not identify which nation is which on his animal farm. *The Memoirs of Alexander Herzen*. London: Chatto & Hindus, 1924; Vol. 3, pp. 74, 95, 96, 100, 186.

[1] Plutarch's *Lives*, Dryden Translation. London: Macmillan 1902. Vol. 4, p. 242.
[2] AP despatch from Moscow, October 22, 1946.

remarked when President Roosevelt referred to the moral leadership of the Vatican: "How many battalions *has* the Pope?"

The Americans on the other hand, insist that they can beat everyone not only with hydrogen bombs but also with their wise constitution, of which the famous Canadian historian George M. Wrong used to say: "It is the worst in the world. *They* think it has been given to them by God." Many of them also think they have invented almost everything. And so do the Russians, while the Germans, Italians, British, and French think they have invented merely the most important things. The French are convinced they beat all comers with the highest logic, the sharpest wits, the best universities, the greatest literature, the most glorious military victories, the sincerest love of peace, the richest of languages, the greatest sense of humour. In short, as the famous critic Jacques Rivière (*The Ideal Reader*, London 1962) writes 'coolly': "French intelligence has no equal; no other is more powerful, more keen, more profound. . . It is the only intelligence that still exists in the world today. . . We are the only people in the world, I repeat coolly, who still know how to think." Not bad, is it?

But this is, of course, what also the British, Italians, Germans, Americans, Russians, think of themselves. After all, is it not always their own jokes that make them laugh most? The Germans, *das Volk der Dichter und Denker*, feel that their Shakespeare translations are superior to the English original, while Englishmen suffer from the suspicion that their equally famous King James translation of the Bible surpasses even the original of the Jews, which is supposed to have been taken down practically on dictation from the Lord Himself. Nor are such lavish claims upheld simply by a bunch of pub characters speaking under the influence of drink. Evelyn Waugh calls English with characteristic understatement – another national identifying feature – "the most splendid language in the world", nothing more, nothing less (*The Sunday Times*, January 7, 1962), while N. R. Ridley, author of *Studies in Three Literatures,* places, in the terms of Harold Nicolson (*The Observer*, January 21, 1962), "in all modesty. . . . the English language above those of Greece and Rome", neither of which possessed " 'the power of reacting to the magic on earth' that has rendered English lyric poetry the finest in the history of literature". No wonder that Mr. Nicolson "found this study a sunshine of enlightenment". So did the people of Vienna with a delightful book of verse, *Wien Wörtlich,* in which Joseph Weinheber proved, sealed, and certified coolly and in all modesty that, contrary to the majority belief of conceited outsiders, the only poetry that counts has been written not in English, German, French, Latin, or Greek, but in the Viennese dialect – the language the Viennese happen to understand best. As he puts it:

"Des hot ka Goethe gshriebn, des hot ka Schiller dicht',
Is von kan Klassiker, von kan Genie,
Des is a Weaner, der mit *unserm* Göscherl spricht,
Und seng S', erst *des* is für uns Poesie."

(No Goethe nor a Schiller wrote this down,
No genius, no poet of renown;
A Viennese in *our* tongue here sings,
That is for *us* where poetry begins).

Yet, were the populous large nations any less convinced of what to smaller ones, or to the treasonably wise, appears as little more than a collection of abysmal absurdities, they would all disintegrate. Such are their Rabelaisian identity requirements that it proved, for example, almost impossible for American public opinion to accept the postponement of the long overdue first attempt to put the standard bearer of their national image into orbit though all considerations of reason were opposed to the flight. But, as Geoffrey Pardoe, head of the British Hawker Siddeley Space Group, at the time said: "To drop this project would mean a loss of face. And where prestige is concerned, rational thinking, scientific logic and engineering sense go overboard." To which the famous Cambridge astronomer Fred Hoyle added: "I would say the whole thing is an absurdity. The social motives behind this flight are precisely the same as in the times of the Roman Empire. It is just a method of exciting public interest; a stunt in which human life is endangered." (*The Sunday Times,* January 23, 1962). Unfortunately it is precisely such stunts, such absurdities which are constantly needed to freshen up the identity of large nations, whose mass is as unstable and fissionable, if left to itself, as is the mass of heavy atoms.

A different picture emerges only when we turn our attention to progressively smaller communities whose dependence on and need for identity-building absurdities begins at a given point of shrinkage to diminish with their size. Below that point, smaller countries need to be less irrational than larger ones, provided that they are neither underdeveloped, afflicted with an indigestable excess of wise men, nor made indistinguishable by too great an affinity with neighbouring communities. Thus, Iceland needs hardly more to preserve her image than the heroes of her sagas, a little hostile memory of the Danes, and an occasional gunshot across the bow of a British trawler. The Swiss have enough with a single hero, William Tell, on whom they are able to bestow their national affection mainly, as the late Professor Rappard never failed to emphasize, because he did not exist. And peoples such as the Danes seem almost wholly rational. Whenever they speak with foreigners, they do not show pride; instead they insist on their total insignificance. So one wonders what their identity game is, until one discovers that this is exactly it. As others are kept together through their faith in their singular national greatness, the Danes seem to build their image around their singular insignificance, as the Salzburgers do with the singular stupidity of their bullwashers. That does make them unique, does it not? In fact, it makes them more unique than others. They are the only ones humble enough to know that they amount to nothing which, of course, is the hallmark of supreme Socratic wisdom. Are they thus not the wisest of nations? The really superior human tribe? With the strangest little jerk in their language? The most enchanting of literatures? With Anderson, Kierkegaard, Niels Bohr, the Ombudsman? And of course what about all the past wars they fought, the empire they had? But halt! They are nothing but a speck in the human multitude, unimportant, insignificant, nobodies, with a twinkle in the eye when they discuss their national image – as if it were a *bêtise*. In larger countries they might be put before the firing squad for this.

4

Now, however, a final important modification must be made. So far, we have treated the irrationalities of national identity building as a riot of nonsense. The reason for this is that we have viewed the process from the point of view of the *individual*. In our capacity as the unindoctrinated rational by-standers watching with fascination the spectacle of make-up being applied to the national image, it strikes us indeed queer to see a perfectly sober neighbour, before settling down for a day's work at court, sling a grass skirt around his hips and stick chicken feathers into his hair. Or to observe him hanging the glistening black robe of a giant bat around his shoulders and putting the wooly skin of a sheep's underbelly on his head. He might just as well have put on curls of maccaroni or tresses of spaghetti. But from a *national* point of view, nothing of this is nonsense. It is only the cue by which a society – a tribe of savages in the one case, a nation of highly civilized sophisticates in the other - recognizes itself as a cohesive entity in an act of utmost social significance: the dispensation of justice. And since man is in his second nature a *social* animal, which makes it impossible for him to exploit his primary nature as an individual to the fullest except within the framework of a group, what has so far been pictured as individually irrational is actually supremely rational if viewed from a communal point of reference.

This means, approaching the subject of identity building this time from the social rather than the individual end, we come back to our starting point: the proposition that the personally unreasonable may in a different context yet be highly reasonable. And this is not all. Since most of us *must* live in society, the collision of what is personally unreasonable with what is socially reasonable modifies on the rebound the concept not only of our *individual* rationality. As Thorstein Veblen has shown when he challenged the classical assumption of an always rationally acting 'economic man', the really reasoning individual strives to accomplish not what is best for him in isolation, by detachedly balancing revenue with cost, but what is best for him within the framework of the group, by feelingly balancing cost with applause. When a brewer sponsors a symphony orchestra, he shows that he is dominated by the public, not the private, image he casts. Instead of maximizing profit by applying the rational laws of industrial efficiency, he tries to maximize acclaim by yielding to the economically wholly unsound demands of his community's fickle irrationality. What guides his conduct is his longing for happiness, which depends on the emotional response of his community, not rationality or wisdom in the absolute, which depends on his relationship with the Lord. He is rather alive and red (in a red environment) than principled and dead. His reason adjusts not to truth but to the prevailing state of collective unreason. In the terms of Egon Ranshofen-Wertheimer's *Victory Is Not Enough*, it pays to be wrong when everyone else is wrong.[1]

It is this group-modified concept of rationality, then, that accounts not only for the readiness with which, in our capacity as citizens, we accept our national conceits as if they were divine revelations. It accounts also for the fact that, even in our capacity as supposedly strictly rational economic men, our behaviour is governed by such rationally indefensible reflex reactions as our pathetic efforts to be in equilibrium with standards set not by ourselves but by the Joneses. If they have two cars, so must we, although this may throw us into debt and wreck our nerves. If they display abstract art, so must we, although we may mistake 'November Morn' for 'Man with Bottle'. If they go to the opera, so must we, although we look forward to nothing except a pint of beer during the intermission. A more modern word for this sort of privately cultivated irrational reflex behaviour towards our social environment is *status seeking*. But the principle is nothing new, though the form is subject to frequent change.

Thus, in the earlier and much poorer decades of this century,

---

[1] The principle involved is the same that accounts for the elimination of the white moths in industrial towns, the sooty air of which made them a too easy target for birds to permit survival. By contrast the dark moth, previously a rare strain, proved now the fitter in the new environment on the simple ground that it pays to be sooty when all else is sooty, just as it pays to be a democrat amongst democrats, a fascist amongst fascists, a communist amongst communists, an intriguer amongst intriguers, an idiot amongst idiots.

the status seeker had to indulge in what Veblen called *conspicuous consumption,* a madly wasteful display of useless assets such as doormen standing idly by in spotless attire, forbidden all day long to lift a finger. For had they been seen working, it would have indicated that payment for their upkeep came from their own labour rather than the splashing surpluses of their employer. In the guilt-ridden though infinitely richer societies of our own time, on the other hand, the top status seeker, provided he has established proof that he can afford everything, seems increasingly to be driven into the opposite direction: towards *conspicuous abstention* rather than *conspicuous consumption.* if he runs for office or desires other forms of public acclaim, he may still secretly go about by private plane. But what the public wants to see in him, always provided there is no doubt about the fatness of his bank account, is the anonymous pedestrian, staying at home when everyone else is on tour, drinking milk while his secretaries guzzle champagne, and delighting in snacks at lunch counters while the local pack of boy scouts frolicks in his swimming pool with pin-up girls from Hollywood. Only at lower levels of status seeking, where it can either not at all be afforded or only on a hectic pay-as-you-go basis, is it still permissible to sport the vulgarity of a brand new car every year, or to turn into a travelling 'culture vulture' during vacation time. But for the rest, the true public image of the Age of Affluence is one not of high consumptio but of austere abnegation just as in ages of abnegation the public likes to identify itself not with frugal saints but with profligate courts. Irrational? Indeed! Yet rational nonetheless.

In conclusion we must therefore take into account two final considerations of relevance in the understanding of the problems of national identity:

In the first place, the description of the full range of human action requires not, as we assumed in the beginning, one but three concepts of rationality: the rationality of the individual in isolation; the rationality of the individual *within* the group; and the rationality *of* the group. All three intersect, and all three contradict each other, so that what is sense from one standpoint may be nonsense from the other. What is reason from the perspective of the isolated individual may be treason, or at least bad citizenship, from the point of view of the nation. What is decent in the privacy of one's home, such as being comfortably dressed, may be indecent in a group, such as wearing a morning coat in a nudist camp. None of these concepts affect the validity of the others. But in the end, all blend into a single amalgam. While individual rationality determines the thoughts of man – his dreams, his spirtual aspirations; the two social rationalities bring him down to earth. They determine his actual behaviour. While the former acts as a steadying beam pointing, like a magnetic needle, always in the same direction, the two latter exert a distorting effect, the strength of which depends on the relative significance of the four variables discussed in the preceding pages: the age of the group, its affinity with other groups, the wisdom of the citizens, and the size of the group.

And secondly, the existing identity of a group is itself not an unchanging concept once it has been defined, but subject to continuous modification, just as the concept of status (as used in the term *status seeking*) is subject to continuous reinterpretation. The only difference is that while the meaning of the latter tends to change with the speed of fashion, the idea of a particular national identity shifts only gradually, with the change of epochs or, in our faster times, of generations. As a result, different generations within the same nations may nowadays have as little in common aside from their descent and their national name as parents and children have within the same family. In fact the *modern* Englishman – who would consider it anything but flattering to be called Victorian in literary, artistic, moral, educational, domestic, public, religious, or political respects – differs more from the *Victorian* Englishman, and the modern American more from the pioneer American, than either of them differs from the contemporary German or Italian. And both would feel as alien and non-belonging if they should suddenly wake up in their home towns twenty years earlier, as Rip van Winkle did when he woke up twenty years later. They would realize that the Victorians were not only a different generation but a different nation. While it is true that all draw on the heritage of those with whom they are loosely linked in linguistic continuity, they use this heritage as the Italians used the monuments of ancient Rome: as a quarry. The only thing suggesting continuity is the stone. But the image carved from it is something completely new every time there is a turnover in the ranks of nation builders – the poets, the artists, the orators, the "mahatma propagandhis". And whenever there is a new team, the irrational identity tags (irrational if viewed from a personal point of reference) used in the make-up of the national archetype will be selected in deference not to tradition but to whatever strikes the current imagination.

But while all nations and, within modern nations, all generations must have their bagful of irrationalities that sets them apart not only horizontally, from their neighbours in space, but also vertically, from their neighbours in time, there is no need for these irrationalities to be of the vicious hatred and war inspiring variety. Imaginative nation builders, particularly in the case of small countries, could just as well make use of a set of less harmful irrationalities without affecting the volume of nuclear force needed to hold their peoples together. The literary and artistic image makers of an emerging nation such as the New Puerto Rico, for example, do not necessarily have to look to Castroite-Cuban anti-American hatred, as so many seem to believe, in their effort to protect their slipping society from losing its face as a result of the Americanizing effect of every modern economic development. By this they will achieve not Puertoricanization but Cubanization or a castrating Castroization which is as much a threat to the identity of Puerto Rico as well as of many other underdeveloped Latin American states as is Americanization. What they can do with an equal chance for success is to adopt as their hallmark for instance a perfect degree of Spanish-English bilingualism.

True, this would in itself not be irrational enough to make them distinguishable from Americans when switching over to the English part of bilingualism. But it *would* be sufficiently irrational to meet their identity requirements if they were to speak English not in the warm drawling American but in the exclusive forbidingly chilly Oxford accent. That would leave neither the Americans nor themselves in any doubt that they are a unique people – *veddy, veddy* different indeed. Or they might become a monarchy in a sea of republican neighbours – like England to be envied by most, and pitied by Malcolm Muggeridge.

X. Meta-Economics

The most fascinating paper read at scholarly conventions is frequently the presidential address. Is it because the president is almost invariably an outstanding member of the profession? This might account for the excellence, but not the *superior* excellence, of his paper. Is it because his office represents the culmination of professional ambitions? Hardly, unless the profession is politics, in which case the presidency is culmination indeed. Rather it seems to be due to the fact that, as Professor John H. Williams has pointed out at a meeting of the American Economic Association, "one of the advantages of a presidential address is that one can appear ... with a topic of his own choosing."[2]

But why should this constitute such an advantage?

Most other topics, whether discussed in conferences or studied at school, are nowadays either assigned or co-operatively determined to fit into the pattern of a larger program. While this avoids overlapping, it has deprived the scholar of the full dimensions of his subject. Caught in the sharp but almost dimensionless focus of his speciality, he is no longer able to leave its confines except on such rare occassions as his election to the presidency of an association of colleagues. When this happens, he is briefly liberated

---

[1] There may be some question about the inclusion of this study, which deals with a new approach to the teaching of economics, in a volume otherwise devoted to the various aspects of a single theme, the impact of social or national size on the problems of communal existence. I might say that the strictly academic field of economics has begun to suffer from the same disease of excessive growth as states and nations, and that it is therefore a fitting subject for a volume dealing with problems of growth, size and form. However, the real reason for its inclusion is that the discernment of the principle which I have applied in the analysis of the problems discussed in all the preceding chapters as well as the understanding of my consistent use of seeming analogies, depends precisely on the kind of educational philosophy which I have discussed in this concluding chapter. While its visible relationship with the practical problem of size particularly in the field of economics may thus appear insignificant, its actual relationship is that of the submerged part of the iceberg. Without it, all I have advanced may be followed, but hardly understood.

[2] *The American Economic Review*, Vol. XIXX, No. 1 (March, 1952), p. 1.

from the narrowing clutch of the plan that governs and coordinates the activities of everyone else, giving him for once the long-awaited chance of making pronouncements on topics strictly his own. Since these are inevitably close to his heart, it is only natural that he should present them with greater competence than if they had been parcelled out to him on the basis of co-operative selection.

However, this is only one reason for the frequent superior excellence of presidential addresses. The principal reason is that anyone gaining temporarily the freedom of topic will almost invariably use it less to choose a particular subject than to choose a particular approach. Emaciated as a result of his long and enforced preocupation with too narrow a field, he will try at least on this one occasion to restore to it the full dimensions of which specialization has divested it, And this is always fascinating, particularly since this is not infrequently done with a feeling of guilt in the face of the relentless currents of our age, as is indicated by so Augustinian a title as *An Economist's Confessions* which Professor Williams chose for his own presidential address.

But this is not all. The uniformity with which the heads of professional organizations, liberated from the fetters of assignment, choose so invariably the full-dimensional rather than the specialist's one-dimensional approach, not only restores temporarily depth and lustre to subjects that have become flat and dull; it also points to the uniformity of their awareness that the basic problem confronting a modern science such as economics is the loss of its third dimension and the frayed condition into which an originally well defined substance has been pushed by the very means by which we hoped to improve it – by growth and specialization. While this process has greatly extended our collective horizon, it has at the same time dimmed our individual vision. For the widening areas demanding attention have not only lengthened the distance between center and perifery but, like the sprawl of a suburbanized modern city, in many instances cut the connection.

However, it would be exaggerated to say that this awareness has produced nothing but a string of nostalgically brilliant addresses.

Repeatedly it has led to practical attempts to reintegrate what modern life has so successfully fragmentized into specialties and subspecialties. In economics it has led to a series of holistic revolutions. Attention was shifted from the special to the general, from the particle to the aggregate, and from the study of individual to that of group behaviour. But each time a revolution had come to an end, it could hardly be said that it had added new understanding. Nor had it reintegrated the subject. On the contrary! To the old were now added new specialities since, as even the macro-economists soon discovered, there are quite as many aggregates as there are particles.

The only thing these revolutions have accomplished was the fashioning of new tools. Since aggregates could be more easily grasped on a statistical basis, *political economy,* with its reliance on deductive reasoning, was abandoned in favour partly of *statistical economy,* with its dependence on quantitive checking, but primarily in favour of *mathematical economy,* with its surrealistic love of symbols and diagrams. Though this transformation of the science, which began in footnotes and ended by supplanting the text,[1] was hailed as a great advance, happening at the very time when further development seemed to have become impossible, mathematical economy did essentially nothing but obscure rather than illuminate the subject. It expressed in a difficult patois what previous theorists had formulated in elegant prose. It is to conceptual economics what bricklaying is to architecture.[2] Not a single new concept can be said to have arisen as

---

[1] Alfred Marshall, who contributed a great deal to the science and was one of the first to use mathematics as a means to illustrate economic principles for the benefit of those well versed in that particular language, remained himself only a footnote mathematician, keeping the tool strictly to where it belonged.

[2] Economics is not the only field that has suffered from mathematically talented imperialists on constant lookout for new territories to be invaded and new disciplines to be subjected. When more than a hundred years ago they began their successful incursion into physics – a field which, to the layman, looks particularly accessible to mathematical penetration – no less a physicist than Michael Faraday came forth with a similar complaint when he wrote in a letter to James Clerk Maxwell: "There is one thing I would be glad to ask you. When a mathematician engages his conclusions, may they not be expressed in common language as fully, clearly, and definitely as in mathematical formulae? If so, would it not

Footnote continued overleaf

a result of the mathematical approach, not the marginal analysis, not the multiplier, not the prospensity to consume, not the quantity theory of money, not the various equilibrium concepts. They all sprang from the realm of philosophical speculation for which the mathematical economists provided not the spark but either proof or illustration. The spark was provided by speculators, by dreamers, or, as Keynes called them, 'academic scribblers'. This is true even of such mathematically gifted economists as Cournot, Walras, Jevons, or Pareto whose philosophical perception was often greatly sharpened by their additional talent, but not created by it.

But now, even the mathematical approach seems to have run its course. Having translated every concept of political economy into a language which illustrates well the complexities of the field to mathematicians but not to economists, a new approach has become necessary. What the mathematicians have obscured must be translated back into a medium that can again be understood by all.[1]

In the 19th century, this medium would have been prose. In our more primitive time it is pictures. Hence, the last mutation of which the science seems capable is pictorial economy or, as one might irreverently call it, *cartoon economy*, a terminal phase whose ascendency becomes more obvious from year to year. There are already film strips illustrating visually the consequences of econ-

---

be a great boon to such as I to express them so? - translating them out of their hieroglyphics, that we might also work upon them by experiment!" From a letter 1857, quoted by Sir Lawrence Bragg, *Nature*, 169, 684 (1952). It goes without saying that the value and glory of mathematics as a discipline in its own right is not contested here. It is indeed perhaps the greatest of all philosophic pursuits, It is therefore not mathematics that is challenged but mahematical economics, if perhaps for no other reason than, as the mathematician Dr. J. Bronowski once said in a conversation with the author, that "only second rate mathematicians are economists."

[1] Wesley Mitchell's argument against mathematical economics was based less on linguistic difficulty than on human behaviour. He thought: "Mathematics is a logical science. Economics is a science dealing with human behaviour. Human behaviour is not logical. Anyone who approaches economics, a science of human behaviour, mathematically, is lost." From Lecture Notes by Anatol Murad of the University of Puerto Rico. See also Allan G. Gruchy, *Modern Economic Thought*. New York: Prentice-Hall, 1947, p. 247.

omic actions, textbooks inspired, if not actually arranged, by cartoonists, and machines showing by means of coloured fluids and glass pipes the flow of national income. As the past generation of economists had to be accomplished in writing, and the present generation in mathematics, the coming generation will have to demonstrate ability in drawing and animating. But as far as a *deeper* understanding of the subject or the elaboration of *new* aspects is concerned, pictorial economy will not contribute more than mathematical economy, since it is the nature of tools that they can work on a substance but not add to it.

Nor will pictorial economy solve the basic problem of the science which is not to illustrate but to integrate. But how can this be done? Through another holistic or macro-economic revolution? The trouble is that, when a field has grown too large, its natural tendency is, as in the case of a state having reached critical size, to diffuse and to fringe, creating thereby simultaneously a demand for integration and the very condition making it impossible. For everything that extends beyond a certain point – separates, and what separates may perhaps be rejoined by a disproportionate effort into an artificial unit, but not fused into an organic whole. Which means that whenever a holistic or macro-economic revolution becomes technically necessary, it becomes organically unfeasible. This is why a number of economists have come to the conclusion that if they are to regain a measure of understanding, they will get nowhere by pushing their explorations still further afield. What they feel they must do is to apply the same device which the previous chapters suggested for the solution of other problems of overgrowth: They must retrace their steps. Evidence of this awareness is their renewed interest not so much in advanced as in basic economic concepts, and their proposals to study them not so much on an elementary as on an advanced level. It is the same philosophy that has induced physicists to seek an understanding of the universe through an understanding of the atom, shedding light on the macro-cosmos through the study of the micro-cosmos, not the other way round.

However, though a revitalized preoccupation with basic economic concepts may increase the understanding of their distant derivations, the new approach falls short in one vital point. It does not retrace its steps far enough. For a concept may be basic in economics, and yet not be basic to the general scheme of things of which economics itself is nothing but a derivation. One must never forget that the greatest phase of the science was its earliest phase, when it began to emerge as a result not of economic but of philosophic speculation. It was then that most of its fundamental principles were discerned and formulated. And its greatest exponents ever since have not been technicians or specialists, but philosophers and thinkers who entered economics not as experts but more often than not as amateurs and dilettantes. Before Adam Smith was an economist, he was a professor of moral philosophy; Thomas Malthus – a minister of the gospel; John Stuart Mill – a scholar of Latin and Greek; Karl Marx – a student of philosophy and history.[1]

But why should these pioneers in the field of economics have had a greater ability to explain its phenomena than their specialized successors who grew up in it? The reason for this seems simple. They were men who did not see one or two dimensions of a problem, but all its dimensions. They were able to explain *economic* phenomena because their training and disposition enabled them to explain *all* phenomena. In their search for solutions they could therefore go *beyond* economics, back into realms where the laws of nature can be more easily observed because of their greater proximity to their ultimate source. Whenever the occasion warranted, they could thus draw from a number of sciences such as biology, physics, or the discipline correlating them all – philosophy. In other words, they were great economists because they were great philosophers. In analogy to a term made famous by the editors of Aristotle, they might also be called *metaeconomists*. Arriving at the limits of physics, Aristotle was likewise driven to elucidate its mysteries by searching for their causes in the field lying beyond, in meta-physics. Like all philosophers, he

---

[1] It is not without significance that Robert L. Heilbronner entitled his book on the great economic thinkers: *The Worldly Philosophers*. (New York: Simon and Schuster, 1953).

tried to find the purpose and end of things in their beginning on the assumption that it is the beginning which shapes, and is shaped by, all the ends. The reader should be warned, however, not to confuse my argument in favour of *meta*-economics with a plea for meta-*physical* economics.

This shows us the direction into which economics must proceed if it is to be saved from hopeless dilution in too far-reaching an expanse. Having run the gamut from political to mathematical and pictorial economy, it must return to the discipline from which it once sprang and become philosophic economy or, to retain the Aristotelian expression, meta-economics. This is not so revolutionary a reversal as it might seem. On the contrary. Though half-hearted and apologetically, the trend in this direction is already manifesting itself in at least two forms. One, as has been mentioned at the beginning of this chapter, is represented by the groping addresses of presidents of economic associations. The other is reflected in the increasing use, in the exposition of economic theory, not of mathematical formulae but of analogies drawn from disciplines beyond economics, *including* the magisterial discipline of mathematics.[1]

This, in fact, would already amount to meta-economics were it not for the timidity with which authors render their own analogies useless by insisting that they are merely expository in nature, but not fundamentally relevant to their propositions. Afraid of being accused of trying to prove a theory by proving an analogy, they

---

[1] Compare the economic application of the mathematician J. Von Neumann's theory of games which "rests on the notion that there is a close analogy between parlour games of skill, on the one hand, and conflict situations in economic, political and military life, on the other." This led in particular to the discovery of a connection with linear economics which "resides in the fact that the mathematical structures of linear programming and game theory are practically identical. Is this pure coincidence? . . . Both game theory and linear programming are applications of the same branch of mathematics – the analysis of linear inequalities – which has many other applications as well, both in and out of economics. The connection is analogous with the connection between the growth of investments at compound interest and the Malthusian population theory." *Linear Programming and Economic Analysis.* By Robert Dorfman, Paul A. Samuelson, Robert M. Solow. New York: McGraw-Hill, 1958, p.2 and 5.

will rather deflate the meaningfulness of their comparisons[1] than defend the one assumption which justifies their use in the first place – the assumption that, if an analogy is meaningful, it must be relevant, and that, if it is relevant, it must be more than a mere analogy. It must be a different manifestation of the same principle it is called upon to elucidate. It must, in fact, to use a biological term, be a *homology*. And if this is the case, it follows that every economic principle may be as vividly argued in its economic as in its physical, chemical, or biological application.

Once this is realized, it becomes possible to draw from knowledge gained in non-economic fields much more effectively and authoritatively than could be done previously. The only question is, would such a new approach, the analysis of economic principles by analyzing their meta-economic manifestations, add to their understanding and shed new, or rather old, light on the seemingly new problems of our time? Yes, for it would provide the only form of integration now needed, the integration of economics not with itself but with its philosophic hinterland. And unlike the mathematical approach, the meta-economic approach would not make things harder but simpler. A student may have difficulty comprehending Gresham's law. But he will at once understand its operation when told that it may be nothing but the economic manifestation of the law of gravity in its terrestrial manifestation. Both explain the same principle, the pull which the lower and denser level invariably exerts on the higher and more tenuous level. And he will understand it still better if he realizes that it applies also to education, where low standards drive out high standards, or to language, where bad accents drive out good

---

[1] An example to this effect is illustrated by the following sequence of assertion and retraction. After using very effectively a biological analogy in an article "Uncertainty, Evolution and Economic Theory", (*Journ. Pol. Econ.*, June 1950, LVII, 211-21), Armen A. Alchian replied to a criticism directed against him by Edith T. Penrose in "Biological Analogies in the Theory of the Firm", (*Am. Econ. Rev.* Dec. 1952, XVII, 804-19), by insisting that his "biological analogy was merely expository", since his theory "stands independently of the biological analogy". (*Am. Econ. Rev.*, Sept. 1953, XVIII, 601). But if an analogy is irrelevant, it is not only useless; it is bad, and should never have been introduced.

accents.[1] The quantity theory of money, which links price level changes to changes not only of the supply but also of the circulatory velocity of currency, becomes infinitely more revealing to both economists and sociologists if it is realized that, *mutatis mutandis,* it applies also to population problems. For, as the preceding chapters have shown, just as inflation, so overpopulation may result from an increase not only in the quantity but also in the velocity factor. At the low velocity of a lazy Sunday afternoon not even New York is overpopulated while at the high velocity of a week-day rush-hour period even the most dreamy community becomes beset with the problem of overpopulation though not a single individual has been added to its mass.

Similarly, most other concepts assume quite a different luminosity when viewed in the light of the various shapes they may take. And, by doing this, they add not only to our understanding but, more importantly, may contribute to the solution of many of our contemporary problems. A concept such as equilibrium, for example, which the suspicion of modern social scientists has rendered almost useless as an ideal to be aspired to, could again be used to constructive ends if, instead of chasing its mathematical magnitudes, economists were to appraise it in the light of the biological principle of ecology, the musical principle of harmony, or the physical principle of balance, of which it seems but a variation. We would then find that, in the first place, there are two basic kinds of balances and not one, each applicable to a

[1] Paul A. Samuelson, in a humorous though not unserious aside during the presentation of his paper before the 64th Annual Meeting of the American Economic Assoc. (Boston, December 1951), alluded to the meta-economic applicability of Gresham's Law, but confined himself to a single example: that bad speeches drive out good speeches. One may say that low in the physical sense does not mean low in the moral sense. But, as will be shown, at a given rate of incidence, quantitative aspects begin to assume qualitative characteristics. A different meta-economic application of the physical law of gravitation is the Law of Molecular Attraction by which Henry C. Carey explained man's gregarious disposition. Noticing the fact that large cities attract more people than small ones, and both more from their neighborhood than from the distance, he thought that "gravitation is here, as everywhere, in the direct ratio of the mass and the inverse one of the distance" (*Principles of Social Science,* p. 38, in the edition of McKean). Much of Carey's fertile originality was due to his meta-economic conviction that both the social and the physical universe are governed by the same fundamental principles.

different universe, and that the difficulty of operating with them is due mainly to our failure to distinguish between them;[1] and, secondly, that one of the main problems plaguing our time is consequently not, as is nowadays so often believed, one of balance versus unity,[2] or of equilibrium versus control or growth. As Henry Kissinger has so clearly perceived, it is one of a good balance versus a bad balance. If this defies solution, it is only because of the belief of so many of our social scientists that a principle applying everywhere else represents in economics or politics at best a bad anology.

Similarly, the law of diminishing productivity could be restored to greater usefulness if it were more consciously correlated with its meta-economic manifestations. Everyone understands its relationship to the Malthusian population principle, according to which a continuously growing mankind must ultimately outrace its ability to furnish the necessary food supply. But it is only now that both are gradually recognised as being variations of a more

---

[1] The two balances are the stable balance for non-moving and the mobile balance for moving and living systems. A sound balance being characterized by its self-regulatory nature, a balance in a non-moving system is the better the larger and fewer its balancing units. A good mobile balance, on the other hand, is the better the more numerous and the smaller its balancing units, so that collisions resulting from the free movement of particles cannot disturb the system as a whole. A living, dynamic, competitive system such as capitalism can therefore, as Chapter V has shown in greater detail, function effectively only as long as its units are both numerous and small. Read in this connection a similar emphasis on a revitalized approach to equilibrium analysis: Keneth E. Boulding's almost classical example of a meta-economic piece of writing, *A Theory of Small Society* (*Caribbean Quarterly*, Vol. 6, No. 4), in which he tells how he was at first baffled, but ultimately not at all surprised to find that the stellar constellations were, at the time when he composed his paper, almost equal in number to that of the member states of the United Nations on earth. Accident? Not at all, says Boulding, for both are the product of the human mind. To encompass the vastness of the universe, as in the case of the vastness of humanity, man has divided the galaxies into small constellations. – pp. 262-3.

[2] This is expressed in such juxtapositions of political alternatives as capitalist competition versus socialist control, or balance of power versus a united world. However, what seems wrong with the world is of course not that its powers are balanced but, that they are badly balanced.

basic biological and physical law of growth and form.[1] Once this connection is generally accepted, it cannot but change the direction of our economic aims. Above all, as this volume has tried to prove from its very outset, it would show that the principal question of our time is not: how to continue growing in an ever expanding economy, but how to stop growing; and that the answer must therefore lie not in union and integration but in splitting and duplication. This is the biological way of advance.[2] It seems to suggest itself all the more as many units of social organization – in the economic field: the big corporations; in the political field: the big powers – have long started to outgrow the requirements of their purpose and their form.

The meta-economic approach would thus suggest what other approaches seem unable to perceive: the urgency for a change in theoretical emphasis away from *growth economics*,[3] which still obsesses our great universities, to *form economics*, whose academic development is as overdue in the 1970's as the shift to macro-economic analysis was in the 1930's. In this it would merely follow a similar development that has set in even in physics which, in its most recent phase, is likewise returning from Newton's dynamics with its emphasis on forces to the ancient Greeks' approach which stressed the primacy of structures, the harmony of proportions, of form.[4]

These few examples appear sufficient to indicate both the nature

---

[1] No one has elucidated the interrelationship between growth and form better than D'Arcy Wentworth Thompson in *On Growth And Form* (Cambridge University Press, 1952). In his paper *Toward a General Theory of Growth* (The Canadian Journal of Economics and Political Science, August, 1953, pp. 226-240), Kenneth Boulding draws heavily from D'Arcy W. Thompson in what amounts to a classical example of meta-economic exposition.

[2] See Julian Huxley, *Biological Improvement*, in *The Listener*, November 1, 1951, pp. 739 ff.

[3] In his pamphlet on *Growthmanship* (Hobart paper 10, 1962), Colin Clark, one of the main inspirors of growth economics, confessed to having had second thoughts about it.

[4] See *"The Harmony and Wholeness in Greek Scientific Thought"* by Professor Sambursky of Jerusalem, read at the triennial meeting of the British Classical Society, Oxford, August 1, 1961.

and the value of a meta-economic approach.[1] It would integrate economics *philosophically* and restore to the science at least some of the depth it possessed at the beginning of its development. Moreover it would seem to be in line with the hidden desire not only of economists but also of representatives of other disciplines. One of the most profound contributions to appear in the last few years in the field of biology was a meta-biological study by a physicist, the Austrian Nobel-prize winner Erwin Schroedinger.[2] *The Nation* devoted an entire issue to an impassioned plea for the meta-disciplinary technique of scholarship penned by the late British mathematician Dr. J. Bronowski.[3] And the dean of an American Engineering College, Elmer C. Easton of Rutgers University, came forth with a similar appeal when, contemplating the basic weakness of modern education, he urged that every teacher be required "to discuss with his students the interrelationships among the basic principles of his field and those of other disciplines." Summarizing the value of the meta-approach he pointed out that:

> "In some instances these interrelationships are fairly obvious. For example, the similarities among the principles of heat transfer, flow of electricity, and flow of liquids are well known to the engineer. It is easy, therefore, to require that they be pointed out in order to integrate courses in the three subjects. On the other hand, some engineers and some sociologists may be surprised to find the concept of entropy applicable both in thermodynamics and in the statistical analysis of group behavior. It requires men of the broadest possible education to detect obscure interrelationships and to design a curriculum so as to utilize them as an integrating device."[4]

[1] Since this chapter does not itself fall into the category of meta-economics, but merely proposes a new approach, a new academic discipline, none of the examples were meant to be advanced here except in the most scetchy manner.
[2] Erwin Schroedinger. *What is Life*. Cambridge: University Press, 1951.
[3] J. Bronowski, *Science and Human Values*. *The Nation*. December 29, 1956.
[4] *Designing a Curriculum*, mimeographed remarks by E. C. Easton, presented at the All-University Educational Conference at Rutgers University, September 25, 1953.

The urge towards a return to philosophic speculation seems thus to arise at the present time in a variety of fields simultaneously. Yet, as an approach to knowledge and truth it is not new. It has been pursued since time immemorial. It represents, in fact, the oldest and most fruitful direction of human inquiry. The greatest contributions to man's advance have been rendered by man's effort to go back, back to the cause common to all consequences. Aristotle's search for the ultimate unity behind everything has made him the most enduring shaper of categories in the sciences that became subject to his scrutiny. Plato's profundity as a scholar stems from his life long dedication to define an *anima mundi*.[1] Pythagoras' – from an extension of his idea of numbers until it embraced geometry, justice, music, and astronomy in a single system. Goethe's pursuits led to the creation of a new discipline, *morphology*, the study of similarities of forms and functions in the various fields of life. Leonardo da Vinci's philosophic speculations resulted in his dramatic discernment of what was hailed as the greatest discovery in mechanics since Archimedes – a unifying law underlying the motion of all waves, be they of water, of wheat in a field animated by an autumn breeze, of sound, or of light.[2] Michelangelo attributed his greatness as an architect to the fact that he knew how to draw nudes, "for the structure of the human body and of buildings is the

---

[1] Plato's Academy encouraged amongst others, less the study of various sciences as the study of similarities. Parts of a work by one of his students, Speusippus, *On Similarities* are still extant, See Wilhelm Nestle's discussion of the Platonic Academy in his: *Griechische Geistesgeschichte*. Alfred Kroner Verlag, p. 280.

[2] This is how Leonardo described his discovery in his diary: "The Law of mechanics is the same in both instances! As waves upon water from the thrown stone, so do the waves of sounds go through the air, crossing one another, without mingling, and preserving as their central point the place of origin of every sound. – And what of light? Even as echo is the reflection of sound, so the reflection of light in a mirror is the echo of light. There is but one sole law of mechanics in all the manifestations of force. There is but Thy sole will and justice, Thou First Mover: the angle of descent is equal to the angle of refraction." – From Dimitri Merejkowski, *The Romance of Leonardo da Vinci*. Garden City, N.Y.: Garden City Publishing Co., 1930, p. 333. A great number of additional examples can be found in J. Bronowski's *Science and Human Values*, quoted above, as well as in *The Springs of Discovery*, a passionate plea for the *Meta*-approach by Professor Herbert Butterfield, Master of Peterhouse, Cambridge (*The Observer*, July 9, 1961).

same". Darwin's achievement, in his own estimate, consisted in his transference of the theories of Malthus to "the whole animal and vegetable kingdom." Spencer's life-long search was devoted to the discovery of a basic principle of evolution common to astronomy, biology, and society. William C. Carey thought the same laws governed mind and matter, the physical and the social universe. For similar reasons, the first school of economists is called the Physiocrats. And, to repeat a quotation from the beginning of this book, Confucius, at the end of a life of rewarding speculation, told a student admiring him for the wide range of his knowledge: "I know only one thing, but this permeates everything."

The one element these pioneers of human knowledge had in common was the approach they applied to their varied pursuits. They all were *meta-scientists*. By stepping beyond the boundaries of their original fields in search of ultimate causes and basic laws, they fertilized along with the disciplines they entered the disciplines from which they came. Does it seem daring to suggest that an approach so fruitful in richer ages should prove fruitful also in our emaciated time? Does it seem irreverent to believe that, what served so well the physicist, might serve well also the silted science of the economist? And is it to the credit of our metropolitan prestige universities that the only institution having undertaken concrete steps towards offering a course in Meta-Economics should have been the University of the tropical island state of 'indolent' Puerto Rico?

Bibliography

BOOKS CITED

Aristotle, *Politica,* Ed., W. D. Ross, Oxford University Press, 1942.
Augur, B.Y., *How to run effective Business Meetings.* New York: Grosset & Dunlap, 1964.
Augustine, Saint, *City of God.* Edition: *Basic Writings,* New York: Random House, 1948.

Bacon, Sir Francis, *Essays.* New York: Walter Black, 1942.
Brandeis, L. D., *The Curse of Bigness.* New York: The Viking Press, 1935.
Brombert, Victor, *The Intellectual Hero.* London: Faber, 1962.

Cadden, V., and Whitbread, J., *The Intelligent Man's Guide to Women.* New York: Schuman, 1951.
Carey, Henry C., *Principles of Social Science,* Philadelphia, 1858.
Clark, Colin, *Growthmanship.* London: Hobart Papers, 1962.
Coyle, David C., *Day of Judgment.* New York: Harper & Brothers, 1949.

Diogenes Laertius, *Lives of Eminent Philosophers.* London: Loebs Classical Library, 1942.
Dorfman, R., Samuelson, P., Solo, R. M., *Linear Programming and Economic Analysis.* New York: McGraw-Hill, 1958.

Farrand, 1 and 2, *Records of Federal Convention 540.*
Ferguson, William Scott, *Hellenistic Athens.* London: Macmillan, 1911.
Fox, Annette B., *The Power of Small Nations.* Cambridge University Press, 1960.

Gruchy, Allan G., *Modern Economic Thought.* New York: Prentice-Hall, 1947.

Harris, S. E., and Schultz, H., *American Public Finance.* New York: Prentice-Hall, 1949.
Heilbronner, R. L., *The Worldly Philosophers.* New York: Simon & Schuster, 1953.
Herodotus, *Histories.* London: Everyman's Library, 1949.
Herzen, Alexander, *Memoirs.* Chatto & Hindus, 1924.

Kohr, Leopold, *Customs Unions.* Washington: Foundation for Foreign Affairs, 1949.
Development Without Aid. Swansea: Christopher Davies, 1973.
The Breakdown of Nations. London: Routledge & Kegan Paul, New York: Rinehart, 1957; *Paperback,* Swansea: Christopher Davies, 1975.
Is Wales Viable? Swansea: Christopher Davies, 1971.
Die Ueberentwickelten. Dusseldorf: Econ Verlag, 1962.
The City of Man. San Juan: University of Puerto Rico Press, 1976.

Liechtenstein, Principality of, *Budget.* Various Years.

Malthus, Thomas, *Essay on Population.* 1798.
Marx, Karl, *Value, Price, and Profit.* Chicago: Kerr & Co.
Mackintosh, J. P., *Devolution of Power.* Penguin, 1968.
Marshall, Alfred, *Principles of Economics.* London: Macmillan, 1920.
Merejkowski, Dimitri, *The Romance of Leonardo da Vinci.* New York: Garden City Publishing Co., 1930.

Müller, Adam, *Elemente der Staatskunst.* Jena: Baxa, 1921.
Vom Geiste der Gemeinschaft. Selected Writings, 1931.
Murad, Anatol, *Lecture Notes,* 1927.

Nestle, Wilhelm, *Griechische Geistesgeschichte.* Stuttgart: Alfred Kroner Verlag, 1944.

Ortega y Gasset, *The Revolt of the Masses.* New York: The American Library, 1950.

Parkinson, Northcote C., *Parkinson's Law.* London: John Murray, 1958.
Pigou, A. C., *The Economics of Welfare.* London: Macmillan, 1938.
Plutarch, *Lives.* London: Macmillan, 1902.

Ranshofen-Wertheimer, Egon, *Victory is NOT Enough.* New York: W. W. Norton, 1942.
Rivière, Jacques, *The Ideal Reader.* London, 1962.
Robinson, E. A. G., *The Economic Consequences of the Size of Nations.* London: Macmillan, 1960.

Samuelson, Paul, *Economics, An Introductory Analysis.* New York: McGraw-Hill, 1973.
Schrödinger, Erwin, *What is Life.* Cambridge University Press, 1951.
Schumacher, Dr. E. F., *Small is Beautiful.* New York: Harpers, 1974; London: Blond & Briggs, 1974.
Schwartz, Harry, *Russia's Soviet Economy.* New York: Prentice-Hall, 1950.
Smith, Adam, *The Wealth of Nations.* Modern Library Edition, 1937.
Simons, Henry C., *Economic Policy for a Free Society.* Chicago: University Press, 1948.
Strachey, John, *The Great Awakening.* London: Encounter Pamphlet Series, 1961.

Temporary National Economic Committee, *Competition and Monopoly in American Industry.* Monograph No. 21. Washington: 1940.
Relative Efficiency of Large, Medium-sized, and Small Business. Monograph No. 13. Washington: 1941.
Thompson, D'Arcey W., *On Growth and Form.* Cambridge University Press, 1942.
Thucidides, *History of the Peloponesian War.* London: Loeb's Classical Library, 1969
Thyme, Alexander, *Regional Manifesto.* Warminster: Longleat House, 1976.

United States, *Government Reports.* Various Years.
Manpower Report, 1964.
Municipal Yearbook, 1951.

Villari, Pasquale, *Life and Times of Savonarola.* New York: Charles Scribner & Sons, 1896.

Weinheber, Josef, *Wien Wörtlich.* Hamburg: Hoffmann & Campe, 1935.

2

ARTICLES AND PAPERS CITED

Alchian, Armen A., Uncertainty, Evolution and Economic Theory, *Journal of Political Economy,* June, 1950.

Bagrit, Sir Leon, Fifth Reith Lecture, *The Listener*, December 10, 1964.
Boulding, Kenneth E., A Theory of Small Society, *Caribbean Quarterly*, Vol. 6, No. 4.
  Toward a General Theory of Growth, *The Canadian Journal of Economics and Political Science*, August, 1953.
Bronowski, Jacob, Science and Human Values, *The Nation*, December 29, 1956.
Butterfield, Herbert, The Springs of Discovery, *The Observer*, July 9, 1961.

Easton, E. C., *Designing a Curriculum*, paper read to All-University Educational Conference, Rutgers University, September 25, 1953.

Huxley, Sir Julian, Biological Improvement, *The Listener*, November 1, 1951.

Keats, John, *Ode on Indolence*.
Kohr, Leopold, Disunion Now, *Commonweal* (New York), September 26, 1941.
  Towards a New Measurement of Living Standards, *The American Journal of Economics and Sociology*, October, 1955.
  The Aspirin Standard, *Business Quarterly* (Canada), Summer, 1956.
  The Fallacy of Size, *Cambridge Opinion*, November, 1962.
  The Convivial Theory of State Origin, *Queens Quarterly* (Canada), Summer, 1957.

Penrose, Edith T., Biological Analogies in the Theory of the Firm, *American Economic Review*, December, 1952.

Sambursky, S., *The Harmony and Wholeness in Greek Scientific Thought*, paper read before British Classical Society, Oxford, August 1, 1961.
Stacey, Tom, Freedom Was Not Enough, *The Sunday Times*, January 28, 1962.

Times, Editorial: *Small is Harmonious*, London, February 26, 1976.

Williams, John H., An Economist's Confessions, *The American Economic Review*, March, 1952.

Note: An extensive bibliography on Smallness is being prepared by the *Institute of Man and Science* (Rensselaerville, New York 12147) since 1975.

3

NEWSPAPERS AND PERIODICALS CITED

American Economic Review.
American Journal of Economics and Sociology.
Associated Press.

Business Quarterly (Canada).

Canadian Journal of Economics and Political Science.
Commonweal.
Cambridge Opinion.
Carribbean Quarterly.

Daily Express, London.

Economist.

Guardian.

Journal of Economic History.
Journal of Political Economy.

Listener.

Monthly Review (Federal Reserve Bank, New York).

Nature.
New York Times.

Observer.

Queens Quarterly (Canada).

Simplicissimus.
Sunday Times, London.

Time.
Times, London.

UK Department of Employment *Gazette*.
US Government Reports.

Index of Names

A
Abbas, Ferhat, 142n.
Achilles, 140.
Alchian, Armen A., 168n.
Alexander, 2n, 157.
Amin, Idi, 141, 143.
Amis, Kingsley, 136.
Amphiclides, 148.
Anaxagoras, 148.
Andersen, Hans Christian 154.
Apollo, 31.
Archimedes, 173.
Aristotle, 12, 19, 22, 22n, 30, 30n, 72n, 82, 83, 84, 87, 166, 173.
Aspasia, 148.
Auger, B. Y., 21n.
Augustine, St., 10, 63, 114n.
Augustus, 140.

B
Bacon, Sir Francis, 129, 139.
Bagrit, Sir Leon, 113n.
Baldwin, Stanley, 144.
Bartholomew, 13.
Battenberg, 144.
Beaverbrook, Lord, 130, 151n.
Betancourt, Romulo, i.
Bismark, 120, 121.
Bohr, Niels, 154.
Boticelli, 12.
Boulding, Kenneth E., iv, 2, 170n, 171n.
Bragg, Sir Lawrence, 164n.
Brandeis, Louis, 75n.
Breycha-Vautier, A., von, i.
Brombert, Victor, 149n.
Bronowski, Dr. J., 164n, 172, 173n.
Bukharin, N. I., 70.
Butterfield, Herbert, 173n.

C
Cadden, Vivian, 38n.
Campanella, 49.
Carey, Henry Charles, 169n, 174.
Castro, Fidel, 129, 130, 141, 143.
Churchill, Sir Winston, 11, 94, 139.
Cicero, 130, 133.
Clark, Colin, 30n, 126.
Colberg, Severo, i.
Confucius, 11, 174.
Cournot, Augustin, 164.
Coyle, David Cushman, 75n.

D
Dante, 12.
Darwin, Charles, 174.
Davies, Sir Alun Talfan, i.
Demochares, 148, 148n.
DesEcherolles, Alexander, i.
Diem, Ngo-dinh, 85.
Diffrient, Niels, i.
Diogenes, 13, 28.
Diogenes Laertius, 148, 148n.
Dionisius, iv.
Disraeli, Benjamin, 141, 144.
Dreyfus, Alfred, 149n.
Dupont, 26, 144.
Duquesne de la Vinelle, L., 120.

E
Easton, Elmer C., 172.
Eden, Sir Anthony, 94.
Edinboburgh, Duke of, 75n.
Eisenhower, Dwight, 22n, 96.
Elizabeth II, Queen, 86n, 132, 135n.
Evans, Gwynfor, i.
Evans, Myfanwy, i.

F
Faraday, Michael, 163n.
Ferguson, W. S., 148n.
Ford, Motor Co., 44n.
Fourrier, Charles, 17n.
Fuéré, Yann, i.
Franco, Francisco, 7, 149.
Freud, Siegmund, 10, 144.

G
Galbraith, John Kenneth, iv.
Gandhi, Indira, 7.
Garibaldi, 150.
Goebbels, Josef, 141.
Goethe, Johann Wolfgang von, 12, 173.
Gonzalez, Dr. Antonio, i.
Gorham, 73, 74, 74n.
Gossen, Hermann, ix.
Graicunas, V. A., 21n.
Gresham, Sir Thomas, 168, 169n.
Gruchy, Allan G., 164n.
Gulliver, 62.

H
Halifax, Lord, 26.
Hannibal, 2n.

Harris, Seymour E., 37n.
Harwood, Lous, 60, 61, 73.
Heath, Edward, 94.
Heilbronner, Robert L., 166n.
Heine, Norma, i.
Heller, Walter W., 39.
Hemming, Margaret, i.
Heraclitus, 148.
Hermodorus, 148.
Hernmarck, Helena, i.
Herodotus, 135, 135n.
Herzem, Alexander, 150n-151n.
Hesiod, 14.
Hitler, Adolf, 2n, 7, 62, 90, 141, 149.
Home, Sir Alex Douglas, 94.
Homer, 140.
Hoyle, Fred, 153.

I
Illich, Ivan, v.

J
Jesus, 147.
Jevons, W. S., ix, 64, 164.
Jewkes, J., 75n.
Jöhr, W. A., 75n, 109n, 110n.
Johnson, Samuel, 85.
Joseph of Egypt, 64.
Julius II, Pope, 62.
Jung, Karl, 10.

K
Katyusha, 77n.
Keats, John, 126n.
Kennedy, John F., 4, 22n, 144.
Kenyatta, Jomo, 141.
Keynes, John Maynard, 66, 71, 164.
Khrushchev, Nikita, iii, 77n, 96, 112, 116n.
Kipling, Rudyard, 141.
Kierkegaard, Søren, 154.
Kissinger, Henry, 170.
Kneschaurek, F., 75n, 108n, 110n.
Kohr, John R., i.
Kohr, Leopold, vi-x.
Kubishta, 144.
Kuh, Anton, 147.

L
Lasalle, 26.
Leonardo da Vinci, 173, 173n.
Lincoln, Abraham, 141.
Lorenzo, the Magnificent, 27n.

M
Mackintosh, J. P., 125n.
Macmillan, Sir Harold, 77n, 94.
Madison, James, 74n.
Malenkov, G. M., 151.
Malthus, Thomas, 33, 166, 174.
Mao, 141.
Margolin, Robert, 44n, 124n.
Marshall, Alfred, v, 162n.
Martin, W. McChesney, 69n.
Marx, Karl, ii, vii, 10, 11, 39, 39n, 65, 67, 70, 71, 112, 166.
Maxwell, James, 163n.
Meade, James E., i.
Meadows, Dennis L., 30n.
Menger, Carl, ix.
Merejkowski, Dimitri, 173n.
Michelangelo, 173.
Mill, John Stewart, 166.
Misham, E. J., iv, 30n.
Mitchell, Broadus, i.
Mitchell, Wesley, 164n.
Moore, Barbara, 108.
More, Sir Thomas, 17n, 49.
Mozart, Wolfgang A., 12, 134.
Müller, Adam, 129, 132, 139.
Muggeridge, Malcolm, 160.
Muñoz Marin, Luis, 127.
Murad, Anatol, i, ii, x, 164n.
Mussey, Barrows, i.
Mussolini, Benito, 149.

N
Napoleon, 2n, 62, 149.
Nehru, Jawaharlal, 7, 129.
Nestle, Wilhelm, 148n, 173n.
Neumann, J. von, 167n.
Newton, Sir Isaac, 12.
Nicolas, Czar, 150, 153.
Nicolson, Harold, 135, 152, 153.
Nixon, Richard M., 130.
Nkruma, Dr. Kwame, iii, 129, 130, 132.
Nordhaus, William D., iv, 42n.
Nyerere, Julius, 142, 143.

O
O'Brien, Dr. Connor Cruise, 7n.
Ortega y Gasset, José, 12.
Orwell, George, 22, 93.
Ovid, 126.
Owen, Robert, 17n.

P
Pace, Donna, i.
Papworth, John, i.

INDEX OF NAMES

Pardoe, Geoffrey, 153.
Pareto, Vilfredo, 164.
Parkinson, Northcote C., 63n, 112.
Pasteur, Louis, ix.
Pausanias, 14.
Pericles, iii, 62, 148, 149.
Penrose, Edith, 168.
Petty, Sir William, 39.
Pigou, A. C., 39.
Plaid Cymru, 105.
Plato, 17n, 49, 148, 173, 173n.
Pliny, the Younger, 122, 123.
Plutarch, 149n.
Prometheus, 14.
Propagandhi, Mahatma, 141, 159.
Protagoras, 148.

R
Ranshofen-Wertheimer, Egon, 156.
Rappard, William E., 154.
Read, Sir Herbert, i.
Rees, Alvin, i.
Ricardo, David, 39.
Ricciardi, Franc M., i.
Ridley, N. R., 152.
Rip van Winkle, 158.
Rivière, Jaques, 152.
Robinson, E. A. G., iii, ix, 21n, 75n, 109n, 110n, 113-114n, 120n, 121, 121n.
Roosevelt, 144.
Roosevelt, Franklin Delano, 152.
Rowntree, Joseph, 119n.
Russel, Bertrand, 149.

S
Saharoff, Sir Basil, 63n.
Sambursky, Shmuel, 171n.
Samuelson, Paul, iv, 43n, 167n, 169n.
Sandberg, Carl, 141.
Saxe-Cobourg-Gotha, 144.
Schrödinger, Erwin, 172.
Schulz, H., 37n.
Schumacher, Dr. E. F., v, 30n.
Schwarz, Harry, 69n.
Seibt, Peter, i.
Shakespeare, William, 12.
Shaw, Bernard, 145.
Shrapnel, Norman, 135n.
Simons, Henry C., 53n, 73, 76, 94.
Smith, Adam, iii, 50n, 132, 166.
Snowdon, Earl of, 135n.
Socrates, 148.
Sophocles, 148n.
Spencer, Herbert, 174.
Speusippus, 173n.

Stacey, Tom, 142.
Stalin, Joseph, 151.
Strachey, John, 116n.
Sukarno, Dr. Ahmed, 129.

T
Tannenbaum, 144.
Tarshis, L., 75n, 110n.
Taunus, 44n.
Tell, William, 154.
Teller, Edward, 10.
Theophrastus, 148n.
Thomas, Brynmore, i, v.
Thompson, D'Arcy W., 29.
Thorne, Alfred, i.
Thucidides, iii.
Thynne, Alexander, 125n.
Tito, 7.
Tobin, James, 42n.
Torruellas, Dr. Luz, i.
Toynbee, Philip, 149n.
Trotzky, Leo, 70, 76.
Truman, Harry S., 96.

U
Ulysses, 140.

V
Veblen, Thorstein, viii, 155, 157.
Victoria, Queen of England, 141.
Villari, Pasquale, 27n.
Virgil, 140.

W
Wagner, 144.
Walras, Leon, 164.
Waugh, Evelyn, 152.
Weinheber, Josef, 153.
Whitbread, Jane, 38n.
Wilde, Oscar, 8.
Williams, John H., 161.
Wrong, George M., 152.

Index of Places

A
Afghanistan, 108.
Africa, 117, 143, 145.
Algeria, 142n.
America, 115n, 121n, 145, 150n.
Andorra, 17.
Annam, 85n.
Arabia, 144.
Arctic, 117.
Asia, 145.
Aspen, i.
Athens, 148, 148n.
Australia, 115.
Austria, 90, 106, 115, 146.
Azores, 47.

B
Babel, 117.
Bavaria, 106.
Belgium, 36n, 37n, 108, 115, 119.
Bern, 89, 120n.
Bremen, 106.
Britany, 125.
Brussels, 120n.
Buffalo, 63n.

C
Calabria, 125.
Cambodia, 131n.
Cambridge, i, iv, x, 153.
Canada, 34, 35n, 36n, 37n, 40n, 43, 106, 115, 146.
Catalonia, 125.
Chicago, 2, 62, 63n.
China, 4, 7, 7n, 93, 96, 131n.
Cornwall, 116, 125.
Corsica, 125.
Cuba, 7n, 131n.

D
Delaware, 26.
Delphi, 31.
Denmark, 36n, 40n, 105, 107, 115, 125.
Dresden, 120n.

E
East Anglia, 125.
East Germany, 120n.
Egypt, 108, 115.
Elizabeth, N.J., 63n.

England, 26, 40n, 44n, 77n, 94, 106, 113, 114, 115n, 116, 128, 129, 149, 149n, 150, 160.
Ephesus, 148.
Essex, 125.
Europe, 150.

F
Finland, 121n.
Flanders, 18.
Florence, 27n, 105, 120n.
France, 12, 37n, 63n, 75, 108, 114n, 115, 117n, 119, 120, 120n, 125, 128, 149, 149n.
Frankfort, 106.

G
Genoa, 105.
Germany, 6, 12, 18, 75, 77n, 92, 108, 115, 118, 119, 120, 120n, 121, 125, 128, 129, 141, 146, 149.
Ghana, 106, 108, 115.
Great Britain, 12, 36n, 45, 63n, 73, 75, 92, 93, 106, 108, 114n, 115, 116n, 117, 119n, 120n, 125, 128, 141, 145.
Greece, 18, 31, 37n, 118, 140.
Greenland, 36n.

H
Hamburg, 106.
Harvard, iv, 33.
Haryale, 90, 131.
Hesse, 106.
Hollywood, 141, 157.
Hyderabad, 7.

I
Iceland, 34, 47, 105, 106, 107, 110, 115, 117, 125, 145, 154.
India, 7, 7n, 8, 115n, 119n.
Ireland, 115n.
Israel, 106.
Italy, 18, 36n, 63n, 75, 114n, 117n, 119, 121, 150n.

J
Japan, 109.
Jugoslavia, 108.

INDEX OF PLACES

K
Kabul, 144.
Katanga, 7n.
Kashmir, 7.
Kent, 125.
Korea, 2.
Kremlin, 10, 12, 58, 76, 116.

L
Lampsakos, 148.
Laos, 108.
Laufen, 146.
Latin America, 117.
Liechtenstein, 17, 88-91.
Lisbon, ii, iii, ix, x, 106, 110n, 113n.
Lombardy, 125.
London, 21n, 101, 119n, 120n, 131n.
Louvain, 120.
Lubumbashi, 7n.
Luxembourg, 37n, 56n, 108, 114n.

M
Madrid, 120n.
Manhatten, 144.
Marocco, 108.
Massachusetts, 73, 74n.
Mercia, 125.
Milan, 103.
Minneapolis, 144.
Monaco, 17, 117n.
Monrovia, 153.
Moscow, 6, 116n.
Munich, 120, 143.

N
Nepal, 7.
Netherlands, 37n, 40n, 119.
New Brunswick, N.J., 100.
New York, 3, 100.
New Zealand, 115.
Northumberland, 125.
Norway, 36n, 40n, 106, 115.

O
Oberndorf, 146.
Oxbridge, 90, 131.
Oxford, 33, 136.

P
Pakistan, 7.
Paris, 103, 111, 112, 120n.
Parma, 105.
Peking, 131n.
Persia, 12.

Perugia, 105.
Plainfield, N.J., 63n.
Portugal, 37n.
Prague, 120.
Prussia, 106.
Puerto Rico, x, 91, 117, 127, 127n, 159n, 164, 174.

R
Rome, 6, 12, 47, 62, 73, 100, 118, 124n, 140, 159.
Russia, 5, 7, 69, 75, 76, 91, 92, 116n, 150.

S
Saigon, 85n.
Salzach, 146.
Salzburg, 134, 146, 147.
San Marino, 17, 117n.
Sardinia, 125.
Savoy, 125.
Saxony, 106.
Scotland, 116, 125.
Sicily, 125, 144, 148.
Siena, 105.
Soviet Union, 4, 7n, 10, 12, 92, 93, 96, 112, 116n, 120n, 126, 131n.
Spain, 75, 149.
St. Gallen, 109n.
Stockholm, 120n.
Sussex, 125.
Sweden, 108, 115.
Switzerland, 34, 42, 89, 90, 108, 109, 109n, 110, 120, 125, 150n.

T
Tanganyika, 142.
Thebes, 118.
Thule, 36n.
Toronto, 144.
Turkey, 37n, 115.

U
United Kingdom, 34, 108, 119n.
United Nations, 7, 7n, 73.
United States, 4, 6, 7n, 22n, 32n, 34, 35n, 37n, 40, 40n, 42n, 45, 51n, 63n, 73, 75, 77n, 91, 92, 93, 108, 109, 114n, 117, 120n, 127, 127n, 128, 129, 130, 131n, 141, 146, 149.

V
Vatican, 152.
Venice, 105.
Verona, 105.
Vesuvius, 123.

Vienna, 153.
Viet Nam, 85n.

W
Wales, i, v, 105, 114, 125.
Washington, 101.
Wessex, 125.
Winterthur, 26.
Wurthemburg, 106, 125.

Y
Yale, iv.
York, 119n.
Yorkshire, 144.

Index of Subjects

Bigness, the curse of, 75n, 185.

This was to be one of the entries of my Index of Subjects had I not myself become the victim of Bigness which this volume has taken such pains to expose as our time's primary cause of distress. As I am sending this final page to press, more than a year has elapsed since, under the auspices of the welfare state, I applied to the biggest local optician for a new pair of spectacles. It took months to obtain my first appointment, weeks to have a specialist examine my eyes with drops that gave me visions of hell for a further week, and more weeks to be issued spectacles which proved worse than the ones I was wearing. When I courteously complained, I was told in a hurt tone to give my new glasses a chance. No one thought of giving *me* a chance. When wear refused to improve them, I was told that, after all, my eyes were *defective*. As if I did not know. There was no suggestion that the new glasses might be defective. When they were finally returned a few weeks ago in the same stage of now customary professional perfection, I decided to give up on them and, lest I lose my sight completely, on my index too. In its place, I put detailed subject listings under each chapter heading in the table of contents, which may be more useful anyway.

As to the Index of Subjects itself, I hope I shall be forgiven, after half completing it, for confining myself to this single entry: *The Curse of Bigness,* confirmed more than ever, alas, in the central contention of this book: that the larger the state, the worse off is the citizen.

University College of Wales
Aberstwyth, 4 January 1977.